THE LAST CHANCE

Also available from *Continuum*:

Sartre: A Guide for the Perplexed, Gary Cox
Sartre and Fiction, Gary Cox
Sartre's 'Being and Nothingness': A Reader's Guide, Sebastian Gardner
Sartre's Ethics of Engagement, T. Storm Heter
Sartre's Phenomenology, David Reisman
Starting with Sartre, Gail Linsenbard
Sex and Philosophy, Edward Fullbrook and Kate Fullbrook
The New Sartre, Nick Farrell Fox
The Sartre Dictionary, Gary Cox

THE LAST CHANCE
Roads of Freedom IV

Jean-Paul Sartre

Translated by Craig Vasey

continuum

Continuum International Publishing Group

The Tower Building
11 York Road
London SE1 7NX

80 Maiden Lane
Suite 704
New York NY 10038

www.continuumbooks.com

© Editions GALLIMARD, Paris, 1981

Translation, Introduction and Commentary © Craig Vasey 2009

Ouvrage publié avec le concours du Ministère français chargé de la culture –
Centre national du livre

This work is published with the support of the French Ministry for Culture –
Centre national du livre

British Library Cataloguing-in-Publication Data
A catalogue record for this book is available from the British Library.

ISBN: HB: 978-1-8470-6550-6
           PB: 978-1-8470-6551-3

Library of Congress Cataloging-in-Publication Data
Sartre, Jean-Paul, 1905–1980.
[Dernière chance. English]
Last chance/Jean-Paul Sartre; translated by Craig Vasey.
   p. cm. – (Roads to freedom; 4)
ISBN-13: 978-1-84706-550-6
ISBN-10: 1-84706-550-3
ISBN-13: 978-1-84706-551-3 (pbk.)
ISBN-10: 1-84706-551-1 (pbk.)
1. World War, 1939–1945–Prisoners and prisons, German–Fiction.
I. Vasey, Craig. II. Title. III. Series.
PQ2637.A82D4713 2009
843'.914–dc22   2009006374

Typeset by Newgen Imaging Systems Pvt Ltd, Chennai, India
Printed and bound in Great Britain by the MPG Books Group

Contents

CONTENTS

Part III *Scholarship and Analysis*

Acknowledgments

I would like to thank Professor Christine Daigle at Brock University for many hours of discussion of these texts between fall 2006 and spring 2008, my student aide Annie Kinniburgh for her editing revisions of the manuscript and several excellent recommendations on wording, my colleague Professor Andrea Smith for reviewing idiomatic constructions with me in December 2008, the University of Mary Washington's Office of Academic Affairs for a Faculty Development Grant in summer 2007 and Sabbatical Leave in spring 2008, Professor Tom Flynn at Emory University for his early encouragement to pursue this project, my wife Wendy (Professor Wendy Atwell-Vasey) for her wonderfully reliable and constant support, and my son Dylan for the inspiration he effortlessly provides.

Craig Vasey, editor, translator

PART I

Introductory Material

CHAPTER 1
Translator's Introduction

Craig Vasey
University of Mary Washington

At the beginning of an interview he gave the day after presenting his now famous lecture, *Existentialism is a Humanism*, Sartre told a journalist in the Café Flore: "I had been hoping to clear up the misunderstandings that those who read badly spread among those who don't read."[1]

It is intriguing to consider this line on the occasion of presenting the fourth volume of Sartre's *Roads of Freedom* in English for the first time. Two kinds of "reading badly" come to mind in this context: one with respect to translation and the articulation of meaning, and another with respect to Sartre as a thinker and author.

1. THE TEXTS OF *ROADS OF FREEDOM*

Sartre stopped work on these texts in the early 1950s, and yet they have remained unavailable to the Anglophone audience for over half a century. The story of the two pieces of the fourth volume is itself an interesting and somewhat complicated one with respect to issues of reading, understanding and translating. Elements of this story will be addressed in this introductory essay, and again in an essay of philosophical analysis presented at the end of this volume, where readers, then familiar with

3

the contents of *Strange Friendship* and *The Last Chance*, will be more likely to appreciate them.

It is well known that Sartre's *Roads of Freedom* is a trilogy. And yet here we present the fourth volume! Not only that, but this fourth volume has not been entirely unknown; the first section of it, "Strange Friendship," was published in French in *Les Temps modernes* in 1949 (numbers XLIX and L). Although in length it cannot appear to be a full volume on par with the other three (each of which runs close to 400 pages), as a completed piece of the story, published by the author, it clearly merits recognition and inclusion. Thus it is peculiar that "everyone knows *Roads of Freedom* is a trilogy."

Sartre's novel has a name at two levels: the whole is called "Les Chemins de la liberté," but each of the parts has its own, completely independent title as well. As a result, in one sense, there is no *text* that has the title "Roads of Freedom"; rather, *Roads of Freedom* is a set (or cycle) of novels, *The Age of Reason*, *The Reprieve*, *Death in the Soul*, *Strange Friendship*, and *The Last Chance*. In 1970, the BBC produced and aired a multi-part series for television based on *Roads of Freedom*, under the title *Roads to Freedom*.[2] We hope the BBC will one day re-release it. But my interest here is to note the use of "to" rather than "of" in the title. This choice was also the choice of the editors of both the Vintage edition sold in the United States, and the Penguin edition sold in the United Kingdom: the book jackets indicate that the novels are parts of Sartre's *Roads to Freedom*.

What difference is conveyed by rendering "de" (which means "of" or "from") as "to," as though it were "à" (or more correctly, "vers" in this case)? Sartre certainly could have entitled his cycle *Les Chemins vers la liberté*, but he did not, and it is worth pondering what the difference is. Sartre's title could be seen as equivalent in meaning to "Freedom's Roads" or "The Paths of Freedom," because in these novels we encounter or cross the paths of many freedoms, that is, the paths of many individuals who are trying to cope with their lives in 1938–1940. This is a compelling suggestion, since in his major philosophical work of the same years he writes that "What we call freedom is impossible to distinguish from the *being* of 'human reality'."[3] His is a philosophy of responsibility, and the novels examine how a set of characters live their responsibility, their freedom, in these particular historical circumstances. Most importantly, in reading this cycle, we are witnessing the development of the main protagonists' freedom; we follow Mathieu and Brunet along the roads that are their freedom. It is in the final pages of *The Last Chance* that the idea of "having traveled quite a road" is, for the only time in 1,400 pages, actually asserted—by both characters.

"Roads *to* Freedom," on the other hand, conveys the impression that at the end of the roads the novel explores we will find freedom; perhaps these roads will include some dead-ends, some dangerous stretches, and so on, but in the end, we will come to freedom. The implication here would be to arrive at political freedom in some form or other, as opposed to exploring the problem of living as a free being. But anyone who has made his or her way to the end of the third volume, where the French forces have been defeated, have been captured, and are now being shipped off to the prisoner-of-war camp in a train—and one of them is shot down on the tracks—would have a hard time thinking that the novel ends with freedom.

However, when we learn that *Roads of Freedom* is more than the trilogy we have always thought it was, and read some of the supplementary texts never before available in English, we gain a perspective that might make "to" more plausible, if still not convincing. Sartre himself provides one source for it. For example, in the 1945 interview, Sartre says these roads are leading his characters to their freedom; but at the same time, in the "Please Insert" comment to the reader for *The Age of Reason* and *The Reprieve* (the first two volumes, both published in 1945), he said that the road they are on will lead them to the liberation of Paris, if not their own. These statements are not consistent with each other (together they suggest that these roads both are and are not leading the characters to their freedom), and this inconsistency itself argues against the choice of "to." Once we know the fourth volume, we appreciate how personal and political freedom are both at stake, and that the movement of the story leads from one stage of the main characters' lives (and freedom) to another, and thus can be said to be leading from an abstract and inauthentic kind of freedom *to* a situated and more authentic freedom. While this distinction is crucially important, it is not a sufficient reason for changing the title Sartre chose for his work.

Conclusion: Sartre's novel cycle is *Roads of Freedom*, not *Roads to Freedom*. In this volume it will be referred to by the correct title. Reading badly, continuing in this sense of the phrase, has had a widespread effect on *Roads of Freedom*, especially with regard to the third volume, known in the United States as *Troubled Sleep*, and in the United Kingdom as *Iron in the Soul*. Neither of these titles is an accurate rendering of *La Mort dans l'âme*, which unambiguously says *Death in the Soul*. In this volume, again, we will refer to the third volume as *Death in the Soul*, and hope that in the coming years these incorrect titles will disappear. Sleep is not even a theme in the novel, which is about the defeat of the French forces in June 1940, in what Sartre called the "drôle de guerre."[4]

The BBC title for the third part was *The Defeated*, which would have been preferable. But in the novel itself, the phrase "death in the soul" occurs three times as Schneider and Brunet argue about why it's so difficult for Brunet to get Frenchmen to join the Communist Party:[5] "Am I to blame if the French are a bunch of bastards with no initiative and no courage?" says Brunet. And Schneider replies that, yes, he (Brunet), Pétain, Stalin, Hitler, are all to blame:

> The whole lot of you are busy explaining that these poor devils are doubly guilty—guilty of having made war, and guilty for having lost it. You're going around taking away from them all the reasons they thought they had for fighting. Here's a poor guy who thought he'd embarked on a crusade for Justice and the Rights of Man, and now you want to persuade him that he was duped into taking part in an imperialist war. He doesn't know what he wants, he's not even sure what he's done . . . There he is, he's fallen outside the world, outside history, with a bunch of dead ideas, he's trying to defend himself, to rethink his situation. But with what? Even his tools for thinking are out of date: you're fuckin' killing his soul.[6]

Just a minute later, Schneider uses this expression again, but about Brunet now:

> You could try to escape, but you don't dare to, because you're afraid of what you'll find out there. You agitate, you organize, you make contacts: but you're running away. The rest of us, we're like stalled machinery, but you, you keep on running, as if that were worth anything anymore. You know it, you know you're out of gas, and you're just like us. You've got death in your soul. You might even have it worse than us.[7]

And a little later, Brunet uses the expression as he reflects: "Death in the soul. Ok, and so what? 'That's just psychology' he said to himself scornfully."[8]

Without dwelling here on where this phrase might have originated, or exactly what Sartre might mean by it, we think it is clear that the phrase "troubled sleep" doesn't capture it. The British translation says "iron in the soul" all three times, changing "death" into "iron." The current US translation does the same, for instance: "He's suffering from the iron that has entered into his soul, and it's you who are to blame."[9] An illuminating rendering.

At the beginning of the passage above, when Brunet calls the French a bunch of "bastards with no initiative and no courage," it may be interesting for the Anglophone reader to realize that Sartre's word choice is "salaud." This is the same word he uses in the lecture *Existentialism is a Humanism* to characterize certain of his philosophical opponents,[10] and that his character Roquentin uses in *Nausea* to characterize the bourgeois of Bouville when he leaves the library. In the UK edition (*Iron in the Soul*), this is rendered as "a bunch of no-goods," whereas the US text correctly says "bastards." Clearly, part of the problem we are drawing attention to here is the moralistic standards of the 1950s distorting the text of the author—the translator or editor choosing to sanitize the text, and spare the reader "strong language." To bolster this argument, consider that "stinkers" was used in the US translation of *Existentialism is a Humanism* to render "salauds."[11]

So these are a few examples of how those who read badly—or translate badly—can spread misunderstandings among those who don't read—in the original. An even more serious example, however, which does not have to do with censorship or propriety, concerns the striking difference between Part I and Part II of the third volume, *Death in the Soul*. Part I is written in a standard literary style, with action reported in the past tense, with indentations and paragraph breaks, and is divided into sections for different days or times of day; but Part II is written entirely in the present tense, with no indentations, paragraph breaks, or section breaks whatsoever: a solid 200 pages of text. The UK translation is faithful to the difference with respect to the indentations and breaks, but does not keep to Sartre's present tense in Part II. The US edition makes the same move of shifting the narration into the past tense, but also introduces paragraph breaks throughout. It is unthinkable that an author of Sartre's skill would produce a text this peculiar without a reason, and therefore it is an astonishing bit of violence to the text to disregard it. Some comment will be offered below on how to interpret Sartre's decision to write in the simple present tense whenever Brunet is the main character, because the reader will find that, here, in *The Last Chance*, the Brunet narrative is always in the present tense.[12]

2. THE BACKGROUND FOR *THE LAST CHANCE*

In order to present the fourth volume to readers, it is undoubtedly necessary to tell something of the story of the 1,200 pages that come before, and to introduce characters whose long history is relevant to the action of *Strange Friendship* and *The Last Chance*. Few of the characters from the first three volumes have any role or relevance here, but the reader must know at least something about Brunet and his relationship with Mathieu Delarue. This summary is probably not superfluous, even for a large number of Sartre scholars, because—and this is another sense of "reading badly"—*Roads of Freedom* is today an often overlooked and unknown text: perhaps because of its length, perhaps some consider it an unfinished work not worthy of attention, or perhaps some philosophers consider that fiction is not of equal value to philosophical texts. The latter, which is all-too-likely, would be a consequence of the institutional professionalization of philosophy, something quite an anathema to a philosopher like Sartre. For whatever reason, one cannot expect that many readers will come to the present text with a fresh memory of the story of the first three volumes.

In *The Age of Reason*, the lead character, Mathieu Delarue, a 34-year-old high school philosophy professor in Paris, deals with the unwanted pregnancy of the woman friend he sees a few times a week, Marcelle. This entire novel, some 400 pages, takes place within a 48-hour period in June 1938. Mathieu's time is divided between trying to find an affordable abortionist for Marcelle, and hanging out in bars and cafés with his student Boris, and Boris' sister Ivich, with whom he is infatuated. Mathieu is preoccupied with being free, which to him means not being tied down. It is the time of the Spanish Civil War, and he does not get involved—he says it is not *his* war. But he does have a painter friend, Gomez, who has gone to Spain, and rises in the ranks to be a General in the anti-Franco forces; Mathieu visits Gomez's wife, Sarah (who is

Jewish), in search of help finding an abortionist, and encounters a friend from his childhood, Brunet. (We never learn Brunet's first name.) Brunet is now a member of the French Communist Party, a political activist, and he urges Mathieu to put his freedom at the service of the Party. Mathieu, preoccupied with being free, will have nothing to do with such commitments.

The title, *The Age of Reason*, comes from the scene in which Mathieu asks his older brother Jacques for money for the abortion, but Jacques will not help unless Mathieu marries Marcelle. He admonishes Mathieu to grow up, saying several times, "You've reached the age of reason." By the end of the book, Mathieu finds himself freed from Marcelle, but only because she decides, with the malicious encouragement of Daniel (another of Mathieu's childhood friends, now a successful investment banker, but also a conflicted homosexual), to keep the child, marry Daniel, and dump Mathieu (who had never seriously considered the possibility of being a father).

In *The Reprieve*, where the threat of war with Germany hangs over the country, we meet other characters: Maurice, a rough working-class fellow who resents Brunet for being a higher-up in the Party. Brunet may be a Communist, but he is educated, and is a columnist for the French Communist Party daily newspaper, *L'Humanité*. An endearing character is Big Louis,[13] an illiterate peasant, who comes in from the countryside to Marseille because he needs work, and comes to find out that he's been mobilized and is to report for service. Through his experiences, North African blacks are introduced into the story, as is the distance between peasants and "good society." Though Big Louis has some money, he cannot get served in a restaurant, and he winds up being conned by some street thugs who rob him. His inability to read is crucial to his experiences, and Sartre explores the consequences of the absence of this taken-for-granted competence.

Sartre spends time examining another usually overlooked subject in the character of Charles, an invalid in a hospital that has to be evacuated for fear of a German invasion. Like the other patients, Charles cannot walk, and spends his life on his back. Angry at having no life of his own and being completely dependent on "the stand-ups," he is unpleasant to everyone until he meets another invalid, a woman, when they are transferred to box cars in a train to be transported to another part of France.

The scenes about them caused some controversy, especially Sartre's treatment of the patients' need to relieve themselves while en route, exacerbated by the porters' oversight in having mixed male and female patients together in the same boxcar.[14]

Sartre includes a character named Birnenschatz, a Jewish businessman in Paris who denies the relevance of being a Jew; his discussions with other Jews, who know something of the persecutions in Hitler's Germany, show a man trapped in the paradox of being made to be, and having to be, what he does not experience himself as being. These ideas are explored more extensively in the 1946 essay, *Reflections on the Jewish Question*. Resistance to the idea of war is expressed in the character of Philippe, a somewhat spoiled adolescent rebelling against a military step-father (a WWI General); Philippe decides to desert, has false papers made up, but then romantically rejects his own cowardice and makes a scene in the streets denouncing war. When some of the crowd begin beating him up, Mathieu, passing by, intervenes, pretending to be a police officer, and saves him. This is the first time Mathieu has put himself out for anyone else. He too, like Big Louis, has been called up, and he is trying to make arrangements for his departure, which includes setting up Ivich, the girl he was infatuated with, in his apartment while he is away.

Hitler, Chamberlain, and Daladier[15] are also characters in *The Reprieve*, which is an effective and uniquely written account of the shattering of everyone's life by the coming of war. The title suggests multiple connotations: suspension, reprieve, deferral, but most clearly refers to what we call the Munich Pact, which is notorious today as the capitulation of England and France to Hitler's aggression against what was then Czechoslovakia. As the volume approaches the end, Mathieu realizes that with the Munich Pact, and no war (apparently) after all, he is now choosing not to go back to the life he had been getting ready to leave behind, using the war as an excuse; he's free, he says, and shall remain so. But his freedom is now freedom from the life that was committed only to being free-from-commitments.

Though it is not crucial to a plot summary, it is worth mentioning that the passage of time in *The Reprieve* is experienced in a unique way, because of the style in which Sartre writes it.[16] The 400 pages begin on September 23, and end on September 30, 1938, with Prime Minister Daladier's return to France after the agreement that has avoided war.

In the final scene, as Daladier sees he is being greeted with shouts of praise at the airport, he turns to his aide and says, "The asses!"[17]

The third volume, *Death in the Soul*, takes place in June 1940, one year and nine months later than the action in *The Reprieve*. The war, of course, has not been avoided. By the end, Brunet is the main character, and how he comes to displace Mathieu is one of the most masterful elements of the novel. Mathieu was stationed with an auxiliary unit well behind the front lines, and they never see any action at all by the time they learn that France is defeated and it is all over. Their officers desert them in the night, and the men are left on their own in the countryside outside a village, where they spend their time bored, reading, waiting, and getting drunk. Then a squad of fifteen French fighters led by a lieutenant arrives, looking to set up an ambush for the approaching Germans, and Mathieu decides to join his pal, Henri Pinette, who has chosen to follow the soldiers and join in the ambush, although they are certain the Germans have won, and that they will all be killed. The final pages of Part I lay out an impressive battle scene in which Mathieu, in anguish, and with the other soldiers, waits in a church bell tower for the German soldiers to enter the town—with the aim of holding them for fifteen minutes. Mathieu shoots and kills two Germans during this scene, and witnesses the death of some of his comrades in the bell tower. In the end a cannon shells the bell tower, and it collapses.

In Part II, which opens the night before this ambush, Brunet shaves in the basement of a home he'd entered, and where he slept, though most unwelcome. When he comes upstairs and outside, he finds thirty Germans working at taking out the bell tower; he is captured along with all the other French soldiers, and "emerges on the main road just at the moment the bell tower collapses."[18] Given that we are now in Part II, and that the writing style has shifted dramatically to all present tense, with no indentations or paragraph breaks on the pages,[19] it seems quite clear that the story Mathieu was at the center of is over; it is now Brunet who is the main character. We hear no more of Mathieu.

Brunet has been a recruiter for the Communist Party, and as the French forces fall into despair at their rapid defeat and capture (thousands follow one another complacently along the road, under the "guard" of a single German soldier), he sets about trying to organize some of the ones he sees as promising, giving them some discipline and morale. One fellow

11

soldier, Schneider, seems to hit it off pretty well with him, and they talk politics. As the novel draws to a close, they are all being transported by train from a makeshift camp in eastern France toward a POW camp inside Germany. On the trip to the camp, one of the men—a printer—jumps from the train, then tries to get back on, and is shot down by the Germans. The hatred the rest of the Frenchmen feel for the Germans at that moment is a revelation for Brunet, and the book ends with him soberly reflecting that tomorrow the black birds will come for the body.

By this time, one has read about 1,200 pages, been through numerous historical moments of the late 1930s, seen fictional parallels to many of the themes discussed in *Being and Nothingness*, and been treated to impressive insights into the upheaval of many kinds of people's lives, at many levels. The reader is full of questions and hopes, and identifies with the despair of the French prisoners. The reader does not, however, feel that these have been stories of roads *to* freedom.

In English, that's as far as one can go, but in French one could read another hundred pages in 1949, when Sartre published *Drôle d'amitié (Strange Friendship)* in his journal, *Les Temps modernes*. (*Death in the Soul* had also appeared in 1949.) In 1981, when Sartre's complete works of fiction were published as *Oeuvres romanesques* in the Pléiade edition, *La Dernière chance (The Last Chance)* appeared for the first time. This is quite a different text from all the others, truly reconstructed after the fact, through the labor of George H. Bauer and Michel Contat, from completely unorganized manuscript pages.[20] It consists of three extended segments, and a series of fragments still at the draft stage. Though the piece called *Strange Friendship* (also consisting of three sections) is a little longer, Sartre made clear in the 1945 interview at the Café Flore, that it was his plan to call the final volume *The Last Chance*, hence the choice of *The Last Chance* for the overall title of this fourth volume.

Once the reader has been through Part II (*Strange Friendship* and *The Last Chance*), he or she may well be interested in a little more context and bibliographical information. To this end, and especially for serious readers of Sartre's thought, I have included several supplementary texts from the Pléiade edition of *Oeuvres romanesques*: the interview at the Café Flore, Sartre's two "Please Insert" notices for the novels (Part I), and four essays of analysis (Part III). One of these is an overview of the place of *Roads of Freedom* in Sartre's life and work, by Michel Contat. Two others address

Strange Friendship (this piece includes an account by Simone de Beauvoir of what Sartre had planned for the end of the novel), and *The Last Chance* specifically.[21] I conclude the volume with a brief essay on one of Sartre's main philosophical concepts, and how it sheds light on the way in which he wrote the Brunet story.

CHAPTER 2
Interview at the Café Flore: 1945, Jean-Paul Sartre and Christian Grisoli

This is the only interview Sartre gave at the time the two volumes The Age of Reason *and* The Reprieve *appeared in French. It was published on December13, 1945 in the journal* Paru. *The interviewer was a young, enthusiastic journalist named Christian Grisoli.*

The Café Flore, six o'clock in the evening, all lamps lit in the evening fog—packed full. People are gathered around tables, and the air is thick with smoke and voices. Faces at once unknown but vaguely familiar—the ambiguous face of "glory" itself—float above the booths at the center of more compact and talkative groups. Chairs stick out into the aisles for the late-arrivals. They sit, but uncomfortably. They feel out of place and indiscrete, useless spectators of a show no one can anticipate.

Sartre has just come in, immediately welcomed by calls and waves. He is hailed, approached, followed; he resists. I can tell he intends to keep the interview he has been good enough to schedule with me. We finally find ourselves sitting in an isolated corner in the upstairs room, not far from a couple who are happily entwined in each other's arms.

Philosopher, novelist, playwright, critic, journalist, able to express himself equally well in any mode, here is Sartre, simple and cordial, open to any and all questions, his mind overflowing, his speech brief and clear, grasping ideas at once and with complete clarity.

Grisoli: How are you doing? It's a banal question, but I ask it having been in attendance last night at your lecture.[1]

Sartre: I nearly died of suffocation there. At least, I hope that, eh . . . warm welcoming crowd wasn't made up entirely of snobs. Snobs for, and snobs against, the curious out to see the curiosity, the great corruptor, the pernicious philosopher, as the chorus of "right-thinking" people like to chant. I had been hoping to clear up the misunderstandings that those who read badly spread among those who don't read. It can seem strange to have to present the evidence . . .

Grisoli: No, not at all, when you consider the wall of misunderstanding and bad faith that you find yourself up against.

Sartre: They stubbornly reproach us, we existentialists, for our pessimism, the darkness of our "philosophy of despair." It's such a surprise. They criticize us in the name of common sense—well, what idea of man does common sense offer? Look at its proverbs, its sayings, its stories, its myths. They all show us man capable of the very worst, pushed to the worst by his very nature. And what does it say, this wisdom of the world, in the face of the weaknesses, cowardice, villainies and the meanness of men?[2] It doesn't say, "How disgusting!" but only, "How human!", as if in man there were some kind of essential, irremediable corruptness which provided an excuse. But we say that there is no human nature, there is no eternal and unchanging essence of man—abstract potentiality, Platonic Form—that would determine individual existences. We say that in the case of man, freedom precedes essence, that he creates his essence through acting, that he's what he makes himself through his choices, that it's his lot to choose and make himself good or evil, and that he's always responsible. Is this a philosophy of despair? Well sure, to the degree that we grant no sense whatsoever to the transcendent hopes of religions and metaphysics. There is no traced-out path to lead man to his salvation; he must constantly invent his own path. But, to invent it, he is free, responsible, without excuse, and every hope lies within him. This morning I met someone who reproached me for being too optimistic! What are you going to do?

Grisoli: From that perspective, what sense do you give to the notions of abandonment and anguish, that are so annoyingly abused these days?

Sartre: These are very basic ideas, and ones that reflection immediately clarifies. Man is free. It is he who makes there be a world. It's by his choice that he decides its meaning. He cannot refuse to choose, because this refusal is itself a choice. And he has to choose on his own, without aid, without any recourse. Nothing is coming to him from outside that he could receive or accept. He has to make himself, down to the slightest detail: that's his abandonment—a consequence of his freedom. As for anguish, that's the consciousness of this freedom, the recognition that my future is my possibility, that it depends on me to bring it into existence and sustain it, that the only thing that separates me from it is my freedom. There's nothing in all this that crushes man, as all-too-many say. Quite the contrary.

Grisoli: What do you think of the morality trial that you're being subjected to on a daily basis because of *The Age of Reason* and *The Reprieve*? Your characters are moved by their most base instincts; they muck about in the filth. Sartre's man is man below the belt, etc.

Sartre: I think that what makes my characters irritating is their lucidity. They know what they are, and they choose to be it. If they were hypocritical or blind, they'd be more acceptable. People were upset that there was a tale involving abortion at the center of *The Age of Reason*. Quite wrongly! Because, after all, abortion was a prosecutable offence back in 1938, it certainly existed. Why should we willfully close our eyes to that? Statistics would undoubtedly show that there are more abortions per year than there are subway workers. Who would get upset over a novel about subway workers? But I'm going too far. Yes, without a doubt, Mathieu is guilty of refusing to have the child. But you can find justifiable reasons for this refusal: fear of compromising Marcelle, of causing her mother pain . . . Haven't those who've gotten indignant about this known women who've refused to have a child just because it would be a lot more convenient to not have one? Sure Mathieu is guilty. But his real fault isn't where people have looked for it. It's less in his proposing abortion to Marcelle than it is in his being committed for eight years in a loveless relationship. And he is not really committed to Marcelle. Not because he hasn't married her—to my mind marriage makes no difference, it's just the social form of commitment. But because he knew very well that this relationship wasn't really a two-way street. They see each other four times a week. They say that they tell each other everything: in reality, they never stop lying to each other, because their relationship itself is false, it's a lie.

Grisoli: In *The Reprieve* there's a theme, an episode that people complain is nothing but a gratuitous obscenity: the one about the paralyzed patient. What's the real meaning of this episode to your mind?

Sartre: Well, there too, I have not made anything up, and I have it from good sources that the relations between patients and nurses are often like that between Charles and Jacqueline. I think there is something very important and very profound here, like a defense mechanism, defiance. A man is his project, his future. Charles isn't a man, because he is the future of other people. He's an object, a potted plant. His life has no future, it's a dead life, deprived of its most essential dimension, the dimension of action. That's why he tries to establish relations with the stand-ups—who are the constant proof of his submission—that will reduce them to the level of instruments, humiliating relations, relations from below. By the same token, I know that the right-thinking have had their stomachs turned by the scene where the patients are relieving themselves. And yet, I think that in this world, where natural needs rule, Charles' attempt to defeat his body, to overcome his needs, is a moving attempt to become human.

Grisoli: The revealing and the elucidation of freedom are at the heart of *Being and Nothingness*. How is the problem of freedom also the principal object of your novel?

Sartre: Man is free in the fullest and strongest sense. Freedom isn't in him as a property of his human essence. He doesn't exist first, and then be free later. He is free by the fact that he exists. There's no distance between his being and his freedom. But man, who is thus condemned to freedom, still has to free himself, because he doesn't immediately recognize himself as free, or, because he misunderstands the meaning of his freedom. This working-his-way-along the road to his freedom is the paradox of freedom, and it's also the theme of my novel. It's the story of a deliverance and a liberation. But it's not finished yet. *The Age of Reason* and *The Reprieve* are only an inventory of false, mutilated, incomplete freedoms, a description of freedom's roadblocks. It's only in *The Last Chance* that the conditions for a true liberation will be defined.

Grisoli: On this theme of failed freedoms, shouldn't we see Mathieu and Brunet as two poles?

Sartre: Exactly. Mathieu is the incarnation of this complete uncommittedness that Hegel calls "terrorist freedom", and which is really a counter-freedom. He's like Orestes at the beginning of *The Flies*, weightless, unattached, unconnected to anything in the world, floating like a thread. He's not free, because he hasn't been able to commit himself. He has not really committed himself to Marcelle, because he doesn't know how to build a life for two with her. He hasn't committed himself to the Spanish Civil War, on the grounds that it doesn't concern him. But nothing concerns me unless I make a beginning. The war in Spain would have become his concern if he'd left for it. He's truly the brother of the worker he meets at the beginning of *The Age of Reason*, who was afraid, who stayed behind, and who is ashamed. Mathieu doesn't commit himself any more genuinely to the war that does become his war, just by the fact that he accepts it. He accepts it, but he doesn't claim it as his own. He feels excluded from the historical adventure that is unfolding. He thinks of the others who've been mobilized for the war with him as either casualties or survivors, and by that he separates himself from them. Mathieu is the freedom of indifference, freedom in the abstract, freedom for nothing. Mathieu's not free, he's nothing, because he's always on the outside.

Grisoli: Is Brunet any more free for always being on the inside?

Sartre: Brunet is the incarnation of the spirit of seriousness, who believes in transcendent values inscribed in heaven—intelligible, independent of subjectivity, given as things. For him there's an absolute meaning of the world, and of history, and that directs his actions. He's committed because he needs certainty in order to live. His commitment is just passive obedience to this need. He escapes anguish at rather low cost. He's not free. Man is free to commit himself, but he's only free if he commits himself to being free. There's another kind of activist life besides the kind we see in Brunet, but Brunet is an activist who lacks freedom.

Grisoli: You have given your novel the title **Roads of Freedom**. If these roads are not dead-ends, they have to lead somewhere. Where are they leading?

Sartre: They lead the characters to their freedom, in fact. Mathieu finds his love, and his life's work. He commits himself, in a free commitment, which will give the world a meaning for him. That'll be the subject of *The Last Chance*.

Grisoli: But from *The Age of Reason* to *The Reprieve*, does he make any progress?

Sartre: No. What he accomplishes is to free himself from his past. When *The Reprieve* ends, his life is in order, he's taken care of everything. Marcelle is no longer a burden in his life. He has given up Ivich for a girl he happens to meet. He's alone, he's ready for his freedom.

Grisoli: So in fact the reprieve is not only the ridiculous reprieve of Munich; it's also a reprieve you request for your characters.

Sartre: Yes, because nothing is ever simply finished. You're not born a hero or a coward, like you are born short or red-headed. You choose yourself a hero or a coward, and this choice can always be put in question again. My characters are suspended. There is no absolute meaning of their behavior, fixed once and for all. Their futures will decide the meaning of their pasts; their futures will save them, if they save themselves. It's too early to judge them.

Grisoli: It is commonly said—and the connection is becoming almost a matter of habit—that your work is very similar to that of Camus. What's your view of the comparison?

Sartre: It's based on a very serious confusion. Camus is not an existentialist. Even though he refers to Kierkegaard, to Jaspers, to Heidegger, his real influences are the French moralists of the seventeenth century. He's a classical man, a Mediterranean. I'd call his pessimism solar, thinking of the blackness in the sun. Camus' philosophy is a philosophy of the absurd, and for him the absurd is born from the relation of man with the world, man's rational expectations and the irrationality of the world. The themes he draws from there are the themes of classical pessimism. For me there's no such thing as the absurd in this sense of scandal and disappointment that Camus sees. What I call absurd is something quite different: it's the universal contingency of the being who is, but who is not the foundation of his being. It's what there is in being of the given, the unjustifiable, the always primary. And the consequences that I develop from this feature of being are developed on a completely different level from where Camus puts himself, which is the level of dry contemplative reason, in the French style.

Grisoli: You are often accused of wearing Marxism's hand-me-downs. Do you feel this criticism is warranted?

Sartre: My position regarding Marxism is clear. I take it to be a situated philosophy, just as is Newtonian physics, Darwinian evolution, and vitalistic biology. This physics, this evolutionism, and this biology are outdated today. Why would Marxism outlive them, closed in on itself like a dogma? It's an open-ended philosophy, and in this sense I am Marxist, because I agree with Marx on the basic idea that man makes his history from within his situation. There is a given, there are conditions of history. But from that, the only way you can infer the negation of freedom is if your thought is led astray by nostalgia for a being that is full and without lack, if your thought refuses to admit that there is nothingness.

Grisoli: Since you are used to hearing yourself described as the great corruptor (*mauvais maître*), you won't be surprised if I ask you the irritating question of your disciples.

Sartre: I have no disciples and I do not wish to have any. Like any philosophy professor, I've had some students who've distorted the meaning of themes that I've taught about. I've said that it's important to be clear, but this clarity is not an end-in-itself, it's a clarity *for*. Some people have taken this insistence on lucidity for a simple-minded complacent cynicism, as if becoming conscious of your imperfection was enough to justify you in having all your little desires. I could multiply the examples.

Grisoli: What are you working on at this point?

Sartre: You know that *Being and Nothingness* ends on the need and the promise of an ethics. I'm working on this existentialist ethics at the same time as *The Last Chance*.

Grisoli: Don't you have a play coming soon?

Sartre: Indeed. And these characters have already traveled the road of freedom. The action takes place in the Resistance, and for lack of a better word, the theme of the play is heroism. I'm trying to show that there is something "total" about heroism, like I will show, in an upcoming issue of *Les Temps modernes*, that there is something "total" about anti-Semitism; it implies a stance not only on Jews, but on children, on trees. I'll be trying, as well, to elucidate the very complex relation that exists, in torture, between the executioner and his victim, the executioner needing to believe in the baseness of his victim in order to feel justified, and the victim, from the other side, needing to believe in his own dignity in order to not be finished off once and for all by his executioner. Torture is truly the battle to the death of consciousnesses.

We go downstairs, again entering the dense enclosed room of lights, rumors and smoke. I take my leave.

Sartre is what we've been waiting for, and a promise we can be sure will ever be fulfilled.

Christian Grisoli

CHAPTER 3

Please Insert 1: 1945, Jean-Paul Sartre

At the time of the publication of The Age of Reason *and* The Reprieve, *in 1945, Sartre wrote the following comment, entitled "Please Insert." When these volumes were translated into English, this comment was not included, hence its publication here.*

My aim is to write a novel about freedom. I wanted to retrace the road traveled by certain people and social groups between 1938 and 1944. This road will lead them to the liberation of Paris, though not necessarily to their own. But I hope, at least, to be able to make it possible to sense the conditions of a complete deliverance, beyond the point at which I end this tale. In this novel, which will take three volumes, I did not think I should use the same technique throughout. In the misleading calm before the storm of 1937–1938, there were still people in certain circles who could harbor the illusion of leading an individual existence, closed off, watertight. That's why I chose to tell the story in *The Age of Reason* as one usually does, showing only the relations between a few individuals. But with the events of September 1938, the walls come down. The individual, without ceasing to be a monad, finds himself caught up in a role that goes beyond him. He continues to be a point of view on the world, but he is surprised by a process of generalizing and dissolving. He's a monad that's taking on water, that will never be able to stop taking on water, without ever going down. To take account of the ambiguity of this situation, I had to draw on the "big picture." In *The Reprieve*, you will find all the same people from *The Age of Reason*, but now they are lost, surrounded by a crowd of other people. I wanted both to avoid speaking of a crowd or of a nation as if it were a single individual—giving it tastes, desires and concepts like Zola does in *Germinal*—and to avoid reducing it to the sum of the parts that make it up. I tried to take advantage of the experiments in technique that certain writers of simultaneity, like Dos Passos and Virginia Woolf, have undertaken. I took up their question at the very point where they had let it lie, and I tried to uncover something new along this path. The reader will say whether or not I've succeeded.

I ask that you not judge my characters on the basis of these two first volumes, one of which attempts to describe the stagnation of France in the years between the two wars, while the other aims to reinstate the disarray that overwhelmed so many people at the moment of the despicable reprieve of Munich. Many of my creations, even those who seem at the moment to be the most cowardly, will prove themselves later on to be heroes, and it is precisely a hero-novel that I am aiming to write. But, unlike our right-thinkers, I do not believe that heroism is an easy thing.

CHAPTER 4
Please Insert 2: 1949, Jean-Paul Sartre

As he had done in 1945, Sartre added this last minute comment at the 1949 publication of Death in the Soul, *the third volume of* Roads of Freedom. La Mort dans lâme *is published in the United States as* Troubled Sleep; *in the United Kingdom as* Iron in the Soul. *Neither title is correct: it means* Death in the Soul. *In the interview Sartre gave in 1945, following the publication of* The Age of Reason *and* The Reprieve, *he indicated that the next volume would be called* The Last Chance. Death in the Soul *appeared in 1949, and he worked until 1952 on manuscripts entitled "Strange Friendship" and "The Last Chance." The expectations raised in the interview for the characters—especially heroism—do not materialize in* Death in the Soul; *some of them are deferred to* The Last Chance. *The expectations raised in the second paragraph of this "Please Insert," especially for Mathieu and Brunet, also do not materialize in* Death in the Soul, *but only in* Strange Friendship *and* The Last Chance.

They're alive, but death has touched them all: something is over. With defeat, the bookshelf of values has fallen off the wall. While Daniel, in Paris, celebrates the triumph of an uneasy conscience, Mathieu, in a village in Lorraine, takes stock of the damage: Peace, Progress, Reason, Law, Democracy, Country, everything is shattered, and no one will ever pick up all the pieces.

But something is beginning as well. Without direction, without references or letters of recommendation, without even understanding what is happening to them, they continue their paths, just because they've survived. Daniel, at his basest and without knowing it, begins the ascent that will lead him to freedom and to death. Brunet undertakes a project, but he is far from suspecting that through it his sword of certainties will be broken, and that he will be left naked and free. Seeking the death that has been stolen from him, Boris flies toward London, but it is not death that he will find there. And Mathieu, especially, timidly has the experience of solidarity. In the midst of all these men who lose themselves together, he learns that no one saves himself alone. In fact, he has the most to lose: the others have lost their principles, but he—he loses his problem. Rest assured, he will find himself another.

PART II

The Last Chance

CHAPTER 5
Strange Friendship

Jean-Paul Sartre

1. FIRST SECTION

Brunet wakes up, leaps to the floor, lights a lamp; cold diamonds cover his skin, the shadows dance, it smells like night and like morning, it smells like happiness.

Outside, in the dark, there are two hundred dead barracks, thirty thousand guys sleeping. Alone, upright, Brunet places a hand on the top of the bunk and leans over a little pile of sleep:

"Get up!"

Moûlu shakes his head without opening his eyes; a large sharp mouth opens in his unseeing face. "What time is it?"

"Time to get yourself up."

Moûlu sighs and sits up, his eyes still closed: "Must have been a freeze last night."

He opens his eyes, takes a look at his watch, and gives his daily stupefied cry: "Jesus Mary! 5 o'clock!"

Brunet smiles; Moûlu cries, his hands in his hair, rubbing his head; Brunet feels like stone, a happy cold stone.

"5 o'clock!" says Moûlu. "There's not a single fucking barracks in the whole camp except for this goddamn one where the guys get up at 5—the Krauts don't even ask us to get up before 6. At this point it's not captivity anymore, it's like jail." He hesitates, he thinks, his eyes suddenly shine and he joyfully fires his favorite morning shot: "Dirty fascist!"

Brunet laughs with pleasure. He loves everything that repeats itself. The cold, the dark, "dirty fascist," six months in this camp but it's one single morning; always the same, returning every morning, darker than the last, colder than the last, deeper than the last, more his than the last.

Moûlu jumps from the bed, whimpering from the cold, puts on his shirt, his pants. Brunet watches without pleasure as he gets to work at the stove: he would have liked to enjoy the cold a little longer. "Don't waste coal, we'll run out."

Moûlu lights some paper, the kindling crackles; he stands up, reddened, and laughs in Brunet's face: "Who do you think your housekeeper is? Has she ever not come through?" He points to a box full of coal. Brunet frowns:

"Where'd you get that?"

"The kitchen."

"I told you not to do that!" Brunet says, irritated.

Moûlu interrupts him, indignant: "Oh sure. You know where it winds up, the mess cooks' coal? In Fritz's Kommandantur! May as well be us gets a little."

Brunet doesn't respond, he's shaving. Beneath his razor's bite his cheeks of stone begin to come back to life. Warmth begins to reach him like a temptation.

"Chocolate?"

"Yeah." The stove sputters. Moûlu places a pot filled with water on top, takes two chocolate bars from his bag, throws them in the pot, and, watching them melt, says:

"You're shaving early."

"I'm going out."

"To do what?"

"New arrivals this morning, workers from France. I'm getting ten of them for the barracks."

"Newbies!" says Moûlu cheering up.

He stirs the water in the pot with the blade of his knife.

"Poor newbies! Not that they're any worse off here than somewhere else, but they'll have to get used to it."

A brown liquid simmers in the pot, the bubbles make it shake, droplets splash on the stove and turn white as they sizzle. Moûlu uses his handkerchief to grasp the pot, and sets it on a box. Brunet sits himself down next to him.

"Come in."

Zimmer, the medic, pokes his frizzy head in the doorway.

"Already up?" says Moûlu.

"Because of these sons of bitches coming in from France. Got to go see if any of them are sick."

He wrinkles his nose:

"It smells like chocolate."

"I got a package," says Moûlu gaily.

"You're lucky."

"Come on!" says Brunet, annoyed. "What did you want to tell me?"

"It's about Cognard. They're taking him down to the hospital this morning. Dysentery."

"Thanks," says Brunet.

The head disappears, the door closes, Moûlu cuts some slices in a hunk of stale bread:

"You want some crusts?"

"No," says Brunet dryly.

"You're wrong," says Moûlu without moving. "You don't know what's good." He gets up, takes the mugs down and pours the chocolate. He points at Cognard's mug, still hanging from the nail:

"That gets me a bit. Not you?"

Brunet shrugs his shoulders: Cognard was lazy.

"Who are you going to replace him with? Schneider?"

"Of course, Schneider."

"I'm for it," says Moûlu. "He won't screw up." Brunet gets up and puts on his cap. Moûlu grabs the broom. Brunet opens the door.

"The door!" cries Moûlu. "You're taking all my heat."

Brunet closes the door and returns to the cold in the long hallway that runs through the barracks. It's an eternal cold; falling from soles and caps; in this tunnel of night and wind, little drifts of eternal snow pile up and harden; I've got to tell them to scrape their shoes outside or they'll end up making the floor rot away; a door slams, the wood cracks; at the end of the tunnel a vague grey fog glimmers—morning.

Standing in the night, in the cold, in the wind, in the snow, on the hills of the morning, Brunet ponders his day: at ten, Chancelier, report on his work at the infirmary: intensify the propaganda and recruitment; Armand at noon, figuring out for good the problem of ink for the copier; at three, committee with Brada: ask the organization to take charge of the Spanish prisoners being isolated and starved by the camp administration; that's some hard work, it'll be a bit risky, but it brings you together. He breathes forcefully, the cold flows into him through his nose down to his veins, a bouquet of joy. Behind doors, rustlings, scrapings, whispers, a crowd waking up. Everyone's asleep except my boys. He pushes a door, nightlights on tables send long shadows to the walls.

"Anyone sick in here?"

Confident smiles, flashes of teeth. "No one's sick."

Brunet opens and closes doors; the place is teeming, one guy is singing, another playing the harmonica. They're happy, the cold and their hate keep them going; see what I've made of them.

In Lambert's bunk a fat naked baby hides in the shadows, Brunet grabs him by the armpit, pulls, and tosses him on all fours in the middle of the floor, everyone laughs, the big guy protests with good humor:

"Can't a guy sleep it off a little?"

"You've had enough sleep, old full-of-soup."

"It's not that, but I was having a nice dream."

"In the sack with your gal?"

"Yeah, right! I was in the watchtower with a machine gun, and the Krauts were in the barracks instead of us."

"Don't worry," says Brunet. "One of these days . . . "

Lambert tugs at Brunet's sleeve.

"The Macaronis—is it true they've been trounced?"

"You bet."

The guys pull themselves up, and turn hard eyes on Brunet:

"So it's true? It's not bull?"

Brunet looks right back at these brutal faces:

"So you didn't catch the news last night?"

"Didn't have time."

Thibaut had set up a radio in a soap box in his barracks.

"Send someone to Thibaut," he says. "There's good news."

Their eyes shine, hate and joy dance on their cheeks. Brunet feels his heart beating—look what I've made of them!

"In Albania, you guys, the Greeks gave it to 'em, they're in full retreat."[1]

He closes the door, touched: they'll start their day in glory. He opens one last door, the good one: 17 out of 18 in here are communists, seventeen cocky young guys, who go everywhere, gathering information and spreading the word. The eighteenth is Schneider. Brunet comes in and smiles; at them he always smiles first.

"Hey guys."

He goes to sit on the bench and they gather around. He has nothing much to tell them, but it's the best part of the day. He takes out his pipe and fills it, looking around. Everything's clean, the floor's already been swept and washed; leaning forward on the bench, Schneider wipes his shoes with a linen cloth.

"Who's on today?"

They point at Dewrouckère.

"Him."

"What about?"

Dewrouckère blushes:

"Miners' life in the black country."

"Very good," says Brunet. "Perfect."

He knows Dewrouckère is waiting for him to leave before he starts, but he doesn't get up. He's with family here—just five more minutes. Toussus leans toward him:

"Hey Brunet, my bother-in-law is here in the camp."

"Your brother-in-law?"

"My wife's brother. I saw his name on the sick list."

"Oh yeah?"

"He's not in the Party, you know," says Toussus, annoyed.

"What's he do?"

"Nonpolitical."

"And?"

"Should I go see him? That's what we were talking about when you came in."

Brunet doesn't respond. Perrin takes a step forward:

"Suppose the guy gets involved with the Francistes; he could give us up."[2]

Brunet gestures to be quiet. Everyone's looking at him, and he takes his time deciding. Their confidence is like warm lips on cold hands.

"You like him, your brother-in-law?"

"Well enough; we get along as long as we don't talk politics."

He makes a little movement to show it doesn't matter much:

"You know, I don't really care about seeing him, it's more just if he's got some news about my wife."

Brunet puts his hand on his arm and says softly:

"It would be better not to see him."

Around his head the circle of eyes lights up; he hit it right, the guys didn't want Toussus to see his brother-in-law either. Smiling, he adds:

"Of course, if you bump into him one of these days, it's no big deal either."

Heads nod, approving:

"That's what we were telling him."

"But I agree!" says Toussus right away. "It was just about my wife."

The case is settled, they quiet down, reassured. Brunet smokes his pipe, he's happy. Abruptly, he's seized by the cold. Not the pure chaste glory of the early morning, but a damp cold that reaches his stomach and his thighs; he shivers.

"You're not lighting the stove?"

"We decided not to light it in the mornings any more."

"I see," says Brunet.

He gets up abruptly, he calls:

"Schneider!"

Schneider gets up.

"Yeah?"

"Come on, I have to talk to you."

Saved, Dewrouckère sighs and comes up to the table, holding a sheet of paper; the guys gather around him, everyone stays standing because of the cold.

"Ok, here we go," begins Dewrouckère, "here it is."

He stops, waiting. Brunet gives a wave of the hand and goes out. Schneider follows, whistling.

"You whistle badly."

"I've always whistled badly," says Schneider.

Brunet turns and smiles at him. Schneider's changed, him too. He looks anemic, and he's coughing, but his eyes are almost happy. Brunet pushes the door to his barrack open: "Come on in."

Schneider enters, salutes Moûlu with two fingers, comes up to the stove and holds his hands out to the fire. He stops whistling. He shivers.

"You ok, buddy?" asks Brunet.

Schneider shrugs his shoulders:

"Coming into this steam bath of yours makes me shiver."

Irritated, Brunet looks at Moûlu, I should have thrown his coal out the window. Moûlu smiles innocently. Brunet hesitates, then simply says:

"Make him a cup of chocolate."

"There's no more chocolate," says Moûlu, apologizing, "you finished it a little while ago."

He's lying. Brunet shrugs his shoulders.

"Make him some bouillon, then."

Moûlu throws a couple cubes of Viandox into some boiling water. Brunet sits. Schneider shivers.

"They're taking Cognard down to the hospital," says Brunet.

"What's wrong with him?"

"Dysentery."

"Poor guy," says Schneider, "he's screwed."

Moûlu makes a face, and speaks up:

"Don't talk like that. Maybe it's his break, you know, maybe they'll send him home." Schneider chuckles wickedly.

"Yeah, right."

Brunet asks him, "You want to take his place?"

Schneider turns toward him:

"Well, just what was he doing?"

"Interpreter."

"I can do that."

"Good."

Brunet points out Cognard's bunk.

"You'll sleep here tonight."

"No," says Schneider.

"No?"

"I'll do the work, but I'd rather sleep back there."

"I don't see why." says Brunet. "It'd be a lot more convenient . . . "

He doesn't dare say: and you'd be warm here.

"I'm good back there," says Schneider.

I should have seen this coming. He's refusing to sleep here because here things aren't so bad, we're not freezing to death; always the same mania for shouldering burdens and refusing any advantages. *But these aren't* advantages: this barrack is my workplace. Brunet gets up, takes a shovelful of coal and throws it violently into the fire. Schneider drinks his bouillon, he's stopped shivering, without raising his voice, he points out:

"You're making it hot as Hell."

"Why not?"

"If we shared our coal with the rest of the barracks, everybody'd get three nuggets," says Moûlu briskly.

Schneider says nothing, he needs to be told off once and for all: this stubborn refusal to have anything more than what others have, it's not even Christian humility, its a pompous way to avoid responsibility. You're just an anarchist, one of these fucking intellectuals who lost us this war because you wouldn't become an officer.[3] Brunet shrugs his shoulders, stuffs his hands in his pockets, and holds his tongue; the warmth breeds a belated sleepiness behind his eyes. Suddenly the light dazzles him; the light bulb hanging from the ceiling has come on. Schneider blinks his eyes.

"Six o'clock!"

With a cry of joy, Moûlu pulls out his sewing box, he takes out a thimble, thread, a needle, he raises the needle to the light, squinting at the eye. Brunet leans over to the lamp and blows it out, blowing out his morning; now it's everyone's morning that's beginning.

The light sweeps the room, scouring and cleansing, crushing the sleep in the back of Brunet's head, sculpting Schneider's wrinkles and his fat heavy lips; the whole night has taken refuge in his eyes. Brunet looks at these sad eyes, and he wants to say "Why do you shut me out?" He stands and says:

"You can sleep where you want as long as you're here every morning at 5."

Schneider nods, Moûlu is busy sewing, pulling the needle, making small delicate precise movements.

"So, what are you sewing?" asks Schneider.

"Curtains for the window," says Moûlu. "It'll cheer the place up." Brunet puts on his coat.

"You can do that later. You're coming with me."

"Where?" asks Moûlu, disappointed.

"Black Square. To get my new guys."

Schneider has gotten up.

"Do you need an interpreter?"

"No," says Brunet.

He looks at this face, still pale from the cold, hesitates, then adds:

"But be sure to stay here. I'll need you when I get back."

Schneider gives him a big smile, almost conspiratorial. All of a sudden his eyes are clear and gay. Brunet looks at him, shakes his head; he thinks: strange friendship.

"Ok, let's go!"

He pushes Moûlu out in front of him. Outside they flounder in the mud, Moûlu moans,

"Oh man, we're gonna catch our death of cold."

"Think of the guys who are waiting down at Black Square."

"That's not gonna warm me up."

He trots along in the dark, puffing, whimpering. Suddenly he stops whimpering, sticks his nose in the air, and in a mysterious but excited voice he says:

"Schneider's wrong to not move in with us."

"Well, he likes his pals," says Brunet matter-of-factly.

Moûlu chuckles.

"That could be, but you know, his pals don't like him so much."

"Oh no?" says Brunet, surprised. "What do you know?"

"They say he overdoes it."

"No one ever overdoes it," says Brunet dryly.

"I'm telling you what they've told me. They say they don't know what he's thinking, and that he doesn't belong with them, because he's not one of yours."

"Well, they can come say it to me," says Brunet.

He's irritated for Schneider's sake, but not surprised really. It'd been going around that the guys don't like people who overdo it, martyrs scare people. Brunet speeds up. He'll wind up making himself hated, which will just complicate the work. He decides all of a sudden: no "ifs," "ands," or "buts," he'll sleep in our place tonight. I'll tell him it's an order.

"Hey, Brunet!"

Thibault steps out of his barracks, moonfaced and laughing. Brunet gives him a friendly smile: he gets his work done, even if he is a radical-socialist.

"Hey!"

Thibaut has stopped, his little eyes watering in his large flat face, suffocating from the cold:

"God! That stings! You going to Black Square?"

"I'm getting myself ten."

"Fifteen for me. What are these bastards thinking, doing this at this hour?"

They press on in silence, a vague yellow glow around them. One by one the barracks emerge from the fog as they go by. The camp is deserted; they glide between two rows of ghost ships. Suddenly the barracks disappear. No man's land, fog. They hustle through the dirty frost, their soles scraping on hard ground. Brunet stops to catch his breath. Shadows fidget. Brunet steps up, salutes Cosmet, Astruc, Rioul, other barracks leaders. They are lively and important in their English jackets; you'd think they were officers.

"So," asks Cosmet laughing, "Coming to the slave market?"

Brunet looks away without answering. A swarm of groans; he looks up. There are the slaves, four or five hundred of them, packed together like a pile of clothes and mud, the last rows of them fading in the fog. He takes a step toward them, their earthy faces all looking the same: the Species. He stares at them one after the other, he smiles at them with kindness, but their nocturnal eyes blink like they can't endure a human gaze any longer. Brunet rubs his hands; he'll make men of them. A loud voice comes from the speaker:

"Surrender your utility belts, your razors, your flashlights. Surrender your utility belts . . . "

Mayer, the toady, comes up; a little rat Brunet can't stand.

"Let's go, everyone take your lot."

Cosmet, facing the crowd, throws his hand in the air and rolls his intimidating eyes:

"On my command! The first fifteen to me!"

Thibaut leans over to Brunet's ear:

"What an asshole!"

A wave of earth, hair, and cloth rolls toward Cosmet, who steps back, screaming in an awful voice,

"I said *fifteen*!"

The wave breaks, and stops.

"In rows of three. Ahead. March."

He pirouettes and walks off without looking at them, fifteen men stumbling behind him. Mayer is getting impatient.

"Come on, the rest of you. We're freezing out here. Let's move it."

Astruc isn't finished making his picks; he passes slowly among the prisoners, examining them, taking the heftier ones by the collar, pulling them out of the rows, and behind him.

"Brunet!"

Brunet looks around, but doesn't see anyone.

"Brunet! Brunet!"

Astruc has just grabbed a big strong guy, blue from the cold, by the shoulder. The fellow frees himself with a blow and smiles at Brunet.

"Hey Brunet! Don't you recognize me?"

"Maurice!" says Brunet. "No joking!"

He touches Astruc on the arm:

"He's a friend."

"Take him," says Astruc courteously, "he's yours."

Brunet shakes Maurice, chuckling:

"Hey little man. Oh that's funny! Let me look at you! You've grown even more!"

"Hi," says Maurice, more serious. "Hey look, Chalais' here too."

"Chalais!" Brunet repeats the name, struck.

"Yes."

"Tell him to come too."

The cold bites. Brunet shivers, and scans the crowd for Chalais' thin silhouette.

"Second from the left, next row."

Brunet gleefully waves his hand, Chalais comes over, pale, red-nosed.

"Hi," says Brunet.

"Hello comrade," Chalais murmurs.

They smile at each other, a little embarrassed. Chalais' teeth are chattering.

"You're frozen," says Brunet.

Chalais shrugs his shoulders, his eyes hard and bleak.

"Not any more than the others are."

Not true. Chalais is always either colder or hotter than others. He doesn't take care of himself like he should.

"Come along with me; you'll warm up a little by walking." No reply from Chalais. Brunet turns back and calls out:

"Eight men with me; whoever wants."

Eight men step out of the rows. Brunet looks attentively at these eight indiscernible faces: for them suffering is not an expression, it's the constant background. I like that better.

"Have you eaten this morning?"

"Nothin.' Haven't had a thing since yesterday."

"Moûlu. Go ask Sevien to get us a bite, five loaves and five tins of sardines. Run!"

Moûlu trots off. Maurice and Brunet walk side by side. Chalais hesitates a second, hangs back a little. Brunet turns and sees he's coming along in the middle of the others, his thick short legs pumping underneath his long torso.

"I'm glad Chalais' here," declares Brunet.

Maurice smiles knowingly.

"You're right. He's an ace. You won't find two like him in the whole Party."

Brunet tilts his head, without replying; you bet, Chalais' an ace.

"Stop!"

Some German soldiers step forward: older men, from the National Guard, peaceful types. They count the prisoners, and a field marshal with a long grey mustache and girlish cheeks smiles at Brunet.

"Guten Morgen."

"Guten Morgen," Brunet replies.

Maurice taps his elbow.

"He speaks French?"

"No."

Maurice gives the field marshal a friendly smile:

"Good morning, you old cunt."

The field marshal smiles again, Maurice snickers.

"That's how we've got to treat them."

Brunet doesn't laugh. They start off, the day arrives. From windows and doorsteps guys yawn as they watch them pass by. Brunet knows them all, but this morning they seem foreign and distant to him. He salutes them with a touch of anxiety, the guys smile back, a bit surprised: inside the camp they don't salute each other. Chapelot, leaning out a window, calls out:

"Hey newbies!"

Maurice yells back:

"Go to hell, old farts!"

He turns to Brunet:

"And *pow*!"

He seems like a Parisian draftee making a crashing entrance into a provincial barracks. Brunet looks at him closely: he's toughened, and slimmed down, lost a little hair, gained some confidence.

"The last time I saw you was in Rue Royale," says Brunet.[4]

"Yeah," says Maurice, "in '38. Since then, we had some rough times; I wouldn't want to go through that again."

He points toward the barracks:

"Is that where you crash?"

"What do you expect?"

Maurice breaks out in laughter:

"That sucks."

"Well, what?" asks Brunet, irritated. "Were you better off back there?"

"In Soissons? We were in a brand new barracks. Some even slept in town."

Brunet whistles as if he's impressed, Maurice smiles at his memories, seeming impenetrable.

Brunet asks:

"So how's your wife doing?"

"It's going ok. She came to see me in Soissons; we had all the visitors we wanted."

Brunet lowers his voice:

"You had 'contacts'?"

"Not me. Chalais did. But," he says proudly, "Zézette got me two issues of *L'Huma*."

"Really!" says Brunet with interest. "It's back out?"[5]

"Since July"

Brunet repeats,

"Since July."

He almost feels sick.

"Every week?"

"Not every week, no. When they can." Then he adds, laughing, "But you know one of these days it's going to be back full force, and you'll be able to buy it at the kiosks, and everyone who thinks we're finished are going to shit themselves!"

"Back at full force? With the Krauts in Paris?"

"Why not?"

Brunet gives it up for the moment: even with the best there's going to be work to do; they've been in France too long, corrupted. Suddenly he thinks, so what's Chalais been telling them? He asks,

"You've got a copy of *L'Huma*?"

"No. Ask Chalais, he might. We tossed them so we wouldn't be caught with them."

"You didn't pass them around?"

"No."

"Why not?"

"Most of the guys don't think like we do."

"You have to work on the guys. Chalais wasn't working on them?"

"I don't know what Chalais' been working on," says Maurice dryly. Brunet looks at him, Maurice smiles.

"But what I can tell you is that it still was our good old *L'Huma*."

They walk in silence. Maurice is enjoying himself. His eyes run everywhere, noting everything, a smile of superiority curls his lip: the camp has a witness. Suddenly he stops: half-naked, leaning over a stone trough, twenty guys are washing quickly under a shelter. Maurice shakes his head, Brunet comes back and takes him by the arm.

"We don't have time to waste."

Maurice doesn't reply. Brunet looks at the guys getting washed, and suddenly he sees them: their bent shoulders, their skinny torsos, their puffed out stomachs, they look like old men. He turns toward Maurice with anger; it feels like someone's attacking his work. Maurice is colder than them, and his hands are trembling, but he looks glorious and hard like he's wearing a flag for May 1st, and he holds himself up straight. Brunet straightens himself up mechanically, buries his fingers in Maurice's biceps, and pulls him along: it's easy to show off when you've just had six months in France; in six months we'll see if you're doing any better than they. He says:

"You seem a bit full of yourself, pal."

"You bet!" says Maurice.

"Let's see if it lasts!"

"Why wouldn't it last?"

"You'll see," says Brunet gently. "Germany's not so much fun."

"Bah!" says Maurice, "we're not going to be staying."

Brunet raises his eyebrows, vexed. He whispers:

"You're planning to escape?"

Maurice looks at him with surprise.

"Me? Why bother, since they're going to let us go?"

Brunet starts, Maurice continues, excited.

"You'll see, comrade! You'll see, one of these days, Papa Stalin's going to be sending them word. He'll say, 'Quit fooling around, you guys. Make peace with France, make peace with England, and send the French workers home.'"

"And the Krauts will make peace?" asks Brunet.

"You bet."

"Just like that, all nice and everything? Just because they've been asked?"

"Oh," says Maurice, "you can count on it. The USSR is calling the shots at this point. The Krauts do whatever they want."

"How about that?" says Brunet. "I didn't even know!"

"Of course not," says Maurice indulgently, "because you've been cut off with no contacts for six months. It wasn't like that at first, but now they've got them."

"And why's that?"

"Good lord! Because they provide all their materials."

Brunet jumps:

"*What* materials?"

"A little of everything. Chalais can tell you about it better than me. I mean, if they stopped their supplies, the Jerries would have no choice but surrender."

"And how have you come to know all this?"

"Well," says Maurice, "it's in *L'Huma.*"

Brunet controls himself, he smiles at Maurice and rubs his hands together.

"So much the better," he says, "so much the better. That's really good news."

They've arrived. The sun's coming up, the day's beginning—fat and soft, full of water—and on this day, which is just like all the others, something is beginning to happen. Brunet's not feeling anger or fear, he looks at Maurice with an icy interest, then he turns to the others:

"Go on in!"

They go in, Brunet calls Lambert:

"Take these guys. Moûlu's getting them a bite to eat. I'll see them later."

He gestures to Maurice and Chalais:

"You two, follow me."

They walk behind him to the end of the hallway, Brunet stops, and before entering the doorway says:

"Everyone here is one of us."

They go in, the guys are putting on their coats; they are heading off to work.

"So, how was the Black Country?"

"Ok," say the guys, "it was interesting."

"It was instructive," says Benin, with a sort of fervor.

Brunet is touched, he turns proudly toward Chalais.

"They have discussions in the mornings; they share what they know."

Chalais has no response, but his teeth are chattering. Brunet adds, on his own: "We've got to get them some books."

He points to Chalais and Maurice:

"Here are a couple of new comrades, just in from France."

All heads turn in their direction with warm smiles. Brunet looks at his guys with satisfaction: with these guys Maurice will fit in. He smiles at them as well, with the fleeting impression that he's about to say good-bye; he puts his hand on Chalais' shoulder and pushes him forward, in a serious strong voice he says:

"This one, it's just like he's me."

The gazes turn from him to settle on Chalais. Brunet looks at these gazes that are no longer on him, he thought he had something else to add, but he forgot what it was. He turns on his heels and says to Chalais, over his shoulder:

"Come see me after you've eaten, we'll talk."

He leaves, he's thinking: something's going on; he speeds up, he wants to find Schneider; with all his faults, Schneider is still family. He pushes the door open: Schneider is there, bent over the stove. Brunet feels relieved.

"I'm back."

He enters and shivers, the warmth begins by caressing him, then rises abruptly to his face in a wave of blood. He takes off his cap and throws it on the bed, he's ashamed of being warm.

"So?" asks Schneider.

Brunet sits, the chair creaks. He sends a violent slap into Schneider's back.

"You old swindler! You old social traitor!"

He laughs. Schneider turns toward him and watches him laugh.

"What's happened? Something bad?"

Brunet stops laughing.

"No," he says, "everything's fine."

He stretches his legs toward the fire, breathes deeply, lights his pipe.

"This will be good."

"Huh?"

"My pipe. I bought it yesterday at the mess; it'll be good."

The pipe is good, and Schneider's good old mug, reddened by the fire, is good to see. He feels at home, at ease.

"I've found two comrades, a kid from Le Flaive, and Chalais."

Schneider raises his head, looks at Brunet with dead eyes, and distractedly repeats, "Chalais . . . Chalais . . . "

"Yeah," says Brunet. "His name doesn't mean anything to you: outside the Party no one knows him, but he's a serious contender. He was a deputy in '39, and they threw him in jail, and from there, sent straight to the front line."[6]

Schneider says nothing. Brunet continues:

"I'm pleased to have him here, very pleased. Deciding everything alone, it's ok, but . . . What to think of a free France at this point? I've told you how that preoccupies me. Well, he should know, he'll have had some contacts."

He stops himself. Schneider, blushing, his eyes half-closed, seems to be asleep. Brunet gives him a heel in the calf:

"Are you listening to me?"

"Yeah," says Schneider.

"Chalais' got lots of experience," says Brunet. "Not the kind I've got: he's a preacher's son, an intellectual. He's never had much to do with the base, and he's always been a bit of a puritan. But he's got his head on right. And he knows what he wants."

He stirs the bowl of his pipe and concludes:

"He'll be very valuable."

He stops. Schneider turns his head, like he hears sounds from outside.

"What's the matter with you?" demands Brunet with impatience.

Schneider smiles.

"If you want to know, I'm sleepy. The cold kept me from sleeping last night."

"After tonight, you sleep here," says Brunet with authority. "That's an order."

Schneider opens his mouth, someone's walking in the hallway, he closes it. A curious smile floats on his lips.

"Do you hear?" asks Brunet.

"We'll see tonight," says Schneider. "If you ask me again, I'll be glad to do it."

Footsteps approach, a knock. He stops, he seems to be waiting.

"Come in!"

It's Chalais. He stops on the threshold, looking at them.

"You're freezing us," says Brunet. "Close the door."

Chalais takes a step inside and stops. He looks at Schneider. He closes the door behind himself with his foot, without taking his eyes off him.

"This is Schneider, my interpreter," says Brunet. He turns to Schneider. "This is Chalais."

Schneider and Chalais look at each other. Schneider is still red. He gets up feebly, slowly. Sounding unsure, he says:

"I'm going to get going."

"Stay a bit," says Brunet. "You'll catch a cold from being too warm."

Schneider says nothing; Chalais, speaking precisely, says:

"I'd like to talk to you one on one."

Brunet knits his eyebrows, then gives a good-natured smile, raises his hand and lets it fall heavily on Schneider's shoulder. Schneider's expression remains dull and expressionless.

"This is my right-hand man," explains Brunet. "Everything I've done here, I've done with him."

Chalais remains perfectly still, he's not looking at anyone now, he's indifferent. Schneider slips out from beneath Brunet's hand and drags his feet to the door. The door closes behind him. For a good moment, Brunet stares at the lock, then turns to Chalais.

"You've hurt his feelings."

Chalais says nothing, Brunet's irritation begins:

"Look here, Chalais . . . " he says rudely.

Chalais raises his right hand, keeping his elbow against his body. Brunet stops, Chalais says:

"That's Vicarios."[7]

Brunet looks at him without understanding, Chalais speaks. His body is cold, but his commanding tribunal voice is not.

"That guy who just left is Vicarios."

"*What* Vicarios?" asks Brunet.

But he's already guessed the answer. Chalais replies without raising his voice:

"The Vicarios that was kicked out of the Party in '39."

"This guy's name is Schneider," says Brunet feebly.

In a single cramped, mechanical gesture he raises his forearm and brings his open palm toward Brunet.

"Take it easy. He recognized me, and he knows I recognized him."

Brunet repeats:

"Vicarios!"

The name bounces around in his head, he thinks: that name means something to me. Painfully he says:

"I didn't know he was Vicarios."

"Of course not," says Chalais.

Brunet thinks he picks up a whiff of condescension in this voice, and quickly raises his head. But Chalais's eyes are dull, he hugs himself and tucks his neck into his shoulders: you'd think he was pulling his body together in order to better control it. Quietly Brunet asks:

"Vicarios was a journalist, right?"

"Hold on!" says Chalais.

Quickly he's across the room and up against the stove. He looks humiliated.

"I can't get myself warmed up again."

Brunet waits: he's not cold, he feels heavy and strong, master of himself and of his body. He waits, he has all the time in the world to wait, he smiles patiently at Chalais, all he's got now is infinite patience. Chalais pulls a chair over and sits down. His voice comes back fitfully.

"Didn't you receive the warning from the Party last winter?"

"About Vicarios?"

"Yeah."

"I think I did," says Brunet slowly. "But I was a soldier, and since there wasn't anyone named Vicarios in the regiment . . . "

"He was editor-in-chief of a paper in Oran," says Chalais. "The paper wasn't really a Party paper, but sympathetic. Vicarios, though, was a member; his wife too. He quit in September '39."

"The Pact?"

"Of course. He published his resignation in his paper, then three editorials against us, and then he joined up. Or he was drafted. I don't remember which."

"No kidding!" says Brunet.

He feels like he's just heard about a death. Chalais is going on, and the life of the late Schneider is being settled. Dying, quitting the Party—same thing.

"No kidding."

He repeats: "no kidding"; he thinks: something is going on.

"Since then," says Chalais, "we know he's been making reports to the Algiers general office. Our guys in Algiers have the proof."

Brunet lets himself fall into a chair and laughs with all his heart. Chalais looks at him.

"I'm laughing," explains Brunet, "because just this morning I learned that my guys can't stand him."

Chalais gravely nods his head.

"The base is never wrong."

Brunet thinks: what do you know about the base? He says:

"Yeah, for this kind of thing, they catch the scent."

Chalais warms himself. Brunet thinks: so Schneider was a spy. That stings. He half closes his eyes, he clenches his teeth, he looks at Chalais' homely face through his eyelids, he thinks: this one here's my friend. He feels quite calm: it's not really unpleasant, but it stings. Every time you discover a good reason for thinking people are bastards and that life's not worth living, it feels good at first. He looks at Chalais: for now we're going to be living together, in this camp, for months and years, day after day.

It stings. Chalais examines him with curiosity and asks:

"What do you think you'll do?"

Confused, Brunet chews on his lip. *Is there something to do?* For a second he feels soft and lazy, then suddenly, anger consumes him.

"You want to know?" he stammers. "You want to know?"

He controls himself, and replies dryly:

"I'm going to throw him the fuck out, that's what I'm going to do. And right away!"

Chalais seems cold and perplexed. He murmurs:

"That's risky."

"What's risky is to keep him in the barracks."

"He already knows you're in the Party?"

Brunet turns away, his anger recedes.

"He spotted that on the first day."

"And the comrades? Does he know they are too?"

"Sure."

"Too bad!" says Chalais.

Brunet explains, animated:

"Had to be that way. He's helped me a lot in my work."

"What sort of work were you doing?" asks Chalais nonchalantly.

Brunet knits his brow:

"We'll talk about it later."

"At any rate," says Chalais, "since he's known for so long, you have to expect the worse. If you throw him out like a turd, he'll turn us in."

Brunet shrugs his shoulders:

"No way. He's not that kind of guy."

Chalais says impatiently:

"But I tell you, he was sending reports to the government."

"Right," says Brunet. "Right, of course. But I know him: he's not that kind of guy."

Slowly, like he's talking to himself, Chalais says:

"I was wondering if it wouldn't be smarter to keep him here. We can tell him we have no intention of bringing up his denunciation, and that we're not qualified for that anyway, but that in the present circumstances . . . "

Brunet laughs:

"He's not crazy. If he was with us for ten years he's not going to start thinking the Party ever forgives: if we keep him, he'll think we're afraid of him."

"Not necessarily," says Chalais. "We can . . . "

Anger overcomes Brunet again. His hands tremble, he burns, he cries out:

"That's enough! I can't breathe the same air as this fucker for another five minutes. He tricked me, and he won't do it again."

"It's your call," says Chalais.

Brunet adds, laboriously:

"I'll send him to Thibaut, who's in charge of the barracks. A good guy, he can keep his mouth shut."

They sit in silence, Brunet calms down bit by bit, he barely understands what has just happened to him. Words without sense float around in his head; when he thinks of Schneider, he wants to smash something. Shady stuff like this drives him crazy.

"Ok," says Chalais. "Call Vicarios, let's fill him in on our decision. You'll tell him that we'll let him off easy, but there'll be trouble if we catch him prowling around the Kommandantur."

A brief silence.

"Call him!" repeats Chalais. "I'm sure he hasn't gotten very far."

Brunet doesn't budge. Chalais frowns.

"What are you waiting for?"

"For you to leave."

Chalais gets up ungraciously. Sure, thinks Brunet. You're going to miss that stove.

Chalais has put his hand on the doorknob. Brunet suddenly says:

"Don't say anything to the guys."

Chalais turns around, surprised.

"Why?"

"Because. He . . . he liked them. There's nothing to be gained by pushing a guy to the edge . . . "

Chalais hesitates:

"There was a warning."

"I'm asking you to not say anything to the others," says Brunet without raising his voice.

Chalais shrugs his shoulders.

"Gotcha."

He leaves, Brunet leaves after him, positions himself on the threshold of the barracks, and looks around for Schneider. He spots him, leaning against the wall of 28. They look at each other, Brunet makes a half turn and goes back inside leaving the door open. Schneider is there almost immediately, stamps his feet against the floor to knock off the snow, enters and closes the door. Brunet sits himself down, without looking at him. He hears a chair creak. Schneider has sat down. Brunet looks up: Schneider is sitting next to him, like everyday, with his good old round mug; nothing has happened.

"I saw that guy in Oran," says Schneider calmly.

"You didn't tell me you were from Oran," Brunet points out.

"No, I didn't tell you that."

"You're Vicarios?"

"Yes."

Vicarios is seated in front of Brunet, speaking. Brunet only sees Schneider.

"But I must have met you somewhere," says Brunet. "Those first times, at Baccarat, I said to myself, I know that face."

"We met in '32," says Schneider, "at the Party Congress. I recognized you right away."

"At the Congress! That's it!"

He looks inquisitively at these heavy features, this large pendulous nose; in Vicarios' place, he tries to find once again the Schneider of June 1940, the vaguely familiar, ambiguous stranger that he could still hate. But Schneider had become Schneider *completely*. Brunet lowers his eyes, he speaks looking at the floor.

"I'm going to sign you up over in Thibaut's barracks. You can take your things there after supper."

"Ok."

"We won't say anything to the guys."

"Ok," says Schneider. "Thanks."

He gets up, he's going to go, he takes a step toward the door and Brunet puts out his hand, his mouth opens in spite of himself, a huge voice comes from it, a voice that isn't his:

"Why did you lie to me?"

Schneider looks at him with surprise, Brunet sits up straight, he's as surprised as Schneider. Firmly, he corrects himself:

"Why did you lie to *us*?"

"Because I know you," says Schneider.

He's cold, like Chalais was, but it's not the same cold. He retraces his steps, reaching his good old big hands toward the stove. Brunet looks at Schneider's good old big hands in silence. After a minute, Brunet asks:

"Why did you have to go gluing yourself to us after you'd already quit the Party?"

"I was sick of being alone," says Schneider.

Brunet looks at him attentively.

"No other reason?"

"None."

He takes a few steps around the room, seeming dazed, he adds, as if for himself:

"Of course, I didn't think it would be able to last."

He awakens himself abruptly, raises his head and smiles at Brunet:

"I'm glad that we're able to end this in a proper way," he says.

Brunet does not reply. Schneider waits, smiling, then his smile fades and, without emotion he says:

"Goodbye Brunet. We did some good work together."

He makes an about-face; he's leaving, we will never see each other again, the blood rises in Brunet's face, anger makes him see red. In a low, rapid voice he says:

"What a bunch of crap. You were spying on us."

He'd fired this at Schneider's back, Schneider turns and looks at him. Brunet fidgets on his chair; he's looking for his anger, but not finding it anymore. Softly Schneider says:

"Is this really necessary?"

Brunet does not reply. Schneider adds:

"I'm heading over to Thibaut's. I'll do my best to get by, and you know that I won't do anything to hurt you."

There had been a warning. Brunet looks Schneider in the eyes and calmly says:

"You were being paid by the government."

Schneider looks at him, astounded, almost laughing.

"Who told you that? Chalais?"

"You were the subject of a warning that I myself read last winter," says Brunet.

"I wasn't aware."

A long silence. Schneider is pale. At this moment, he is Vicarios, irreparably. Brunet finds that anger again, and with anger he watches the suffering on Vicarios' face, a suffering that flows like blood, and that makes him want to make him bleed even more.

"So what did your warning have to say?" asks Vicarios.

"That you were a traitor. Comrades in Algiers have the proof."

Vicarios throws himself forward, Brunet thinks he's going to strike, and jumps up, fists ready. Vicarios doesn't strike. He's right up against Brunet, so they're in each other's face. Vicarios' eyes are sightless, they are two beckoning mouths. Brunet is dizzy, he throws his head back, from Vicarios's bad breath.

"Brunet! You can't believe this!"

Brunet doesn't know if it was Vicarios' mouth or eyes that spoke. He wants to shut away all the mouths that beg forgiveness, in a single stroke. He says:

"I believe what the Party says."

Vicarios straightens up. His eyes are black and hard in his chalky face, but now they *see*. Brunet takes a step backwards, but he forces himself to repeat himself *before these eyes:*

"I believe what the Party says."

Vicarios looks at him a long time, then he turns away and heads for the door. May as well go all the way: it serves a purpose. Brunet yells at his back:

"If you talk to the Krauts, there'll be trouble."

Vicarios turns around, for the last time Brunet sees Schneider.

"My poor Brunet!" says Schneider.

The door closes: it's over. The stove's out, thinks Brunet. I'll catch my death of cold. For a moment he looks at the box of charcoal, then he turns away and leaves. Too bad for you, all you had to do was not lie. At the end of the hall he stops, opens the door. Chalais is sitting on the bench. Toussus, Bénin, and Lamprecht are bent over him, all talking at once; over by the window, Maurice, arms crossed, is put out. When Brunet enters the room, everybody stops.

"So you're not working today?" asks Brunet.

"The Field marshal is sick," Toussus explains. "They sent us back to the barracks."

"Good," says Brunet. "Good, that's good."

Angrily, he adds:

"Make a fire, for Christ's sake!"

Chalais looks at him attentively. Brunet says:

"Come along, let's have a chat."

Chalais gets up without a word. In the hall, Brunet says:

"It's taken care of."

"I can see that," says Chalais.

They walk in silence, then Chalais asks:

"He'll behave himself?"

Brunet breaks out laughing:

"Like an angel."

They go into Brunet's place, where the fire has died and is out for good. Chalais seems disappointed, he pulls his collar up, puts his hands in his pockets and sits down. Brunet looks at the cold stove and almost laughs.

"You know I've had some contacts?" says Chalais after a minute.

Brunet starts, and looks at Chalais intensely:

"Serious ones, frequent?"

Chalais smiles:

"I think you know Buchner personally, don't you?"

"You bet."

"Last time I saw him was Monday."

Brunet continues looking at Chalais, but no longer sees him.

"What's the Party's position?" he asks.

"It's ok," says Chalais. "In the beginning there were mistakes: Soviet radio asked our activists to not leave the Paris area, but most of the guys had an old fashioned patriotic reflex: and they left anyway because they couldn't stand being co-opted by the enemy. As a result, *L'Humanit*é could have come out before the Germans arrived—the copy was ready, but nothing happened because the workers weren't there. Today, the guys are on the job, it's all set."

Brunet listens with a mix of respect and boredom: he's disappointed. He has questions he'd like to ask, but he can't bring himself to formulate them. He says:

"Between the arrests and the exodus, there must have been quite a change in personnel. Who's on the Central Committee these days?"

Chalais's smile is thin.

"To tell you the truth, I don't have any idea. Probably Gromaire, that's about all I can say. Times have changed, old pal: the less you know, the better it is."

"I see," says Brunet.

It wrings his heart. Without knowing why, Chalais clears his throat, then raises his head and looks at Brunet a minute.

"So this guy Bénin," he asks, "is he one of us?"

"Yep."

"And Toussus, and Lamprecht?"

"Oh sure."

"Where are they from?"

"Hold on a second," says Brunet.

He thinks a second, then says:

"Bénin's a designer from Gnome et Rhône. Lamprecht is at the city slaughterhouse in Nantes, and Toussus's a locksmith in Bergerac. Why?"

"I was surprised by them," says Chalais.

Brunet raises his eyebrows. Chalais gives him a kindly smile:

"They're a bit worked up, don't you think?"

"Worked up?" repeats Brunet. "Not particularly."

Chalais starts to laugh:

"Toussus talks like there's a cache of arms under the barracks; he wants to take the camp by storm when the Soviet troops enter Germany."

Brunet laughs as well:

"He's from Gascogne," he says.

Chalais stops laughing. In a neutral voice, he points out:

"The others all seem to agree with him."

Brunet gets out his new pipe and fills it.

"Maybe they are a bit excited," he says, "I have to admit that I don't keep track of all that. But in any case, it can't do them any harm; it helps them pass the time."

Without raising his eyes, in a heavy voice that he doesn't even recognize, he adds:

"They know that they're fucked if they give up, so they live on edge; they have nothing but time to spend, all their reactions are exaggerated. You know, Chalais, the oldest one of them is barely 25."

"I noticed that," says Chalais. "You all seem under a lot of strain."

With a little laugh, he adds:

"They told me some good ones."

"For example?"

"The war isn't over, the USSR will crush Germany, the workers have the right to reject any armistice, the defeat of the Axis will be a victory for the proletariat."

He stops, to watch Brunet's reaction. Brunet says nothing. Forcing his smile a bit, Chalais adds:

"One of them even asked me if the workers in Paris had gone on strike, and if they were shooting at the Germans in the streets of Paris."

Brunet continues to say nothing. Chalais leans toward him, and asks him quietly:

"Are you the one who's put these ideas in their heads?"

"Not in quite that form," says Brunet.

"That form or another, but it's you?"

Brunet lights his pipe. Something is going on.

"Yes," he says. "It's me."

They sit quietly. Brunet smokes his pipe, Chalais reflects. A sad yellow light comes in from the window: it's going to rain, for sure. Brunet glances at his watch and thinks: It's only eight thirty. He gets up suddenly:

"I'll have to explain all that to you," he says. "Did they say anything about our organization?"

"Just a word or two," says Chalais, distracted. "Is that your doing?"

"Yeah."

"On your own initiative?"

Brunet shrugs his shoulders and starts pacing.

"Naturally," he says. "You know, I didn't have any contacts."

He paces, Chalais' eyes follow him.

"It was quite a current to swim against, I'll tell you," he continues. "The guys were at a total loss; the Nazis and the priests were doing whatever they wanted with them. Do you know there's even a Franciste Party in here, officially recognized and patronized by the Jerries? So I used desperate measures."

"What measures?" asks Chalais.

"There are four factors that matter," says Brunet. "Hunger, being transferred into Germany, forced labor, and patriotic reaction. I've made use of them all."

"Of all of them?" repeats Chalais.

"Yes, all of them. The danger of death was real, and I couldn't pretend it wasn't. Furthermore, my job was clearly defined by the circumstances: all I had to do was transform their unhappiness."

"On what basis?"

Brunet puts his palm up against the wall, quickly turns and walks to the opposite wall:

"I gave them the ideological basics," he says. "Oh, just the beginnings, an A,B,C: sovereignty comes from the people, Petain is usurping our power, his government had no right to sign the armistice. The war isn't over, the USSR will get involved sooner or later; all prisoners should consider themselves soldiers."

Suddenly he stops. Chalais asks:

"So is that what you were calling your work?"

"Yeah, that's it," says Brunet.

Chalais shakes his head. Sadly.

"Of course."

He looks at Brunet and smiles at him openly:

"There are times when you'd just die if you weren't trying to accomplish *something*, no matter what, right? Anything at all. And since you had no resources, you were flying blind."

"That's enough," says Brunet. "Take it easy."

His voice is hard, he doesn't know if he's talking to Chalais or to the Party, he asks:

"So, in two words, what did I do wrong?"

In an even harder voice, the Party replies:

"It has to all be taken back, old man. You were completely off the mark."[8]

Brunet shuts up. Chalais leans over and taps on the stove helplessly.

"It's out."

Brunet taps on it as well.

"Yeah," he says. "It's out."

"Have you heard talk about Gaullism in these parts?"

Brunet thinks: as much as you. He's about to say: we have a listening post. He stops himself.

"Vaguely," he says.

"De Gaulle," Chalais says, in his worst didactic voice, "is a French general who got out of Bordeaux at the last minute, taking the political insiders and freemason leadership with him."

"Ok," says Brunet.

"They're all in London today. Churchill provides radio time for them, and they attack the Germans everyday at the mike. Of course, it's the London stock exchange that's footing the bill."

"And?"

"And? Do you know what they are saying?"

"That the war isn't over yet, I guess."

"That's right, and that it's going to spread to the whole planet, which is a clever way to bring the USA and USSR into the mix. They're saying France has only lost a battle, that the Vichy government is illegitimate, and that the armistice was an act of treason."

Brunet shrugs his shoulders, Chalais smiles:

"They don't go so far as to talk of the sovereignty of the people, no. But that will come one of these days, when his Majesty's government finds it necessary for its propaganda."

"I can't say I'm moved," says Brunet.

He puts his hands together, cracks his knuckles, and continues calmly.

"I'm not impressed. I told you my program here was an A, B,C. Later, we'll move ahead. There are guys, here in this barracks, who I will bring into the Communist Party by the hand. But there's no rush; we're here for a long haul. As for your little friends over in London, well, what do you want? Coincidences are inevitable. The English are fighting the Axis to protect their interests, we're fighting Hilter because we're anti-fascists. So what if for the moment we have the same enemy; so it's not surprising if we sometimes say the same things."

He looks at Chalais and starts to laugh as though he was about to tell him a whopper, but his throat is tight:

"Until new orders say otherwise, I'm thinking that antifascism is not a deviation from the Party line."

"No," says Chalais, "that hasn't become any sort of deviation. We're against fascism in all its forms, like we've always been. But you'd be wrong to conclude from that that we'll be aligning ourselves with the bourgeois democracies."

"I never thought that," protests Brunet.

"What you think hardly matters. Objectively, you're a streetwalker for Churchill's valets."

Brunet leaps up. He says: "Me?"

He calms himself, he smiles, he sees that he's closed his hands into fists, he opens his hands and lays them flat on his knees. He says:

"I'd be surprised."

"Suppose," says Chalais, "that the guys you've indoctrinated are freed. They return to France, they don't recognize anyone or anything, Vichy propaganda makes them want to puke. Where are they going to go?"

"Oh for Christ's sake . . . " says Brunet.

Chalais' eyes burn into him:

"Where will they go?"

"Well," says Brunet bitterly, "up till now I'd always figured they'd come into the Party."

Chalais smiles, and continues calmly:

"They'll throw themselves headfirst into Gaullism, they'll risk their lives in an imperialist war that has nothing to do with them, and it'll be on the basis of your authority, Brunet, that they'll have fallen for this mystification."

His gaze dies, Chalais tries to smile, but his face won't obey him anymore. From this violet mask and reddened nose, all that comes forth is a warm and persuasive voice:

"This isn't the time, Brunet. We've won, our worst enemy is on his knees . . . "

"Our worst enemy," repeats Brunet, uncomprehending.

"Our worst enemy, yes," says Chalais forcefully. "The imperialism of our French generals and of two hundred some families."

"So *that's* our worst enemy?" asks Brunet.

He clenches his hands on his knees, in a neutral voice he manages to say:

"The Party has changed its position."

Chalais looks at him attentively.

"And when it does? What will you do?"

Brunet shrugs his shoulders:

"I'm just asking you if it has changed its position?"

"The Party has not moved one centimeter," says Chalais. "In '39 it took a stand against the war, and you know what that cost us. But you agreed, Brunet, and the Party was right. It was right because it expressed the basic pacifism of the people, communists or not. Today all we have to do is reap the benefits of that stance: ours is the only organization that can make itself the spokesperson for the masses of workers' wish for peace. Where is the change? While you, all this time, are playing on your comrades' nationalism, and expecting us to commit to a policy of war. It's not the Party that's changed, Brunet, it's you."

Brunet listens, fascinated by this loud-speaker voice: it's the voice of no one, it's the voice of the historical process, the voice of truth.[9] Fortunately, Chalais's eyes begin to water. Brunet jumps up and asks dryly:

"Is this your opinion that you're sharing with me, or is this the Party's current policy?"

"I never have opinions," says Chalais, "I'm giving you the Party line."

"Good," says Brunet, "so go ahead, I'm listening, but no commentaries, we're wasting time."

"I'm not adding commentaries," says Chalais, surprised.

"That's all you're doing. You say: in '39 the CP expressed the pacifism of the masses. That's an *opinion*, Chalais, nothing but an opinion. Some of us in the Party know that in September, the reversal was 180 degrees, and that we very nearly blew it. Some of us have learned, at our own expense, that the masses weren't particularly pacifist at that point in time."

He raises his forearm and hand like Chalais, he smiles like Chalais, tight and precise.

"I know you've never had much contact with the base, that wasn't your business, and I used to see how you'd speak rather romantically of 'the base'. But I—I had tons of contacts, that was my job, I worked in the thick of it, and I can tell you that the guys were not pacifists to start with: they were anti-Nazi in the first place. They hadn't digested what happened in Ethiopia, or in Spain, or in Munich. If they stayed with us in '39, it's because we told them that the USSR needed time, and that it would enter the war as soon as it was armed and ready."

Chalais returns his smile. Brunet has not even managed to make him mad.

"The USSR will never enter this war," Chalais simply says.

"That's your *opinion*!" cries Brunet, "That's your *opinion!*"

He calms himself, and adds, laughing:

"I happen to have the opposite opinion."

"*You*?" says Chalais. "*You, me* . . . what do we have to do with it?"

He looks at Brunet with crushing surprise, like he's seeing him for the first time. After a minute, he continues:

"I don't get the feeling you care much for me . . . "

"Oh drop that," says Brunet, irritated.

"Oh, I say it to remind you. It's not going to keep me from sleeping at night. But make no mistake, this is not a matter of a difference of opinions. I've had contacts, and you haven't, and I'm filling you in, and that's it. Neither of us as a person makes any difference. And we will do absolutely no good if we let ourselves get caught up in issues of individuality."

"That's exactly what I think too," says Brunet dryly.

He looks at Chalais, trying to not see him; he thinks: his individuality is not what matters. It is not Chalais the individual who is looking and judging; Chalais the individual doesn't judge, doesn't think, doesn't see. Mustn't make this about the individual, mustn't make this about pride. He says:

"So, the USSR won't join the war. Why not?"

"Because it needs peace. Because for twenty years, being at peace has been the number one objective of its foreign policy."

"Yes," says Brunet, bored. "I've heard that one before in the July 14 speeches."

He laughs. "Maintain the peace! What peace? There's fighting from Norway all the way to Ethiopia."

"Exactly," says Chalais. "The USSR will stay out of the conflict and do everything it can to make sure it doesn't spread."

"How do you know?," says Brunet ironically. "Is Stalin keeping you up to date?"

"Stalin, no," says Chalais calmly. "Molotov."

Brunet looks at him, opens his mouth, then stops. Chalais continues:

"On August 1, before the Supreme Soviet, Molotov affirmed that the USSR and Germany have the same fundamental interests, and that the German-Soviet pact is based on this common interest."[10]

"Ok," says Brunet. "Sure, sure, and then?"

"In November, he visited Berlin, and received an enthusiastic welcome. He denounced the efforts of the British and Allied press; he said—this is just about a quote: 'The bourgeois democracies are putting their last hope in the supposed differences that separate us from Germany. They will see soon enough that such differences only exist in their imagination.'"

"Bah!" says Brunet. "He must have been forced to say that."

"Three weeks ago," says Chalais, "the USSR and Germany signed a commercial agreement. The USSR will provide 2.5 million tons of wheat, 1.5 million tons of fuel oil, lubricants, gasoline."

"A commercial treaty," repeats Brunet.

"Yes."

"Ok," says Brunet. "I see."

He gets up, he goes to the window, he puts his forehead against the frozen pane, he watches the first drops of rain falling. He says:

"I didn't . . . "

"Excuse me?" asks Chalais behind him.

"Nothing. I was wrong, that's all."

He turns around, sits back down, taps the bowl of his pipe against his heel to knock out the ashes.

"If you look at the situation concretely," says Chalais cordially, "you'll see that it is just not in the interests of the French workers for the USSR to get involved in the conflict."

"The French workers," says Brunet, "are right here in this camp. Or in others just like it. And those who aren't are doing forced labor for the Krauts."

"Exactly," says Chalais. "And that's why the USSR has to pursue its own agenda independently. Quite simply, it is on its way to becoming the decisive factor in European diplomacy. At the end of the war, the other nations will be exhausted, and the USSR will dictate the peace agreement."

"Ok," says Brunet. "Ok, ok."

Chalais is no longer shivering: he's gotten up, he walks briskly around his chair, his hands come out of his pockets and he opens them over his head. Brunet is leaning over, picking up a stick of wood to clean out his pipe, he's cold to his bones, but it doesn't matter. Cold and hunger don't matter anymore.

"Given that," says Chalais, "what should the French working class call for?"

"Good question," says Brunet without raising his head.

Chalais' voice rolls on above the nape of his neck, now closer, now further off, Chalais' shoes creak slightly.

"The French workers, he says, should call for four things: A) an immediate peace treaty, B) a Franco-Soviet non-aggression pact, on the German-Soviet model, C) a trade agreement with the USSR to protect the proletariat from famine, and D) a general settling of the European situation with the USSR's full participation."

"And domestically?" asks Brunet.

"In all ways and by all means, re-establish the legal standing of the Party, and authorize the publication of *L'Humanité*."

"The Nazis would allow *L'Huma* to come back?" asks Brunet, dumbfounded.

"They're treating us with kid gloves," says Chalais.

Casually, he adds:

"And what else can they do? The political parties are disbanded, the leaders have flown the coop."

"They can encourage a fascist movement."

"They can try. And to be honest, they are trying. But they're not crazy, they know it's never going to take with the masses of people. No, the only organization that came out against the war, the only one that defended the German-Soviet pact, the only one that the masses still trust, is ours, and you can be sure that the Germans know it."

"You mean they're reaching out to us?"

"Not yet. But the fact is that their press does not attack us, and you can bet they signed secret agreements with the USSR about European communist parties."

He leans over Brunet, he's speaking to him in confidence:

"Our party has to be both legal and illegal at the same time—that defines its structure and its action. Circumstances have forced us to be semi-clandestine; we'd brought together the advantages of being both legal and illegal, but now all we've got are the problems of being both: when we lose our status as the officially recognized Party, we lose the possibility of making our claims heard publicly or of holding, as communists, key positions. But at the same time, we're too well known: Party officials are followed, the enemy has lists, addresses, it knows our tactics. We've got to change this as soon as possible. But how? By pissing off the Germans? By writing 'Kill the Krauts' in public bathrooms?"

Brunet shrugs his shoulders, Chalais lifts his hand to keep him silent:

"Sure we can organize riots, outbreaks, and strikes, but whose interest is served by that? English Imperialism's. And not for long either, since England's virtually beaten. But if we become a legal party, with a program and responsibilities, we can proclaim a popular government seated in Paris, and go after those who instigated this war. Then and only then should we consider the question of new illegal action, better adapted to the new circumstances."

"And you imagine that the Germans . . . ?"

Chalais interrupts him maliciously: "You know *The People's Voice*? The Belgian CP's paper?"

"I know it," says Brunet.

Chalais takes a minute, smiles, and in a detached tone adds:

"*The People's Voice* has been back on the streets since June."

Brunet sinks in his chair, slides his hand in his pocket, and closes it on the bowl of his pipe since it's still warm. He says:

"So *here*, what should we be doing?"

"Just the opposite of what you're doing."

"Meaning?"

"Attacking the imperialism of the bourgeois democracies, attacking de Gaulle and Petain, affirming the working masses' wish for peace."

"And vis-à-vis the Germans?"

"Wait and see."

"Ok," says Brunet.

Chalais rubs his hands together. He's done good work, and he's pleased.

"Now the two of us," he says, "are going to divide up the work. The comrades have to be brought in line a little at a time, but it would be better if you aren't the one to do it: I'll see to them. You'll take care of those who aren't in the Party."

"And what is it that I should do?"

Chalais looks at Brunet attentively, but doesn't seem to see him: he's thinking.

"For the moment," he says, "your little organization is more dangerous than it is useful. But it's not a bad thing that it exists, it will be useful one of these days. The best thing would be to put it on ice rather than kill it off. Only you can handle that."

"Poor guys," says Brunet.

"Huh?"

"I said poor guys," says Brunet.

Chalais looks at him surprised:

"So who are these guys anyway?"

"Some are radicals," says Brunet. "Some are socialists . . . Then there are some who aren't part of any party."

Chalais shrugs his shoulders. "Radicals!" he says with contempt.

"They're good workers," says Brunet. "And, you know, life's hard here, if you don't have hope anymore."

He stops. He recognized the foreign voice that was speaking through his mouth, the voice of a traitor. It was saying: "Don't go acting like you're Dr. Death." It was saying, "Poor guys, they've got death in the soul."

"They're fucked anyway," says Chalais. "Just let 'em die."

He smirks:

"Radicals! I prefer the Nazis. They're dogs, but at least they've got a social sense."

Brunet thinks of Thibaut. He can see his big smiling mouth, he thinks: He's fucked, he's worth less than a Nazi, he doesn't have a social sense. He thinks: We used to have a radio. He starts to tremble. He thinks: *Our* radio. He gets up; he walks; they're standing face to face. He says:

"It all fits."

"You're telling me," says Chalais, rudely cordial. "You bet it all fits."

"Everything always does," says Brunet. "It can be proved."

"You want proof?"

Chalais reaches into his inside coat pocket. He produces a soiled and rumpled newspaper:

"Here!"

Brunet takes the paper: it's *L'Huma*. He reads: issue 95, December 30, 1940. The sheet is so worn that it tears halfway when he unfolds it. He tries to read the editorial, he can't. He thinks: It's *L'Huma*. He runs his hands like a blind man over the characters in the banner and the head-line. It's *L'Huma*, I used to write for it. Carefully, he refolds the page and gives it back to Chalais:

"It's ok."

He'll leave and go find Schneider, he'll say to him "You told me so." The bubble bursts: Schneider is gone, there's only Vicarios, the spy. The light fades before his eyes, he takes a slap on the shoulder and jumps. It's Chalais: Chalais' mouth flashes a childish smile, his hand comes back with mechanical precision, and falls at his side.

"So there it is!" says Chalais. "So there it is, old pal."

"There it is," says Brunet.

They look each other in the eyes, they nod their heads and smile. In '39 he was afraid of me.

"I better go speak with Thibaut," says Brunet. "You can stay here." Chalais shakes his head, his features are fading, in a childlike voice he says:

"I think I'd rather roll myself up in a blanket and stretch out on my bed."

"Blankets are behind the stove," says Brunet. "Take two. I'll see you later."

He goes out into the rain. He runs to warm himself. The fog gets inside his head, there's no inside or outside anymore, nothing but fog. Thibaut is alone, there's a card game on the table.

"You're playing solitaire?"

"No, I was listening to the radio. I leave the cards on the table in case someone comes in."

He smiles maliciously: there must be some news, he waits for Brunet to ask him. Brunet doesn't ask: he's not interested in British Imperial-ism's victories. He says:

"Do you still have some space in your henhouse?"

"In with the Dutch guys, sure," says Thibaut.

"I'm going to send you up one of my guys. Quietly."

Thibaut's eyes shine.

"Who's that?"

"Schneider."

"He's having problems?" asks Thibaut. "Are the Germans looking for him?"

"No," says Brunet, "not for the moment."

"I see," says Thibaut. He shakes his head. "He'll be bored as Hell, these Dutch guys don't speak a word of French."

"Just as well."

"Well, he can come whenever he's ready."

"Is it warm in there, where the Dutch are?" asks Brunet.

"It's a furnace. One of them's a mess cook, they have all the charcoal they want."

"Perfect," says Brunet. "Oh well, I'm off."

He doesn't go. He's put his hand on the door handle and he's looking at Thibaut the way you look at a town you have to leave. Already, he has nothing more to say to him. A radical, already fucked . . . Thibaut smiles at him confidently; Brunet can't stand this smile: he opens the door and goes out. Outside the rain is falling heavily, he can barely make out the barracks. Brunet slogs through the mud and the melted snow. The guys in 39 have left a bench outside, someone is sitting on the bench, head lowered, the rain trickling down his hair and his neck. Brunet comes up:

"Are you nuts?"

The fellow raises his head: it's Vicarios. Brunet says:

"Thibaut's expecting you."

Vicarios doesn't reply. Brunet sits down next to him. They sit in silence, Vicarios' knee touching Brunet's knee. Time flows, the rain flows, time and the rain, it's all the same. After a minute Vicarios gets up and goes off. Brunet stays there alone, head lowered, the rain trickling down his hair and his neck.

2. SECOND SECTION

Brunet yawns: noon, two hours to kill. He stretches, and his strength stifles him; I must be dying. Starting tomorrow, gymnastics till I can't do it anymore. Someone knocks, he gets up: a visit always helps pass a little time.

"Come in."

It's just Thibaut. He comes in and says:

"You're alone?"

"As you can see," says Brunet.

"I see it, but I don't believe my eyes. Chalais' not here?"

"At the Dentist's," says Brunet yawning.

Thibaut chuckles.

"She's always got something wrong, this little miss."

He takes a chair, pushes it against Brunet's chair, sits.

"You two never leave each other's company."

"I need him here all the time," explains Brunet. "He's my interpreter."

"Wasn't Schneider the interpreter before that?"

"Well, yes, it was Schneider."

Thibaut shrugs his shoulders:

"You're like a pretty girl with her crushes. Last month, it was all about Schneider. Now, Chalais is everything. I liked Schneider better."

"Question of taste," says Brunet.

Thibaut throws his head back and considers Brunet through his lashes:

"You and Schneider aren't pals anymore?"

"Sure we are."

"Then you'll be pleased," says Thibaut with a thin smile. "He asked me to do an errand for him."

"Schneider?"

"He wants to see you."

"Schneider?" repeats Brunet.

"Yes, Schneider. He told me to tell you that he'd be behind the 92 at one o'clock."

Brunet says nothing, Thibaut watches him with curiosity.

"So?"

"Tell him that I'll try to be there," says Brunet.

Thibaut doesn't leave. He opens his large mouth, he laughs, but his eyes remain uneasy:

"I'm happy to see you, old girl."

"Me too," says Brunet.

"Don't see much of you these days."

"I have a lot to do."

"I know. Me too. But you can always find the time, if you want. The guys ask me ten times a day what's become of you."

Brunet doesn't answer.

"Of course," says Thibaut, "I took down the radio post. We don't know anything anymore, we're flying blind: everybody's pissed about that." Brunet chafes beneath this steady gaze.

Dryly he replies:

"I explained this to you. Somebody was talking too much, the Jerries are watching. For now we have to meet less often, it's the simplest form of prudence."

Thibaut doesn't even seem to have heard him. Calmly he continues:

"Some of them are saying you didn't have to make such a fuss if you were going to drop us all the first time things got rough."

"Ho! Ho!" says Brunet jovially. "That's just how it is in politics: you move forward, you step back, and then you take off even better."

He laughs, Thibaut looks at him without laughing, someone kicks at the door, Brunet gets up quickly and goes to open it: it's Moûlu, his arms filled with jelly jars. Cornu and Paulin come in on his heels, they have loaves of bread wrapped up. Moûlu puts the jars on the table, steps back and considers them with satisfaction, crossing his hands on his belly.

"Today it's sardines."

Thibaut gets up:

"So, see you soon. When you have the time."

"There you go," says Brunet. "See you soon."

Thibaut leaves, Moûlu moves toward the door:

"I'll go call the guys."

"No," says Brunet.

Moûlu looks at him puzzled.

"Why not?"

Turning away, Brunet says:

"Today we're going to pass these out in the barracks."

"But why?"

Why? Because Chalais' not here. In a guilty voice Brunet says:

"No reason."

"We've never done that," says Moûlu.

"Exactly, it'll be a new experience. I think we can save some time."

"Whatever we're going to do with saved time here!"

"Oh, get going!" says Brunet impatiently. "Follow me."

They go from room to room, like in the old days. Brunet pushes the doors and goes in, Moûlu comes in on his heels announcing:

"We are serving you at home today, you lucky dogs. Tomorrow it will be hot chocolate in bed."

The guys don't reply. They're coming back from work, they're tired, with slow looks and heavy gestures. Most are seated on the benches, they have their big hands out on the tables, they're looking at no one and saying nothing. Brunet thinks: it just took one month. A month later and this barracks is just like all the others. It used to be that they'd be singing at noon. He hesitates in front of his comrades' room: he never goes in there anymore without Chalais, it's like he's coming back from a trip.

"So," says Moûlu, "you'll open the door, right?"

Brunet doesn't reply. Cornu turns the handle with his left hand, they go in leaving the door open. Brunet stays in the hall. Astonished faces turn towards him, he has to go in. He crosses the threshold, he thinks, "I shouldn't have, this is a big mistake."

"Hey," say the guys, "it's Brunet."

"Yeah," says Brunet, "it's me."

He searches their eyes, but he only sees half-closed lids, the guys surround the table, their hands reaching for the bread and the jars of sardines, a voice says:

"Shit, sardines again."

"Lucky dogs," says Moûlu, "we're serving you at home . . . "

"Shut it!" says Brunet. "Change the record."

He spoke too forcefully: looks turn to him, quickly covered up again by eyelids, blind men's faces again. Brunet takes a step forward. Lying on his back in bed, Maurice watches him, lazy and insolent.

"So guys?" asks Brunet. "How's it going?"

"It's going ok," they say. "It's ok."

Eyelids open, some guys are looking at Brunet, and others are looking at the ones looking at him. Everyone seems to be waiting for something, and afraid. Brunet feels his power, and then all of a sudden, fear grips him. He shouldn't have come, it was a mistake. Now speak! Say anything, quickly. The silence itself is a revelation. He says:

"Chalais is at the Dentist."

"Yeah," say the guys, "at the Dentist."

"That's why he didn't come along," explains Brunet.

"Yeah," say the guys, "yeah."

"He told us yesterday that he wouldn't be doing his course today."

"His course on the history of the Communist Party?"

"That's it. On the history of the Communist Party in France."

A silence. To what degree has Chalais won them over? How long will they still believe me? He raises his head, encounters a look, and turns away, intimidated. *They wish I'd leave.* Anger takes him by the nape of his neck; he jams his hands in his pockets and sits on the end of the bench, like in the old days. In the old days, the guys surrounded him. They don't move. In a reassuring voice he says:

"He'll start up his course again tomorrow."

He'd taken the same tone to tell them: "The USSR will enter the war in springtime." Sénac nods his head.

"Maybe he'll have to go back."

Sénac had said: "Maybe it won't be ready. Maybe it'll have to wait another year."

"I'd be surprised," says Brunet. "I think he's having that tooth pulled this morning."

"It's a wisdom tooth," Maillard explains proudly. "It's coming in sideways."

Brunet gets up. Smartly, he says:

"Well, see you guys! Enjoy your food."

"Thanks," they say. "You too."

He turns around and goes. He walks down the hallway. Moûlu passes him running, followed by Cornu and Paulin. They're laughing; they dive outside, into the sun. Brunet sees them, light against the clear sky, whirling, grabbing each other, releasing, falling down to pick up some snow. He speeds up, positions himself on the threshold of his barracks, and watches them. They disappear behind number 18, pushing each other along; he feels alone. He puts his hand on the door handle. It would open; Vicarios would smile at me, sitting by the stove. What can he want with this rendezvous? In any case, the prudent thing is to not go. He squeezes the handle, he doesn't enter: he knows the place is empty. Someone taps him from behind:

"Brunet!"

It's Toussus. With Bénin.

"What do you guys want?"

Toussu is pale, his eyes don't see, he's trying to find his voice at the back of his throat. Behind, at an angle, Bénin looks like he's ready to run away. Finally Toussus finds his voice:

"We wanted to talk to you."

Brunet leans up against the closed door.

"To me?"

Brunet knits his brow.

"About what?"

"About everything."

Brunet pushes against the door, it creaks. He hears Bénin big coal-miner voice, speaking without looking at him.

"We want to understand."

"Understand!" says Brunet with a mocking laugh. "Understand! How about that?"

He looks at them coldly: he doesn't know if he's pissed because they've come for an explanation, or because they've waited so long to come, or because they're the only ones who've come.

"Talk to Chalais!"

He recovers and gives them a childish smile.

"I'll take a pass. Too much work."

"You're the one we want to talk to," says Toussus patiently. "Don't you have five minutes?"

"Five minutes! If I added up all the five minutes people asked me for during the day," says Brunet, "I wouldn't have the time to find you guys food. I send everyone to Chalais: we've divided up the work."

Bénin speaks, looking down at the tips of his shoes:

"I don't have anything I need to ask Chalais about. He never stops talking, and I could tell you what he'll say before he says it."

"I'd say the same thing as him."

"If we hear it from you, maybe we'll be willing to believe it."

Brunet hesitates. Refuse? That will seem suspicious. At the same time, they've turned to him, both cautious and demanding. Brunet says:

"I'm listening."

Their eyes dilate, they glance around bewildered, and they say nothing. Brunet reddens with anger. He throws the door open, turns his back on them and enters with heavy steps. Behind him the door closes softly. He goes over to the stove, he turns around, he doesn't invite them to sit.

"Well?"

Toussus takes a step forward, Brunet takes one back: no complicity.

Toussus lowers his voice.

"Chalais seems to be saying that the USSR is not going to get into the war."

"What of it?" asks Brunet loud and clear. "Why's it bothering you? Haven't you learned that the country of the working class would never let itself be drawn into an imperialist conflict?"

They stop. They exchange furtive glances to encourage one another. Suddenly Bénin raises his head and looks at Brunet, man to man.

"That's not what you used to say."

Brunet's hands tremble, he forces them into his pockets:

"I was mistaken," he says.

"How do you know that you're the one who was mistaken?"

"Chalais has been in touch with people."

"That's what he says."

Brunet breaks out laughing.

"What, are you suggesting that he's sold out to the Nazis?"

He takes a step forward, he lays his hands on Toussus's shoulders, he speaks in a severe tone:

"You were still in diapers when Chalais joined the CP, my friend. Don't be stupid, guys: if you start acting like your leaders are betraying you every time you don't agree with them, you'll end up telling me that Papa Stalin is working for Hitler."

With these last words he laughs knowingly, looking Toussus in the eyes. Toussus doesn't laugh. Silence, and then Brunet hears Bénin's slow defiant voice:

"It's funny, though, that you were wrong on just that point."

"These things happen," says Brunet lightly.

"You're one of the leaders too," says Toussus. "You were in the Party already when I was in diapers too. So? Who are we supposed to believe?"

"I'm telling you that we are in agreement!" shouts Brunet.

They hold their tongues. They don't believe him. They will never believe him. The walls spin before Brunet's eyes. All the guys are there, all the guys looking at him, he has to say something to quell the disorder. He stretches out his trembling hands, with his palms open, and makes a public declaration:

"I made a mistake because I thought I was clever, and so I made a decision based on bad information, I was wrong because I gave in to an old reactionary stupid patriotic instinct."

He stops, drained. Under his knitted brows, his eyes go from one to the other, rolling with hatred: he'd like to rip their ears off. But the two faces remain lifeless and pale: his declaration hasn't registered with them; they weren't even listening to it. The words dissipate in the air, Brunet calms himself: I've humiliated myself for nothing.

"If the USSR is for peace," says Bénin, "then why has it thrown us into war?"

Brunet straightens up, he looks at them hard:

"Bénin," he says, "watch yourself, you're off the mark. I know where you got this argument, in the trash can. I've heard it out of the mouths of fascists a hundred times, but this is the first time I've heard it from a comrade."

"It's not an argument," says Benin, "it's a question."

"Ok then, here's the answer. If Stalin hadn't acted quickly, the bourgeois democracies' plan would have been to turn the Germans against the USSR."

Bénin and Toussus look at each other, frowning. Bénin says:

"Yeah. Chalais told us about that."

"As for the war," says Brunet, "how can you possibly wish for it to continue? The German soldiers are workers and peasants. Do you want the Soviet workers to be fighting against other workers and peasants just for the profits of some London bankers?"

They stop, more mystified than convinced. They'll head back pitifully to their barracks, to their pals, throw themselves on their bunks and through the evening they'll have the din of banging kettles in their heads and they won't even have the guts to look at each other, and each will be saying to himself: I don't get it. Brunet's throat tightens, these guys are just kids, I have to help them. He takes a step forward; they see him approaching, they understand, and their dull eyes light up for the first time. He stops himself: the Party is their family, the Party is all they have in the world, and the best way to help them is to just shut up. Their eyes go out. He smiles at them:

"Don't think about it too much, guys. Don't try to understand. We don't know anything. This wouldn't be the first time that it looked like the CP was wrong, but look, every time we found out afterwards that it

73

was right. The CP is your party, it exists for you and by you, it has no other goal but the liberation of the workers, it has no other will than the will of the masses. And that's why it is never wrong. Never! Never! Get that into your heads. It cannot be wrong."

He is ashamed of this voice, violent and weak, he'd like to give them back their innocence, he wishes for his old strength. But the door opens, and Chalais bursts into the room, out of breath. Toussus and Bénin scatter. Brunet steps back, he hates how they're acting like caught school boys. Everyone smiles, Brunet smiles and thinks: "He ran, someone must have gone and warned him."

"Hey guys!" says Chalais.

"Hi," they say.

"How's your tooth?" asks Toussus.

Chalais smiles, his face is like plaster: it mustn't have gone so well.

"Done, pulled it out!" he says gaily.

Brunet is irritated to find his hands sweating, Chalais never stops smiling, his eyes going from one of them to the other, he speaks with some difficulty:

"My face is like a block of wood. Well then," he adds, "you came to see me?"

"We were in the area," says Toussus.

"You didn't know I was at the Dentist?"

"We thought you'd already come back."

"Oh well, here I am," he says. "You had something you wanted to ask me?"

"Two or three little questions," says Bénin, "about your course, but there's no rush!"

"We'll come back some other time," says Toussus. "We don't want to disturb you now; you need to be left alone."

"Whenever you'd like," says Chalais. "I'm always here, you know. What a shame you came on the only day I wasn't here."

Backing up, they take their leave, smiling and saluting. The door closes again; Brunet takes his hands out of his pockets and wipes them on his pants, then lets them fall along his thighs. Chalais takes off his cap and sits down; his breath and color beginning to come back to him.

"Nice guys, these two kids," he says. "I like them a lot. They been here long?"

"Five minutes."

Brunet takes a step forward and adds:

"It was me they came to see."

"That's what I figured," says Chalais. "They have a lot of confidence in you."

"They asked me questions about the Party," says Brunet.

"And what did you tell them?"

"What you would have told them yourself."

Chalais gets up, walks up to Brunet and tilts his head to look at him. Smells from the pharmacy escape from his smiling mouth.

"This morning, you passed out the food in the barracks, didn't you?"

Brunet nods his head.

"Christ, Brunet!" says Chalais.

He takes him by the elbows, he tries to give him a friendly jostle. Brunet makes himself heavy, Chalais can't make him move. Chalais' hands open and fall away, but his cordial smile stays.

"I know you're not doing it deliberately. But you don't imagine how much you get in the way of me doing my work."

Brunet says nothing. Word for word, he knows what Chalais is going to say.

"What authority," asks Chalais, "can I have over the guys if they need your permission to believe what I say?"

Brunet shrugs his shoulders: unconvinced himself, he says:

"What does it matter, since we agree about it all?"

"The truth," says Chalais, "is that they don't think we do agree. You repeat to them what I say, but they can't forget that you used to tell them just the opposite. How can I get anything done under these conditions?"

"What more can I do?," asks Brunet. "It's been a whole month now that I've been laying low."

Chalais laughs back at him.

"Laying low? My poor Brunet, a guy like you can't *lay low*. You're too big, you carry too much weight. And if you say nothing, or stay away, you're just even more dangerous. You polarize them into resistance, it's as if you've become the leader of the opposition."

Without any joy, Brunet laughs:

"The opposition in spite of himself."

"Exactly. The fact that you exist, that they know you're in here when they walk by, is all it takes. It just doesn't make any difference if you shut up for good: being objective, they can't hear me over your voice."

Quietly Brunet says:

"And it won't work for you to kill me."

Without raising his eyes, Chalais says:

"That wouldn't solve anything. On the contrary."

That's it. Brunet has no more illusions, he knows in advance that he has lost, but there are still Toussus, Bénin, all the others: got to make another try. He puts his hands on Chalais' shoulders, and, just as quietly, he says: "You know, all this is partly your own fault."

Chalais raises his head but says nothing. Brunet continues: "Your mistake was contacting them yourself. You do a great job teaching recruits, but with these young guys you don't seem to find the right words."

Now it's fucked: Chalais' eyes light up with an icy anger, he's jealous of me. Brunet lets his hands slide down along Chalais' arms, but his conscience makes him continue: "I had them in my hands. If you'd stayed in the shadows, you could have given the orders and I'd have done the work, they'd have only been dealing with one guy, and we could have turned them around without them even knowing it."

Chalais' eyes die down, his mouth smiles. Brunet says:

"It wouldn't have been as hard on them either."

Chalais doesn't reply, Brunet looks on this dead face and, without any hope, adds:

"Maybe there's still time."

"There was never time," Chalais says violently. "You are, in the flesh, a huge mistake, and the best thing would just be for you to disappear: that's for certain. You're out of luck, don't you see? If you stop, if you hide out, you continue to have power. But if you'd spoken, if you'd said what I've been telling them, they'd laugh in your face."

In a sort of stupor, Brunet looks at the little man in front of him: I could crush him in one blow, I could ruin him with one word; but here I am, paralyzed, I've signed my own warrant and I'm just letting it happen, I half agree with Chalais. Without raising his voice he asks:

"Well then? What do I have to do?"

Chalais doesn't say anything yet. He goes to sit down, with his forearms on his thighs and his hands together. He's reflecting, it's very rare to see Chalais reflect. After a minute he says thoughtfully:

"In a different place, with different comrades, you could get a new start."

Brunet looks at him in silence. Chalais is listening to his inner voices, suddenly he snaps out of it:

"Nearly every day some are sent to concentration camps . . . "

"I see," says Brunet.

He smiles:

"I won't go, don't count on it. I want to work, I'm not going to waste my time with a bunch of clodhoppers who fall for whatever the priests tell them."

Chalais shrugs his shoulders.

"You do what you want."

They stop, one standing, the other seated, thinking about how best to get Brunet out of the picture. In the hallway, guys come and go, looking at the closed door, thinking: he's in there. I went along, but now Brunet objects; I'm hiding and he sticks out like a sore thumb.

"You send me to the concentration camps and the guys will see it as an exile."

Chalais gives him a perplexed look.

"That's what I was telling myself."

"How about if I escaped?"

"That would be the worst. Then they'd think you'd gone to Paris to protest."

Brunet stops, he scrapes his right heel against the floor, he lowers his eyes, he breathes, he thinks: I'm in the way. His hands have started to sweat again. No matter where I go, I'll be in the way. Here or Paris, I'll cause disorder. He hates disorder, lack of discipline, putting yourself first. I'm the weak link, the sand in the gears.

"We could get them all together: you present your critique of what I said, and I'll acknowledge you're right in front of everyone."

Chalais quickly raises his head:

"Would you do that?"

"I'd do whatever it takes to get back to my work."

Chalais sits there incredulous; all at once Brunet senses something moving deep inside. He knows what it is, he's afraid. He must speak right away, quickly.

"We'll need to have a vote," he says from behind clenched teeth. "When they themselves have judged me . . . "

"No judging," says Chalais laughing. "Nothing dramatic, that would just muddle things. Here's how I see it: nothing heavy, a friendly discussion, between pals, and at the end, you get up . . . "

Too late, the rocket hisses, whirls, explodes, lights up the night: *the USSR will lose*. It won't stay out of the war, it'll go it alone, with no allies, but its army is worthless, it will lose. He sees Chalais' eyes, stupefied: did I say that? He gets control of himself. A long silence. Then Brunet chuckles:

"I had you going, didn't I?" he says painfully.

Chalais is pale, says nothing. Brunet says:

"I will not make a public confession, old pal. There's a limit."

"I didn't ask you to do anything," says Chalais softly.

"Of course you didn't. You're too clever for that."

Chalais smiles, Brunet looks at him with curiosity: how is he going to handle getting rid of me? Suddenly Chalais gets up, puts his cap under his arm and goes out without saying a word. Brunet follows him out, plunging into the sunlight. It will lose. They'll have demoralized the comrades, and then it'll lose anyway. He contemplates, deep inside, this stubborn thought that returns a hundred times a day, this small shiny fragile bubble, glued to the floor, defenseless: you could crush it with your heel, a thought is so soft, so transparent, so fleeting, so private, so complicit, it doesn't seem to even really exist: and that's what I'm getting screwed for! Do I really think that the USSR will be beaten? Am I just afraid to think so? And if I were to think so, so what? A thought in a head, it's nothing, an internal hemorrhage, nothing to do with truth. Truth is something practical, something proven in action; if it were true, it would be known, it could change how things are going, influence the Party. I can't do anything, I must be wrong. He picks up the pace, reassures himself: none of that matters much. So much for ideas. He'd always had them, like everyone, they're just mildew, leftovers from brain activity; but he never used to pay them any mind, just let them sprout like mushrooms in the basement. So let's just put them back in their place, and everything will be alright: he'll tow the line, follow orders, and carry his ideas around inside without saying a word, like a shameful disease. This will go no farther, this can go no farther: we do not think in opposition to the Party, thoughts are words, words belong to the Party, the Party defines them, the Party controls them; Truth and the Party are one and the same. He walks, he's content, he forgets himself: barracks, faces, the sky. The sky fills his eyes. Behind him, forgotten, words are gathering together, talking among themselves: *since it doesn't count, since it doesn't matter, why not think it through anyway?* He stops suddenly, feeling out of sorts. This must be what it's like for the guys who think they're Napoleon: they reason with themselves, prove to themselves that they aren't the emperor. And as soon as they're done, a voice behind them says "Hello Napoleon." He goes back to his thought, he wants to look it in the face: If the USSR were beaten . . .

He blows through the roof, flying in the dark, explodes, the Party is below him, a living jelly covering the globe, I never saw it, I was inside it; he turns above this perishable jelly: the Party can die. He's cold, he turns: if the Party is right, then I am more alone than a madman; if it's wrong, *we're all* on our own, and the world is fucked. The fear dissipates; he turns in a circle, stops out of breath and leans against the barracks wall for support: what's happened to me?

"I was wondering if you were going to come."

It's Vicarios. Brunet says:

"You can see, I'm here."

They don't shake hands. Vicarios is sporting a beard, growing grey at the moment. He stares feverishly at Brunet's forehead, just above the eyebrows. Brunet turns away: he can't stand the sick, his gaze glides between the barracks and suddenly, in the distance, he catches a flash of light between two half closed eyelids, then a back running away: Maurice. "He's spying on me, he must be the one who went to the infirmary and warned Chalais." Brunet straightens himself, this cheers him up and makes him feel better. He turns back to Vicarios:

"What do you want with me?"

"I want to escape," says Vicarios.

Brunet starts: he'll die in the snow.

"In the middle of winter? Why don't you wait till spring?"

Vicarios smiles. Brunet sees the smile and turns his eyes away.

"I'm in a hurry."

"Well then, get a move on."

The sad heavy voice glides over the nape of his neck:

"I need civilian clothes."

Brunet makes himself raise his head, with boredom in his voice he replies: "There's an organization in the camp that helps guys who want to escape. Go talk to them."

"Do you know who it is?" asks Vicarios.

"No, but I've heard talk of it."

"Everyone's heard talk of it, but nobody knows anything about it. Truth is, it doesn't even exist."

He fixes his inky gaze on Brunet's eyebrows, he seems like a blind man, half-heartedly he forces his large soft voice out of his mouth:

"Sorry, but you're the only one who can help me. You have men everywhere. Manoël works in the store, and there are tons of clothes in there."

Brunet asks:

"Why do you want to escape?"

Vicarios raises his hand, and smiles at his nails. As if talking to himself, he says: "I want to defend myself."

"From who? Before who?" asks Brunet without interest. "The Party has changed its tune."

Vicarios' laugh is low and hard.

"We'll see!" he says. "We'll just see!"

Brunet feels tired and conciliatory: he'll die out there in the snow; I'd rather know he's here in the camp.

"What do you care what we think of you anyway? You quit on us over a year ago, so leave us alone now."

"My wife is still with you," says Vicarios.

Brunet lowers his head, and doesn't answer. After a minute, Vicarios adds:

"My oldest boy is ten: to him, the Party is God itself. I'm sure someone has let him know he's the son of a traitor."

He chuckles softly, looking at his fingers:

"Not exactly how I'd have wished he got started in life."

"Why are you telling me all this?" asks Brunet, irritated.

"Who do you want me to tell?"

Brunet raises his head, pushing his fists into his pockets.

"Don't count on me."

Vicarios says nothing: he waits. Brunet waits too, then loses his patience and forces his eyes into the unseeing ones before him:

"You're against us," he says.

"Neither for nor against. I just want to defend myself, that's all."

"You're against us no matter what you do."

No reply. Brunet continues:

"And besides, now's not the time to reopen your case. You provide arguments for the enemy; you're a slogan all by yourself: the fierce communist who's fed up with the Party. The comrades don't exactly have all their confidence right now: even if you're part innocent, they need you to be completely guilty. Later on, we'll see."

"Later on!"

Vicarios lowers his eyes slightly, looking right into Brunet's.

"No, Brunet: not you!"

They stare at each other. Neither one will lower his eyes.

"Not you. You're the only one who doesn't have the right."

"Because?"

"Because you know full well I'm not a traitor: if you won't help me you're willingly preventing the comrades from knowing the truth."

The truth is what the Party says it is. The truth and the Party are one. If the Party goes wrong, all men are on their own. If you're not a traitor, then everyone's on their own.

"You dropped us when we were in deep shit," Brunet says rudely; "you tried to discredit the Party in your rag. It's just as criminal as if you'd sold out to the government."

"Maybe it's as criminal," says Vicarios, "but it's not the same crime."

"I don't have time for that kind of nuance."

They look at each other. Suddenly the rocket spins: the USSR's going to lose. Brunet looks at Vicarios' ashen face, and what he sees is his own face. It's going to lose and everyone's on their own, Vicarios and Brunet are on their own and they're just the same. In the end, if he wants to die, that's his business.

"I'll get you your clothes."

The heavy face is unexpressive. Vicarios simply says:

"I'll need some crackers too."

"You'll have 'em." Brunet thinks. "I'll try to get you a compass too."

Vicarios' eyes light up for the first time:

"A compass? That would be great."

"I can't promise anything," says Brunet.

They turn away from each other at the same time. Brunet breathes deeply. Time to go. He stays, he wonders why Vicarios doesn't go. All at once he hears a timid sad voice:

"You've aged."

Brunet looks at Vicarios' grey beard and doesn't say anything.

"You doing alright?" asks Vicarios.

"Ok."

"And the guys? What did you tell them about me?"

"That you were sick, and I'd transferred you over to Thibaut's because it wasn't as cold there."

"Good."

He turns his head and says, in a neutral voice:

"Nobody's been to see me."

"Just as well."

"Right, naturally."

"Did you have anything else to tell me?"

"No."

"Ok."

He goes off, walking, he turns in the snow, Vicarios's feverish eyes follow him and move with his eyes. He locks himself down, his eyes go out: whether he dies or not, he's fucked, like the printer, he was fucked, the Party has its rejects, it's normal.[11] He makes a fist, turns around: well, nobody's going to make a reject out of me. He walks: a friendly discussion, Chalais will point out my mistakes cordially, then I'll stand up in front of everyone . . . On the barracks threshold, Moûlu is enjoying a gold-tip cigarette. Brunet stops:

"What do you have there?"

"A cigarette."

"A gold-tip? They don't sell them at the canteen."

Moûlu flushes:

"It's a butt. I picked it up by the Kommandatur."

"You make me sick, picking up butts," says Brunet. "You'll wind up catching syphilis."

Red all over, eyes half-closed, head tucked between his shoulders, Moûlu continues to smoke. Brunet thinks: *before*, he would have thrown his cigarette away.

"The guys are at work?"

"Not yet. They're inside with Chalais."

"Go find Manoël for me," says Brunet. "Quickly. And make sure no one knows about it."

"Understood," says Moûlu importantly.

He runs. At the other end of the hallway a door opens, Sénac and Rasque leave in a hurry. They spot Brunet, their eyes go out, they stop, stuff their hands into their pockets and walk off nonchalantly. Brunet smiles as they pass, and they nod their heads sanctimoniously. They go off. Brunet watches them distractedly, thinking: I always liked Sénac better. Someone tugs his sleeve, he turns: it's Toussus.

"You again!" says Brunet annoyed. "What do you want?"

Toussus has a funny look to him. He asks:

"Is it true that Schneider's name is Vicarios?"

"Who told you that?" asks Brunet.

"Chalais."

"When?"

"Just now."

He looks at Brunet suspiciously, he repeats:

"Is it true?"

"Yes."

"Is it true that he left the Party in September of '39?"

"Yes."

"Is it true that he's working for the Algerian government?"

"No."

"So, Chalais's wrong?"

"He's wrong."

"I thought he was never wrong."

"He's wrong about that."

"He's says the Party put out a warning. Is that true?"

"Yes."

"So the Party's wrong too?"

"Comrades have been misinformed," says Brunet. "It's not very serious."

Toussus nods his head:

"It's pretty serious for Vicarios."

Brunet doesn't reply. Without interest, Toussus comments:

"You liked Vicarios, didn't you? He was your friend before."

"Yeah," says Brunet, "before."

"Whereas now, you wouldn't give a crap if someone cracked his skull?"

Brunet takes his arm:

"Who wants to crack his skull?"

"You didn't just see Rasque and Sénac? That's where they're going."

"Did Chalais give them an order about it?"

"He didn't give any orders. He came in with Maurice, and told his little story."

"What story?"

"That Vicarios was a traitor, that he'd sucked you in, and that you stood by him; that he was dangerous, and that we'd all wake up one day and be turned in."

"What did everyone say?"

"They didn't say anything, they listened. And then Sénac and Rasque got up, that's all."

"And did Chalais say anything to them?"

"He made it seem like he didn't even see them."

"Ok," says Brunet, "thanks."

Toussus holds him back:

"Don't you want me to come along?"

"Absolutely not," says Brunet. "This is a trap, and it's been laid just for me."

He runs; behind number 18, no one; he stops, catches his breath, and takes off again. He's running to his own ruin, he's never run so hard in his life. In front of Thibaut's barracks, he spots Vicarios with Sénac and Rasque. They're out in the sun, black figures in the middle of the empty road, Rasque is talking, Vicarios is quiet. Now Sénac and Rasque come closer and they're both talking at once, Vicarios has put his hands in his pockets, not responding. Brunet runs faster, Rasque raises his arm and strikes Vicarios in the mouth. Vicarios takes out his hand and wipes his mouth, Rasque tries to strike again, Vicarios grabs his wrist, Sénac jumps in and lands a punch, Vicarios turns his head and Sénac's fist gets him behind the ear. It's like Chinese shadow boxing, no sound, and no depth; he can't believe it. Brunet throws himself in and with one paw tosses Sénac against the barracks wall. Vicarios is bleeding, Rasque's eyes are sparkling. Brunet sees the blood, the hate, the trap closing in on him, the hate surrounding him: he believes it.

"What are you doing, you idiots?"

Vicarios lets go of Rasque's arm. Rasque turns toward Brunet and looks him over:

"We're showing him our way of thinking."

"Ok, and you'll share it with the Jerries if they come along, and you'll show them your Party ID card for good measure? Let's go, run along, clear out."

Rasque stays put, watching Brunet with a shifty morose look. Sénac comes back up slowly to join them, he doesn't seem intimidated.

"What do you say, Brunet ? This guy's a traitor, isn't he?"

"Go on back home," says Brunet.

Sénac turns red, he raises his voice.

"He's a traitor, isn't he? C'mon, what do you say? You're defending a traitor, aren't you?"

Brunet looks him in the eyes and calmly repeats:

"I told you to get going: that's an order."

Sénac chuckles:

"That doesn't work any more."

"You don't have any orders to give us, Pops," says Rasque. "It's not your place anymore to give us orders."

"No?"

Brunet thinks: this is it. One move and the spider's web he's caught in will tear open from top to bottom.

"No, Brunet," says Rasque with a calm firmness, "you can't give us orders anymore, that's over."

"Maybe so," says Brunet. "But I can still put you in the hospital for two weeks. Yeah, I can still do that."

They hesitate. Brunet watches them, laughing impatiently: they know they won't win, but which one will save face and say the words that seal this? Sénac twists his mouth and blanches, afraid of what he's going to say. So it'll be Sénac, that's fine: he's the one I'd prefer. The trap is working well.

"From the moment you began colluding . . . " says Sénac.

Brunet throws his fist and it lands joyfully in Sénac's right eye; Sénac lets himself go limp in Rasque's arms, while he backs off. Brunet watches them with interest, then he pops him again in exactly the same place to make sure to finish the job. Sénac's eyebrow rips open and begins pissing blood. Brunet pulls back and laughs: the pile of dishes is on the ground, everything's broken, everything's finished. Rasque and Sénac take off limping away, supporting each other; they'll give their report and then things are going to really warm up in the barracks, the trap has worked well, Brunet rubs his hands together, Vicarios wipes his mouth, his lips trembling, a stream of blood coats the grey beard. Brunet looks at him stunned, he thinks: I did that for him.

"You hurt?"

"It's nothing."

The handkerchief rubs, the beard rasps. Vicarios says:

"You'd promised me you wouldn't say anything to the guys."

Brunet shrugs his shoulders. Vicarios turns his big empty eyes towards him and says, seeming preoccupied:

"They didn't like me, did they?"

"Who?"

"Everybody."

"No," says Brunet, "they didn't like you."

Vicarios shakes his head:

"They're going to make my life hell."

"Nah!" Says Brunet. "You'll be gone in no time."

Vicarios has turned around, his eyes are following Sénac and Rasque.

Brunet sees the end of his nose, and his hairy cheek that's bleeding.

"Friendship," says Vicarios, "it really ought to be possible."

"It is possible," says Brunet, "between guys who are members of the Party."

"As long as they both stay in line."

He speaks from far off, without turning around:

"In Oran, last year, three comrades went to see my wife, and they shoved a document under her nose that they wanted her to sign: they'd written that I was a piece of garbage, and that she had to disavow me. She refused, of course, and they called her a slut and threatened her. These guys had been my best friends."[12]

Brunet says nothing; he gently rubs the knuckles on his right hand, not understanding very well anymore what he's done.

"However," says Vicarios, "if we've fought this much, if we fight again, isn't that about friendship *too*?"

Brunet thinks: and if I popped Sénac, if I fell head first into Chalais' trap, don't you realize that was about friendship? He wants to touch him on the shoulder or squeeze his arm; he wants to give him a smile so it isn't all in vain. He doesn't smile, or reach out his hand: between them there will never be friendship.

"Well, yes," he says, "to make it possible one of these days, after we're gone."

"After we're gone? Why? Why not today?"

Brunet explodes all of a sudden:

"Today? With a billion slaves, and with fires burning in every corner of the planet? You want friendship? You want love? You want to just be able to be a man, just like that? Well, we're not men, old pal, not yet. We're miscarriages, botched goods, half-animal. All we can do is work to see that those who come after us are nothing like us."

Vicarios comes out of his dream, he looks at Brunet attentively, softly he says:

"It's true. You've had a taste of it too."

Brunet laughs:

"Me?" he asks. "No. I'm just talking in general."

"Oh right, oh sure," says Vicarios in a lively, sassy voice. "I know what's going on. Thibaut was telling me that no one sees you anymore, that you made them take down the radio, you let Chalais keep you in your room . . . "

Brunet has no reply. Vicarios' large eyes sparkle, then die down, he looks straight ahead, surprised, he softly says:

"I thought it would make me happy . . . "

"Happy?" repeats Brunet.

Vicarios chuckles:

"You have no idea how much I hated you!"

He turns around suddenly and his eyes go blank.

"From the day I quit, all I've been able to do is survive: but that wasn't good enough for you, you've had to ruin me. It's like you'd established a special prosecutor inside me: I was the grand inquisitor; I'd always been your accomplice, and you knew you could count on me. At times, I was crazy: I didn't know who was talking anymore, whether it was me or you; you'll know what that's like. And it's worse: you made me learn to think like a traitor, to live like a traitor: I felt like a suspect, I was ashamed, I was afraid. It all works out, you know: when someone throws you over, he's got to either hate you or be horrified at himself. If he hates you, you've won, and he becomes a fascist—that's what I had to prove. I held out as long as I could, but you guys kept on knocking, you knocked like you were deaf. And at that point, there were others, who opened their arms to me. No matter what I did—turn my back on them; insult them—it worked to their advantage. I was writing *for you* in my paper, I was begging you to understand, I was trying to warn you, to explain myself: they reproduced my article in a completely distorted form, and you guys rushed to get these fake quotes in print in *Alger Rouge*. I made corrections, I contradicted it all in their own columns; they congratulated me on my loyalty, on my dignity—it didn't cost them a thing to paint me as virtuous: the more virtuous I was, the more criminal you were. And right away, what you guys did was announce to the comrades that I was writing for reactionary papers. You said that I'd gone over to Doriot, to *Je Suis Partout*, and to prove it you just pointed out their praises. You conspired with them to provide me with an image of myself that both made me sick and fascinated me, it made me dizzy, I was going to fall . . . "

He looks at Brunet with somber pride.

"So I went to ground, I held my tongue. I may have hated you, but no one knew; my hate was to no one's advantage; I won, but at what a price! You're strong, Brunet, but I was strong too: look what I've become."

Brunet, without conviction, mutters:

"You should have thought about that before quitting."

"You think I didn't? I knew it all in advance."

"Well then?"

"Well, you see. I quit."

He smiles at his memories; the red trickle in his beard has dried, weaving a small black tail in the middle of his whiskers.

"Oh yes, I hated you! In Baccarat, I was cold, I was a shadow, I came to you because you were alive and warm; I fed myself from your life, I was your parasite, and hated you all the more for it. When you started telling me about your plans, I knew you were screwed, and I said to myself: I've got one. I worked with you—I enjoyed the work we did together: we helped these guys, gave them back the taste for living, it was clean—and I said to myself: one of these days, he'll be like me. And I wanted to be there to see the look on your face. I celebrated in advance."

He shakes his head, he looks deliberately at Brunet, after a minute he says:

"It doesn't make me happy at all."

"You know," Brunet says calmly, "you may not be wrong: it may be that I've run into some little difficulties these past few days, but I would never quit the Party. If I have to give in, I'll give in; if I have to take back what I said, I'll take it back. I'm nothing, what I may have believed or said is of no importance."

Vicarios reflects: "Yeah," he says slowly, "that's one way to handle it. What does it change though? The worm is already in the apple."

There's a long silence.

"Vicarios," says Brunet all of a sudden, "do you know that you're in pretty poor physical shape? If you escape, you've got a pretty good chance of staying that way."

"Of course I know that," says Vicarios.

They stop talking, they eye each other furtively, in a friendly but ashamed way, then Brunet goes off with heavy steps. When he gets to number 27, he runs into Manoël.

"I was looking for you," says Brunet.

"You wanted to ask me something?"

"Yeah," says Brunet. "I need to get two sets of civilian clothes."

3. THIRD SECTION

The wind beats against the window panes, they all creak. Brunet fidgets on his back and sweats; outside, and deep down inside him, it's cold. The night awaits him. He listens: Moûlu's already snoring, not a sound from Chalais' side, where hate keeps watch. Brunet's body stays perfectly immobile while his head turns slowly toward the glowing ashes dying in the stove. He watches the familiar shadows dance, the soft red light becoming softer and softer; watching full of reproaches. Put your faith in the warmth, go to sleep: it would be so easy; after all, it's been pretty good here.

A little hiss, pedantic and steady, he jumps: that's it, no more hate, no more Chalais. He brings the back of his hand to his eyes, he makes out two pale glowing dots: ten past ten, I'm late. He glides out of bed, dresses in silence to the dying gleams of the fire. As he slips on his coat the stove crackles and goes out, the back of his eyes is covered with crocuses; he bends down, feels for his shoes, takes them in his left hand and makes for the door. He has to fight to open it; the wind pushes against it like it was a man. He slips outside, putting his shoes in his right hand, clutching the door handle with his left and returning the latch to the jamb. Got it. In the hallway, it's torture, he steps in a puddle, both feet. He puts on his shoes, bends over to tie the laces, the wind pushes him so he nearly falls over. As he gets back up the cold strikes him in the mouth and on the ears, and sits on him awkwardly like a glass suit of armor, he stays still, his eyes see nothing, not even the night: bunches of mauve flowers blind him. From out of the wailing of the wind, he makes out a festive sound: Bénin's harmonica. Goodbye. Goodbye. Tottering and reeling, he plunges, around him the enormous black drape flaps, he reaches out his hand, the night suffocates him, he finds the wall of the barracks and follows it, leaning against it with his shoulder. His hair dances, a wave carries him, he arrives at the road, the night is everywhere: nothing protecting him, he feels naked, the deep night is a whole people, a million eyes that see him. He walks on, fighting the wind, the night splits open: a flashlight in the distance, a stream of gold runs along the black water to his feet, Brunet glues himself to a wall and holds his breath. A wave of footsteps, two men pass by, their overcoats leaping and whipping wildly around their waists. The night closes in again, Brunet starts up again, slogging; he'll be slogging all through the night. He bumps into a first barracks, then another: this is the one. He enters without knocking. Thibaut and Bouillé look at him with surprise. Once they recognize him, they break out in laughter. Brunet lets out his breath and smiles at them: this is the relay point. He blinks his eyes, shivers, shakes off the cold and the night.

"What a wind! It's enough to blow you away."

"Nice job," says Thibaut reproachfully, "you just had to pick this awful bear of a night!"

"Deliberately," says Brunet. "When the wind blows, the barbed wired creaks."Bouillé takes a devilish tone:

"Get ready, there's a surprise."

"What surprise?"

"Close your eyes," says Thibaut. "There, open them."

Brunet opens his eyes and spots a civilian.

"Isn't he cute like that?"

Brunet doesn't respond, but keeps looking at the civilian, intimidated.

"Where were you?"

Vicarios smiles at him:

"I jumped under the blankets when you came in."

He looks like he just came out of placard, or a tomb, but he doesn't know it. He's shaved his beard, he's wearing a white shirt with no collar and seems cramped in his dark maroon suit. He sits, crosses his legs, puts his elbows on the table, at ease but a little stiff, like his body remembers vaguely having lived once.

"I didn't think you were that heavy," says Brunet.

"Gimme a break. I've got bread stuffed in everywhere I can: you'll have to as well."

"Where are my threads?"

"Under the bed."

Brunet undresses, shivering he slips on a blue shirt with attached collar, striped trousers, and black jacket. He laughs:

"I must look like a notary."

He stops laughing: Vicarios is taking his turn at being stupefied as he looks at him. Brunet turns away and asks Thibaut:

"No tie?"

"No."

"Too bad."

He puts on the civilian shoes and can't stop a grimace.

"A bit tight."

"Keep your boots."

"No way. That's how Séruzier got caught. No, no, these are supposed to do, and they will."

They're face to face in their anachronistic disguises, smiling at each other a bit mystified. Brunet turns toward Thibaut and Bouillé, who's knocking out his pipe: these two look real.

"That's enough," says Thibaut.

He holds out two flat flasks:

"This is for water."

Brunet slides it in his back pocket, he says:

"The overcoat . . . "

"Here you go!"

Playing like butlers, Thibaut and Bouillé help them slip on their over-coats, then they back away and have a laugh:

"Oh! La, la. Check these two out!"

Thibaut takes a critical look at Brunet:

"Careful not to get your coat caught on the barbed wire. You haven't done this in a while!"

"Don't worry," says Brunet.

They laugh a second, and then are quiet, and their heightened spirits settle down. Brunet slips the map, flashlight and compass into his pockets. He suddenly realizes that he's ready, which sends a chill down his spine.

"And there we have it!" he says.

Vicarios gives a start and says:

"There we are."

His clumsy hands slowly button up his overcoat. Brunet waits, trying to turn time backwards. There it is: the last button in its hole, now nothing stands between them and the night. Brunet raises his eyes, sees the bench, the cots, the lamp's oily filament, the red flower that dances at the tip of the filament, the black smoke that makes its way toward the ceiling, the large cozy shadows that play against the walls: it's warm, it smells like men and like dust; it feels like he's abandoning his home. Thibaut and Bouillé have gone completely pale:

"Lucky devils!" says Thibaut.

He pretends to be envious; generously, Vicarios nods his head and says softly:

"I'm scared."

"Nah!" says Brunet. "You'll get over it. Once we're on the other side, everything will take care of itself."

"That's not why I'm scared," says Vicarios.

He licks his dry lips: "What are we going to find out there?"

Brunet feels a small unpleasant pinch, and says nothing. The night: Paris is at the other end of it. We'll have to return to living. Thibaut speaks quickly, nervously:

"Once you're in Paris, don't forget to write to my wife. Madame Thibaut, Saint-Sauveur-en-Puisaye, that's all you need. Give her my best, tell her I'm well, that I don't have the blues, and that she must write me when you've arrived. All she has to say is: the kids have arrived."

"Understood," says Brunet.

The plank is standing there, leaning against the wall. He feels it: solid and heavy. He puts it under his arm. Thibaut comes up and awkwardly claps him on the shoulder:

"Lucky devils! Lucky dogs!"

Schneider heads toward the door, Bouillé follows him.

"One of these days," says Bouillé, "maybe we'll be doing the same."

"Maybe," says Thibaut, "you'll be seeing us come marching home."

Schneider smiles at them:

"My wife," he says, "lives at 13, rue Cardinet."

Brunet turns around. Thibaut and Bouillé, hugging each other, look at them. Thibaut's smile is sad and tender; he brings his big flat face, ravaged by the goodness of his heart, toward them, his large mouth laughing love and impotence: his face is a useless gift.

"Oh, shit on you!"

"Shit! Shit!" Bouillé repeats, wide-eyed.

"And think about the guys once in a while."

"You bet we'll be thinking of 'em," says Vicarios.

"And don't be an ass if you see you're caught. Don't try to get away, cause they have orders to shoot you down."

"We're not getting caught," says Brunet. "Put out the light."

The night swallows up the twin heads and their final smiles once and for all; the window is engulfed in the dark and the cold. Blows from the wind right in the face, the taste of steel in their mouths, violet disks turn in their eyes. Behind them the door locks, the retreat is cut off: before them, a tunnel, enormous patience, and, far off, an uncertain dawn; mud sticks to their boots. Brunet is happy to have Vicarios walking close by. From time to time he reaches out a hand and touches him; from time to time he feels the touch of another hand. A squall stops them in their tracks, they flatten themselves against the barracks for cover but they see nothing. Brunet's plank bangs against a window and bounces off: luckily the glass held. He hears a curse, a muffled blow: Vicarios hits his knee against one of the steps. Brunet helps him up and yells in his ear:

"You hurt yourself?"

"No, but we can't go on like this."

They throw themselves back out into the road. Brunet doesn't feel at ease there: too open, they're vulnerable from every direction. A bit worried, he figures that by now they should have reached the *Entlausung-sanstalt*[13] : but his eyes search in the darkness in vain. A hole opens up in the night, a door opens upon a dimly lit space: the Kommandatur, shit! We went too far to the left. With his free hand Brunet grabs Vicarios and steers him to the right. They rush off; the plank hits a wall, Brunet leaps to the side and almost knocks Vicarios over; they run. Brunet straightens his plank and tries to carry it vertically, it's back-breaking because it scrapes on the ground. He runs, his left arm out, palm open, throwing himself against the wall of the night, the wall recedes, but now and then Brunet can sense it at the end of his hand, and feels like he's going to crash into it, fear flows into his legs and takes over. For a long time the soles of his feet slap into mud, then they hit solid ground, an island emerges: Black Square, a first landmark. Brunet's getting hot, his shoes are hurting less than he thought they would, he pokes Vicarios in the ribs and hears him laugh. Got to get oriented. He grabs his arm, they walk against the wind, suddenly they feel themselves buffeted, they sprout wings and fly.

"We're going in circles," says Vicarios.

They change direction, back to the wind, arm in arm, wind howling, an insect's chirp pierces this useless bombast, it swells louder: Brunet's heart beats faster: the barbed wire. He thinks: now we've got to locate the latrines. At that very moment the wind throws a stench of ammonia and sleet into his face. Guided by the sound and the smell, they glide along the latrines, they squat down behind a trash pile, a meter away the barbed wires whip the air, turning like jump ropes, making an unholy racket. There are two nights now: the one that's sliding down behind them, a large angry weight, already out of play, and another, quite refined, complicit, which begins on the other side of the wall, a black light. Vicarios squeezes Brunet's hand: they are overjoyed. Brunet carefully runs his fingers along the plank. Three rows of barbed wire cover a meter twenty; his plank is a meter thirty, it'll work. Suddenly Vicarios grabs his wrist, Brunet gives a start: the guard's marching along the road. Brunet listens to the invisible steps, and icy joy goes through him: everyone's at their places, we can get started. Three nights in a row he had hidden behind the latrines, watching the guard: he leaves his sentry box, right across from them, covers a hundred meters, and returns to his position. The round trip takes about two minutes: they'll have thirty seconds. He hears the steps fade away, he counts under his breath, the first numbers sticking to the footsteps, then silence, the guard has dissipated, he's everywhere, he's the night itself, on the watch, the numbers fall into the void and ring empty. At 119 the steps are reborn, the guard comes back together, plunges to the bottom of the night, reduced suddenly to this solitary and wearisome lapping, passes in front of them, stops, starts off again. One, two, three, four . . . This time he's back at 127, the next time at 122, let's bet on 120 to be safe. He starts counting again, at 45 he puts his hand on Vicarios' shoulder and is moved to feel the hard fingers squeezing his wrist: these are the fingers of friendship. They get up. Brunet holds out his hand, a whip of steel leaps across it and grazes his palm, he slides his fingertips along the wire, avoids another barb, touches a post without stopping his counting, raises the plank and gently lowers the front end: it holds, a raft softly tossed on the triple waves of barbed wire, Brunet's hands are covered with mud, he takes the time to wipe them on the post, 57, he puts his left foot on the barbed wire on the bottom, jams his shoe against the post, pushes off and up, gets his right foot on the second string of wire, raises his left knee, scrapes it on the way against the head of the post, finally reaching the plank, 59, now he scrambles on his hands and knees, time slows down, 60, over there the guard is making his turn and looking at him, to Brunet's right the night is a searchlight. Moving ahead he reaches out his hand and touches the second post, moves ahead some more despite the lurching, and reaches the third post, moves back a little and turns around on the plank, it almost capsizes, then rights itself, Vicarios has grabbed onto it. Brunet reaches out a foot into empty space, finds a fence wire, 62, he wants to jump so he won't eat up Vicarios' time, the bottom of his overcoat is snagged on a barb, too bad, impatience gets the better of him, he leaps and the lining of the coat rips. He grabs the plank with both hands and moves it back and forth gently to indicate that he's over. The wires groan, the plank rolls, Brunet holds it tight, thinks of the guard, can feel him coming down on them, he thinks of Vicarios angrily: what the fuck is he doing? you asshole, you're going to get us caught, he puts out his hand, touches a head, Vicarios turns around with difficulty on the plank, Brunet hears his breath, and then nothing. A shoe scrapes against his sleeve, he grabs it and lowers it gently to the wire, Vicarios leaps to the ground, a flash of joy goes through them, free! Above the lookout tower another flash blasts them, they blink their eyes uncomprehending, the road is white from the sun at the end of a circle of shadow, the puddles gleam, diamonds sparkling everywhere. Brunet grabs Vicarios by the shoulder and pushes him to run, shots!, they run, bullets whistle, they're being fired on from the lookout tower and the sentry box. *From the sentry box*: they had someone hidden inside, we've been given up. Brunet runs, the road is wide like the sea, everyone can see him, it's a nightmare, bullets whistling. Suddenly Vicarios goes limp and collapses, Brunet's grip brings him back up, he falls again, Brunet pushes him, pulls him: here's the edge of the forest, with what's left of the night, he pushes him between the trees, falls on his back, they roll in the snow, Vicarios howls.

"Shut up," says Brunet.

"You're hurting me!" howls Vicarios.

They roll down the slope, Vicarios whimpers, Brunet doesn't let go, anger strangles him, we've been given up. Above, cries and shots. They keep rolling, Brunet's head hits a wall, his eyes jumping out of his sockets, this isn't the time to lose it, he makes a violent effort, his fingers scrape the snow, he gets back up. His head had banged into a tree root, he's caught between the trunk and Vicarios' body, he moves a little, his arm hits against Vicarios' shoulder, and he yells out in pain:

"Get the fuck off!"

Brunet gets up on his knees. Now he knows he's lost, but he's going to see it through to the end, he slips his hands under Vicarios' arms to lift him and carry him, but Vicarios pushes him away, Brunet tries again, they fight without being able to see each other: suddenly Vicarios vomits on his hands, Brunet lets him go, he falls back down. Above them it's like the dance of the fairies: the tree trunks dance in the light. Brunet brings his face up close to Vicarios.

"Vicarios!" he says, begging him.

"Get the fuck away!" says Vicarios. "It's all your fault."

"I'm not going anywhere," says Brunet, "I escaped so I could come with you."

"It's all your fault," says Vicarios.

"We'll start over, by God! I'll talk to the guys in the Party. I'll . . . "

Vicarios yelps:

"Start over? Can't you see I'm dying?"

He makes a violent effort, then adds, with difficulty:

"The Party's killed me."

He vomits in the snow, he falls back down, silent. Brunet sits, pulls him to him, gently raises his head and rests it on his thigh. Where was he hit? He runs his hand over the suit jacket, over the shirt, it's all soaked, is it snow or blood? Fear freezes him: he's going to die in his arms. He puts his hand in his pocket and pulls out his flashlight, above them there's shouting and calling, Brunet gives a fuck. He pushes the button, a ghastly face comes out of the darkness, Brunet looks at it. Fuck the Jerries, fuck Chalais, fuck the Party, nothing counts anymore, nothing even exists anymore except this awful face flashing before him, eyes closed. Under his breath he says: please don't die. But he knows that Vicarios is going to die: little by little, despair and hate overtake the course of this wasted life, to spoil it all the way back to birth. This absolute suffering cannot be erased by any victory mankind might achieve: it's the Party that's killing him, even if the USSR wins, men are alone. Brunet leans over, plunging his hands into Vicarios' soiled hair, crying as if he could still save him from the horror, as if two lost men could, at the last minute, vanquish solitude.

"I don't give a fuck for the Party: you're my only friend."

Vicarios hears nothing. His bitter mouth gargles and bubbles form, while Brunet cries in the wind:

"My only friend!"

The mouth opens, the jaw drops, the hair whips: the squall that lifts it and is gone, is death. He's hypnotized by this now-blank face, he thinks: I'm the one this death is happening to. The Germans rush down the slope holding onto the trees, he gets up and walks to meet them: his death is only just beginning.

CHAPTER 6
The Last Chance

Jean-Paul Sartre

1. FIRST SECTION

On his way up the stairs, Mathieu had to stop three times to catch his breath. Slowly he walked down the hallway. As he passed the second room, two German soldiers came out: one holding himself up on crutches, the other sporting a bandage over his forehead. On seeing Mathieu they broke out in a huge guffaw, but not maliciously; Mathieu laughed too, the soldiers shook their heads and went off. Mathieu watched them for a minute, then slowly started off again.

He stopped on the threshold of the "French Room": someone had opened the door and all the windows.

"Hey guys," said Mathieu. "Shall I close the door? There's a draft."

He waited a minute, then repeated, louder:

"Shall I close the door?"

A choking voice came from the end of a bed:

"Don't be an ass; we opened it cause it stinks."

Mathieu went in, his nose on the alert, walking between the beds. In the ones in the back were the guys with dysentery, brought down from the camp the night before, sleeping. They'd been flat on their backs since they'd arrived, and Mathieu hadn't been able to get a word out of them. He went over to a window, taking in the hill for a moment—blue in the sun, off in the distance—and smiled. Then he continued on. Bollard, in the bed next to his, watched him with his set twinkling eyes. When Mathieu came closer, Bollard started laughing affectionately.

"There you go again. We're going to have to kill you to get you to stop smiling."

"Sorry," Mathieu said, smiling.

"Idiots are that way: they laugh and laugh all day, and when you ask them why, it's because the soup is good, or they had a haircut that morning."

"Sane enough things to be happy for," said Mathieu, sitting down on the bed. "I don't see why anyone would refuse them that."

"Why were you smiling?"

"Like the idiots," said Mathieu. "Because it's a nice day, and I feel better."

He stopped suddenly. But Bollard didn't seem to have heard him. He smoothed the covers with a flattened hand, he seemed nervous and agitated.

"I'm leaving," he said abruptly.

"When?" said Mathieu.

"In a bit."

Mathieu stopped smiling. Without looking up, Bollard added:

"They're sending the invalids back home, no more Stalag. There's a convoy heading out later, and I have to meet them at the train station."

Mathieu looked at his lowered head, and didn't know what to say.

"I feel weird because you're staying here," said Bollard.

"Well, of course I'm staying here," said Mathieu. "What did you expect?"

His throat tight, he thought to himself: well, we're still the lucky ones.

"They'll send you up there," continued Bollard. "And then to a concentration camp in Germany . . . "

"If it's just that, no need to worry yourself for me," said Mathieu: "I'll be glad to go up there."

Bollard raised his head.

"Oh, you, sure!" He said disdainfully. "What wouldn't you be glad for? But not everyone's the same as you, thankfully." He asked: "You're not too tired?"

"No," said Mathieu. "For what?"

"To get me dressed."

Mathieu got up:

"Where are your clothes?"

"At the foot of the bed." He added: "The orderlies should be back, but I don't want them to touch me."

He had unbuttoned his shirt, Mathieu took it off, and admired Bollard's muscular torso.

"Man! Looks like you could wrestle a bull."

Bollard smiled, and flexed his biceps:

"Feel that!"

Mathieu felt it and whistled, then he took the khaki shirt from the bed and helped Bollard slip it on.

"So how are we going to do the pants?"

"You lift me up," said Bollard. "Bend over a little."

Mathieu bent over, Bollard put his arms around his neck; with a brisk effort, Mathieu picked him up: he was disagreeably light, like a dumbbell made of wood when you expected it to be cast iron. Mathieu almost fell over backwards. He regained his balance, and with his free hand picked up the pants from the bed.

"You all right?" asked Bollard.

"Why not? You know, a vine doesn't hold on with legs. It grabs on, dummy. Hold tight cause I'm letting go."

Bollard fastened onto his neck; Mathieu let go, took the pants in both hands and tried to slide them along his stumps.

"Oh Christ!" he said.

"It's tough, huh?"

"It's tough because I can't see anything. Wait a sec."

He placed one hand on Bollard's stomach and pushed him back a little; with the other hand he pulled the pants up. Thankfully the two thighs were cut off at the same height.

"There we go. Don't move."

He buttoned the fly: the pants held.

"They're tight," said Bollard. "I must have gained some weight. The shitty thing is I'm going to get fat."

Mathieu was already leaning over to put him on the bed.

"Now," said Bollard, "if you're not too tired, carry me over to the window. I want to see this hill at least once."

Mathieu walked toward the open window; Bollard looked and smiled:

"I'd hear you all looking at it, I'd hear you talking about it; you couldn't help it, you'd walk by the window, you'd glance out at it. But I'd never seen yet, y'know?"

He looked at it with excitement:

"You'll be up there. I thought it was higher. Is the white building the Headquarters?"

"Yeah."

"But can you see your camp?"

"It's behind the HQ."

"So you've never seen it either?"

"Of course not."

"Look at the road down there between the trees."

Mathieu looked at the road and saw a blackish mass flowing on it slowly.

"That's them," said Bollard. "That's the invalids, on their way down."

He seemed agitated all of a sudden.

"You can put me down."

It was time; Mathieu's heart was beating hard in his chest. He set Bollard on the edge of the bed; the legs of his pants, flat and empty, spread out on the sheet. Bollard looked at them:

"Gross isn't it? Do you have any pins?"

"Why would I have pins?" said Mathieu, shrugging his shoulders.

"If you had some, you could pin the legs of my pants to my jacket. It wouldn't be so gross."

They were quiet. A new look was forming on Bollard's happy, pretty face: a look of excuse, of crafty and thoughtful suffering.

He said:

"The view from up there—shouldn't be too bad."

"Not at all," said Mathieu.

"Before the war," continued Bollard, "there might have been a restaurant there, or a tavern."

Mathieu didn't respond.

"Oh well, there you have it," said Bollard. "For now, you see the hill from the hospital; once you're there it'll be just the reverse."

He bit his lip carefully, and said, for his own sake:

"In the end, you get tired of even the prettiest point of view."

Mathieu was silent. Then suddenly from Bollard's mouth came a cool stream, a gay, reasonable, reassuring voice:

"You'll escape. I know you, you won't be able to stop yourself."

"Hmm," said Mathieu.

"You'll see!" said Bollard passionately. "You'll see. It's going to be irresistible. First off, it's so easy. When you're so close to the border . . . "

Mathieu interrupted him: he didn't need reassuring.

"Why do you want me to escape?" he asked, smiling. "I told you I'm looking forward to being up there."

"To being up there?"

"Yeah."

Bollard shook his head:

"If I didn't know you, I'd be getting pissed off. You don't have the right to talk like that."

"Because?"

"Because of everything. You're a prisoner, you escape. That's what they do, that's what they're for."

He looked at Mathieu hard:

"I know what you're gonna say, that we have to be reasonable. I know the song and dance. But me, if I was in your place, I wouldn't be reasonable. If they weren't sending me home, I'd be screaming, I'd go on a hunger strike."

"What good would that have done you?"

"To make a point. There are some things you just can't accept. The Krauts are men, just like us. They don't have any right to take away our freedom."

Mathieu didn't want to respond: but Bollard had followed his gaze. Enraged, he cried out:

"It's not the same. The shell fell there by chance."

He turned red, and irritated by Mathieu's silence, he added:

"They didn't even know there was anyone in the woods, they were just firing for the sake of firing. No one took my legs from me. No one. It was an accident."

He turned his eye on Mathieu with such a look of anger and anguish that Mathieu quickly replied:

"If you say so."

Bollard tried to smile:

"You're saying that to make me shut up."

It had been hate, and hate alone, that had knocked him to the ground, and torn off his legs with its iron hand. Mathieu was familiar with this hate; Bollard had the right not to be.

"Really," Mathieu acknowledged, "everyone is responsible for you being wounded. But you can't be mad at everyone. And it's the same for me; the only reason I'm here is because of everyone else."

"Bull! There's these soldiers whose job it is to stop you from leaving, and later on, there'll be the ones whose job it is to beat you if you don't work for them. They're people you'd say hi to if you saw them in the street, and they'll take away your freedom, down to the tiniest detail, from one day to the next."

"For all I did with it anyway," said Mathieu smiling.

"Even to go take a shit," said Bollard, "you're going to have to ask permission."

And you, thought Mathieu, you're going to have to be carried. He turned his head away: Bollard was a man; he didn't deserve to be insulted by Mathieu's pity.

"You mean you've forgotten? Sunday mornings when you'd be thinking about whether to go for a drive in the country? And then in the evenings, coming home from work, taking your time, smoking your pipe . . . "

Mathieu clenched his teeth: I'm not the one who's losing all that, he is. And it's for good. How can he not see that yet? But Bollard insisted on singing the praises of this now-dead world, because he was ashamed of leaving, because he didn't want to think that he'd be leaving these resigned slaves behind. Mathieu, pretending to be cross, interrupted him:

"It's a crap shoot," he said. "Sure, we were free. So what. Free for what? Free from what? Were we able to stop Franco's victory, or this war? In a sense," he continued, "I've never felt as free as since I've been here."[1]

Bollard shrugged his shoulders:

"I don't get it."

"Nothing to get: that's how it is."

Bollard said nothing, and Mathieu added, softly:

"The thing of it is, I've got a bunch of pals over in the Stalag. I haven't seen them since the end of June, and I really want to find them."

"Pals from the regiment!" said Bollard with disdain.

"If you like. The guys I went through the war with."

"It's funny," said Bollard. "The guys from the regiment don't mean a thing to me. Now in Bordeaux, there I have some real friends: guys who may as well have been born with me. The one guy—for the last ten years, hasn't been a day we didn't get together. These guys here, I'll forget all their names in a few days once I'm free."

"Well, there you go," said Mathieu. "For me, these guys are the real ones."

("The real friends are the ones you aren't ashamed to be around with your legs gone"), he thought to himself.

Mystified, Bollard looked at him:

"So you don't have any friends?"

Daniel; Brunet. Mathieu raised his shoulders:

"Bah!"

"What about women? No women?"

"I've had some, like everyone."

"And you didn't like that? A pretty little thing in your bed?"

"Oh no, I liked it a lot. An intellectual, you know, what the hell's he to do? Talks with the guys, screws with the girls. I'll take screwing."

"I'm with you there."

"Yeah, well, better than nothing," said Mathieu.

"Better than nothing?"

"There ought to be more."

"Oh, you think?"

"In June, there was more. We didn't talk a lot. We waited for the Germans, we were together. Y'know, when our officers cut out . . . "

"What?"

"Well, we were together. If it was always like that with the guys, I'd give up screwing except once a month."

"In June, yeah . . . because we'd been beaten. But . . . "

Mathieu interrupted him:

"Up there, it's got to be the same. I'm sure it's the same."

He took a step back, turned toward the hill, and repeated: "I'm sure it's the same."

They were quiet for a moment, then, without looking at Mathieu, Bollard said:

"My wife and I screwed every day. Once in the morning, twice at night. Never stopped once from the day we got married until I got called up."

"Oh well then," chuckled Mathieu, "you'll be back at it!"

"You can bet on it," said Bollard. After a pause he added: "You can't imagine how it was. Sundays, we'd leave the theater before the play was over to go home and make love. Something to be happy for," he said laughing, "the shell didn't blow my balls off."

"You'll be back at it," Mathieu repeated mechanically. "Right back at it."

"She's fine too, my wife, you know," said Bollard. "She plays tennis and basketball; you disrespect her, and she'll put your lights out in two seconds. There were times, in bed, when she'd hold me up at arm's length. And slim: to look at her you wouldn't know she was an athlete."

He stretched out his muscular arms and looked at them smiling: "She especially loved my arms. My arms and my chest. She'd caress my shoulders and my chest. All the time. Sometimes with her fingers, sometimes with her lips. If someone had asked her which she'd prefer I keep, my arms or my legs, I can tell you she'd have said my arms. So you see, after all, it could have been worse."

He raised his eyes, feverish, sparkling, toward Mathieu, and both of them broke out laughing.

"You know what I worry about at night?" said Bollard. "I lie on my stomach and try to see if I can still make the moves. Because I can tell you, I'm not worried about her taking care of things, she'll do it all. But there's no chance she'll go on top. She doesn't want to, it disgusts her."

"And?" asked Mathieu. "Can you?"

"I don't know, it's complicated," said Bollard. "Maybe if I push with my arms. It's hard to get much leverage."

He looked off in the distance, and looked like he was afraid.

"She doesn't know yet . . . "

He got hold of himself quickly, and added:

"I'm not worried about her, y'know. She's strong. It's everyone else who'll drive me crazy. My parents, hers, friends. They'll be all 'Ooh,' and 'What a shame!' I really like Rouen,[2] but you know, it's funny to say it, but I'm glad it got bombed. From my point of you, y'know, an invalid won't attract so much attention in a city that's half-destroyed. People get used to it, and I don't know, I'll blend in with their buildings. Now Marseille, there's a place I'm glad I don't live. They haven't understood it yet, they'd pity me, like someone who got injured on the job. I don't want pity, I just want to fit in. We're going through Switzerland, you know," he said, getting agitated.

"Through Switzerland?"

"Yes, sure, through Switzerland. They'll be giving us chocolate and little cakes, for sure. Three days from right now . . . "

He gave Mathieu a look of surprise:

"It makes me laugh."

No reply from Mathieu.

"I was happy, y'know," said Bollard. "My wife and I, we played sports; never sick, never even a boo-boo. We weren't rich, but we kept things together. I put everything on being happy. Love, sports, my job . . . we'd go camping in the summer. D'you like that, camping?"

Mathieu smiled:

"No, not so much."

"Fathead! You don't like hiking?"

"Hardly."

Bollard laughed:

"There's no justice. I'm not the one who should be a legless cripple. You are!"

Mathieu laughed too:

"No," he said, "there's no justice."

Bollard became serious again:

"Will I ever be able to be happy again?"

Mathieu hesitated. Bollard looked him right in the face and added:

"You see, happiness, now, for me, it's a must."

"I think you will," said Mathieu.

They were quiet. Two German orderlies entered with a stretcher and some blankets. Bollard turned and looked at them with his big eyes; he'd gone pale, and his hands were shaking. The Germans came right over to him without a word, took him by the shoulders and the buttocks, lifted him up and rolled him into the blanket. He looked like a little package. Mathieu wanted to speak, but the words wouldn't come. Bollard looked at him for help; he opened his mouth, but all he said was:

"Goodbye, little guy."

Mathieu took a step, took Bollard from the orderlies and hugged him against himself without saying a thing; again he felt the awful lack of weight; then he leaned over and set him on the stretcher.

"Take care at night on the train," he said. "Don't catch cold."

"Don't worry, no chance I'll catch a cold; I always caught them from my feet up!"

The orderlies lifted the stretcher and set off.

"Goodbye," cried Bollard, "goodbye, and . . . .shit!"

"Shit to you too," said Mathieu.

The orderlies were already out the door. Mathieu thought: he's heading to hell; and for a moment he was horrified to think of the world Bollard was heading back to. Rue LaFayette at 6 PM, crisscrossed by thousands of solitary trajectories. From above, they make a crowd . . . Each one free, certainly, free and impotent. They're responsible for everything that happens to them, and they can't even raise their little finger. Bollard was heading back to that. Just as free, free with both legs cut off at mid-thigh; freedom only gives you something to be sorry for. Free, cut off from themselves and from everyone else by their freedom. Mathieu took a couple of steps toward the window, he looked at the green and darkened hill, at the column of invalids beneath him on the road; gently he felt his happiness coming back, he thought: "I'm no longer free." Thirty-six years of abstract solitude. Thirty-six years of thoughts about *nothing*. He looked up at the barracks wall; on the other side of it his friends were waiting for him, united by a single misfortune, a single destiny, by the same fatigue, the same hunger, the same anger. On the other side of it, encircled by barbed wire, a home town had been constructed and populated just for him.

2. SECOND SECTION

Mathieu was poking about in its belly with his horns, a large heavy eye watching him reproachfully: *Do you realize what you've done?* Mathieu wanted to explain, but in vain; bulls don't talk. *Do you realize what you've done?* He made a violent effort, cried out "No!," and his eyes opened, in darkness. Everything had vanished, except his confusion, this old stupor he'd had since June 18, and that didn't bother him, except when he'd wake up, do you realize what you've done? Far away, toes began moving: were they his? Was this long stretched out, scaly, larval body his? Partly in pain, partly insensitive? Not a bull, certainly, maybe a dead fish, belly up. He tried to get up, banged his forehead against the lid of his coffin, and fell back, dead, buried. It smelled like straw, like sweat, sour, indoor odors. He groaned, then gently, cautiously, lifted his arm and reached out in the night: it was true, there *really was* a sort of ceiling three inches from his nose. His arm fell back, discouraged. He turned his eyes, without moving his head, and could just make out a faint fog around his feet; to his right, a creature stirred, a large vermin; he could hear its nervous breathing. It must be pushing its snout into his side: he felt a heavy living warmth on his side that didn't belong to him. He put out his hand and felt, which brought a laugh and an unknown loud voice:

"So you're awake, little head?"

Mathieu woke all the way up and shook his head, but this time the scene didn't change. His eyes were filled with this darkness like ink, no getting rid of it, except by looking toward the end of the tunnel, at the light from the basement window. The voice went on alone, next to him:

"Boy, you were sound asleep! Everyone's gone, y'know. Just the two of us."

Another voice came down from above:

"Not true. I'm still here."

"Who said that?" said the first voice.

"Hubert, dumb ass!"

"Hey!" They both said at the same time.

Mathieu tried to turn onto his side, but only succeeded in wedging himself between the lid and the bottom of his coffin. His eyes hurt, but they were beginning to get used to the dark. Finally, to his right, just next to his armpit, he could make out a monstrously compressed face: a smiling mouth beneath a large round nose: no forehead, no eyes, no hair; a deformed chin extended by a goiter, fading into the shadow. The mouth moved, the voice came out, but between the words and the lips there was a delay like in the first talking movies.

"You must have arrived during the night?"

"Yeah."

"I heard you when they brought you in."

Christ! thought Mathieu. I'm just seeing this guy's head upside down! The owner of the head must be rather small; he was stretched out on his back; what Mathieu had thought was his nose was really his chin.

"You're getting out of the cooler?" the guy started again.

"No, the hospital, down below."

"Dysentery?" asked the voice from above.

"A slug in the lung."

"Ah! Ahahahah!"

The voice above had become respectful and distant. Next to Mathieu the other guy echoed respectfully:

"Ahahah!"

There was a brief silence.

"If you listen to'em," said the upside down mouth, "they'll all tell you they took down their Jerry. But, to be honest, there aren't many who've really fought."

Mathieu yawned and fell back on his back.

"I didn't fight," he said, "I was in the auxiliary. I caught this kind of like you catch a cold."

The guy chuckled.

"Me neither, I didn't fight either," he said complicitly.

"So, just like that, you're just out of the cooler?" asked Mathieu.

"Since yesterday." He called:

"Hey Hubert?"

"Yeah?"

"I had a cell all to myself," he said triumphantly.

"Prick!"

The guy explained to Mathieu:

"In the camp, you're never alone. Not even to shit."

"What had you done?" asked Mathieu.

"Hey! I got away!"

Now it was Mathieu's turn to feel respect. Deferentially, he asked:

"And where did they catch you?"

"At the border: I'd done the hardest part."

"Bad luck!"

The voice rang out in the dark:

"I've got no regrets."

"The cops beat up on you?" asked Hubert.

"You bet! Yeah, they beat on me pretty good, and brought me back in a truck, hell of a ride. But it doesn't matter, even if they'd kicked the shit out of me on the train, I would have no regrets. Once you get your foot outside, you go crazy! You can't believe what it does to you."

He had lifted himself up on an elbow, and considered Mathieu with interest. Mathieu smiled at this large friendly moon shining in the sky above him, and remembered the countryside and the night.

"You tempted?" asked the guy.

Mathieu laughed:

"Hey, gimme a chance: I just got here!"

"You pulled two months in the hospital?" asked Hubert. "You must have been pretty bad off?"

Mathieu laughed again:

"Pretty bad!" he said.

He lifted his arms, one after the other, with satisfaction. Escaping was out of the question: escaping was for prisoners. Mathieu wasn't a prisoner yet, he had just been born. The morning light spread between his feet; outside, around the barracks, there was an unknown city, and men were walking around in it. He suddenly burned with the desire to be among them, like in the past when he would awaken in Grenada or Meknès after a night voyage. He glued his palms to the board and pulled with his upper arms. His moist hands stuck to the wood like suction cups, his back slid slowly toward the light, the back of his head scraping the bottom of the coffin, it was quite funny. After a minute he stopped: his legs were hanging in the air, feeling around for a support, but no luck; he twisted to turn onto his stomach, but he couldn't do it, a crab stuck on its back.

"Who's making all the racket?" asked Hubert.

Mathieu heard his neighbor chuckling:

"It's the new guy, getting some exercise."

He said to Mathieu:

"Let yourself slide out, you won't get hurt."

"Ok," said Mathieu

He pushed himself forward and jumped, eyes closed.

"There you go," said Hubert kindly, "it's a little tight, but you get used to it pretty fast. You know what we all call them? Coffins."

"I'm not surprised," said Mathieu.

He opened his eyes, and saw *nothing*. He was nowhere. Between two wooden frames with rectangular holes, there were a table and benches, but it was nothing, not even furniture, not even utensils, not even things; the inert underside of a few simple gestures; suspended in emptiness. The emptiness enveloped Mathieu with a glassy dissolving look, penetrating his eyes, gnawing at his flesh, all there was was a skeleton: "I'll be living in emptiness." The skeleton took a seated position. Luxurious and golden, the September light came in through the open window but, finding nothing to illuminate, it died in midair and fell into a soft fog on the table. Mathieu was having trouble breathing. He thought: "I still get winded fast."

"So," said the voice from above, "what do you say?"

Mathieu quickly raised his head and saw two animal eyes shining from inside one of the holes.

"It's like a morgue," he said.

It looked to him like one of the holes was sticking out its tongue at him, but it was just a pair of legs. They flowed out, wriggled about, and blossomed into a large backside; a short chubby guy in a khaki shirt fell to the floor like a ripe apple. He smiled at Mathieu and looked about the room with objectivity:

"This place here," he said, "is a way-station, for clients on their way. They put you here when you get out of jail or the hospital, until you find a job."

"And then?" asked Mathieu.

"Then you go to another barracks, with the guys who have the same job as you."

"And the other barracks, are they nicer than this?"

"Of course," said the chubby fellow.

"So what else do they have in them?"

"They don't have anything else, but, y'know, it's your place, home."

Mathieu put on his jacket:

"I've got some friends in this camp," he said. "Any idea how I go about finding them?"

The short fellow laughed a bit:

"There are thirty thousand of us," he said simply.

"I see," said Mathieu.

"What are their names, your pals?," asked Hubert.

"There's Charlot," said Mathieu, "and then Lubéron, and Longin. All from the 68th."[3]

"Don't know 'em."

"And Pierné?"

"No," said Hubert, "not familiar."

"Try the infirmary," said the short one, "they see so much that happens, maybe they'd know them."

"Where is it?"

"You take the Grand-Rue, you follow it along, you can't miss it."

"Ok, good," said Mathieu, "so long."

"So long," they said.

He opened the door and stepped out. He expected light and warmth, but he found himself in the cool shade of undergrowth. He was in the middle of a tunnel, light shining from each end. He started walking, and the boards bounced and creaked under his feet; he went by closed doors without stopping; he knew now that they each opened onto emptiness, but it was the outside that drew him; out there thirty thousand idlers were dawdling in the sun; he would walk among them, visit the monuments.

A golden froth sputtered in his eyes, blinded him, melted into violet patches which faded, disappeared, and then once again he saw *nothing*. Nothing. No more a city than a horse's ass: a couple of big boxes left on a vacant lot. Between the boxes, open space, and then some more boxes beyond them. The ground was grey and tortured: dried mud. A tidal wave of flotsam and arks must have crashed against the hill and withdrawn, the arks remaining. Far off, to the right, stood a large wooden door, closed and solitary, in the emptiness; he turned around and, far off to the left, he saw another door, just the same, against the sky. Between these two barbaric portals set down in the desert, facing one another like the remnants of some ancient disaster, was a swarm. Churned by various currents, a crowd flowed along the barracks; one might almost have thought it a human crowd. Mathieu's gaze followed one of the currents, the chaos of the abandoned arks organized itself as they passed; they seemed to border a busy boulevard. But it was counterfeit, a fake crowd on a fake boulevard. As soon as Mathieu turned his eyes toward the barracks, they fell back into isolation, the boulevard fell apart, the space froze, nothing was left but the boxes, separated by an undifferentiated void. Mathieu's heart sank. The current brought a couple of these strange creatures that looked so much like men toward him. From up close, their cotton eyes and inert faces betrayed them; among themselves, they spoke in a foreign language, and from time to time a hard and exaggerated animation lit up on their cheeks, fading out just as quickly, like the brief springtime of a polar land. They seemed neither old nor young, neither happy nor unhappy. Or perhaps, in each other's eyes, they seemed young, happy, or unhappy, and Mathieu just could not read their expressions. As they passed, they stared him full in the face, a brutal laugh distorted their mouth and disappeared; ill at ease, Mathieu thought:

"I must seem like a tourist."

"Hey! . . . " he started to say.

But already their eyes were gone, their conversation began again like a downpour: the unknown language turned out to be French: "Why couldn't I hear it right away?" Because he'd just left the hospital where only German was spoken? Because French had already gone the way of dead languages? Or because these captives, forgotten in a strange land, were deforming their native language a little more each day? He listened closely, caught some rude and raucous, nearly mechanical, sounds.

"Was on the *Paris*.[4] Elevator operator. Saw some places."

And then: "Arizona . . . Painted Desert . . . "

They moved along and Mathieu repeated: "Painted Desert, Arizona," for the pleasure of assembling these beautiful little objects of painted wood, these Russian Easter eggs that resembled words but meant nothing, and shone for themselves alone. Again he repeated "Arizona, the Painted Desert," and by the hundreds, eyes came forth from the crowd and pushed against him, caressing him as they passed and leaving damp traces on his face and hands, the desert, Arizona, and it became a poem, which filled him with its odor: "Here words don't have meaning anymore, they have odors." Words struck, others, and still more, "radio," "English overcoat," "lottery," "semaphore": these strange animals that seem to talk are poets. They flowed against him, bumping and jostling him, yet he remained *outside*, and their behavior seemed inexplicable to him. They were not loafing, but they also were not going anywhere. They were flowing, seriously, deliberately, ceremoniously. Even though they filled him with a slight repulsion, and even fear, like crazies he had seen in Rouen in 1936, he knew perfectly well that he was not in an insane asylum: rather, he was in a breeding ground of crabs and lobsters. He was fascinated by these prehistoric crustaceans who crawled around on the tormented ground of an unknown planet, suddenly his heart sank and he thought: in a few days, I'll be one of them. He would have these same eyes, airs, and gestures, he would understand these incomprehensible creatures from inside, he would be a crab, and that would seem atrociously natural to him. He rocked on his heels, he watched his destiny unfolding before him: one step and he'd be in it, but he didn't dare, he remained torn between desire and fear; he hesitated as though it was an extremely grave commitment; my words will freeze, my eyes will go sightless, strange flowers will blossom in my head. "Let this be over as quickly as possible!" he thought, and he threw himself forward. Nothing happened, except a little turning of faces he'd provoked by pushing in. Faces turned toward him, sniffing, curious and brutal, like the faces of those born blind. He walked a moment, out of place, undigested, a rock in a pond, the crowd quieting around him. Fortunately he spotted a group of buildings on his left, surrounded with barbed wire; on the façade of the largest he read *Krankenrevier*. He pulled himself from the crowd and moved along the barbed wire; his jacket caught on an iron star, he pulled away and pushed the gate open.

"Hold on there!"

Mathieu stopped, forbidden. A large mustachioed man wearing a Red Cross armband hurried toward him:

"You can't come in here. What do you want?"

"I want to see an orderly," said Mathieu politely.

"Which one? Why?"

"Any one at all. It's for some information."

The mustachioed man eyed him from head to toe. He was a simple soldier, but he had the arrogance of a captain:

"No entry. Prisoners have no right to enter the infirmary."

"So what are you doing inside?"

The mustache looked at him sideways:

"I'm not a prisoner," he said.

He turned his back and headed back to the *Krankenrevier*. Behind Mathieu someone started to laugh. Mathieu started, turned around suddenly and saw a gaping mouth: the laugh was coming from it, awkward, distant.

"Hey?"

The guy gestured with his hand and lowered his eyes, his mouth stayed open beneath his closed eyes and the laughter continued to roll about inside. Discouragingly, this made him seem incommunicably delighted.

"That's how it is," he said, "that's how it is."

He rested his hand familiarly, almost tenderly, on the cable of the barbed wire, and played with a rusted star with his finger.

"Not like us, the orderlies. Not guys like you and me. Sleep in beds. Not prisoners."

"They aren't prisoners?" asked Mathieu with surprise.

"Aren't prisoners."

It was hard to tell if he was responding to Mathieu or if he was just repeating the words for his personal pleasure. Laughing, he added:

"Why doncha go tell 'em they're prisoners? You'll see."

"Oh yeah?" said Mathieu, annoyed. "But why?"

The prisoner did not seem to have heard him. He meditated a moment, mouth open, then words exploded from between his teeth, and his face was covered with red splotches:

"Apart from that, half of 'em who have the armband are orderlies about as much as I am!"

"What did they do?" asked Mathieu, interested. "Fake their papers?"

No answer. The prisoner cleaned the nail of his index finger on one of the points of the star.

"That's how it is!" he said finally. "That's how it is!"

He raised his eyelids and seemed to just discover Mathieu's presence: "You're not from here," he said in a defiant tone. "Where'd you come from?"

"From the hospital."

The guy nodded:

"Y'can tell right away you're not from here."

He winked, reassured:

"I'm Chomis."

"Delarue," said Mathieu.

"What do you want with the orderlies?"

"I'm looking for friends from my division, they were captured at the same time as me."

He blushed and stopped. He had just realized he'd been yelling, as though he were talking to a deaf man. He lowered his voice to add:

"They should have been here for about a month."

The prisoner looked at him proudly:

"Well," he said haughtily, "you've got your work cut out for you. 'Cause I can tell you, there's a couple of guys in this camp."

"I thought," said Mathieu, "that maybe the orderlies would know them."

The guy shook his head.

"Nobody knows nobody. It's Babylonia I tell you. You couldn't even find your brother."

A fellow exited the infirmary, svelte and fresh, in a stunning uniform, with pink cheeks and human eyes.

"There's Stoegler," said the prisoner. "Go ahead and ask him."

Stoegler opened the gate and came out through the fence. Before plunging into the crowd, he paused for a moment to put on his gloves.

"Hey, could I have a word!" said Mathieu.

Stoegler pulled on his right glove. He lifted his head and considered Mathieu, amused.

"What?"

"I just got here from the hospital," said Mathieu. "I have some friends in the camp and I want to find them."

"So? What's that got to do with me?"

"Somebody told me," said Mathieu patiently, "that maybe the orderlies would know their names."

"I don't know any names. Talk to Chauviré; he has a list of the sick."

"I can't go inside."

"Then wait till he comes out."

He turned and left with a spring in his step. Chomis watched him walk off and said, sadly:

"Wasn't a bad guy. But he's too good for us now."

"Oh well," said Mathieu, "I'll just wait."

"That's all there is to do," said Chomis.

He laughed:

"Time doesn't cost anything here, right?"

"Seems about right."

In fact, Chomis didn't go. He stayed there like a post, without even looking at Mathieu; he just let time pass.

"You wouldn't know them, by chance, would you?" asked Mathieu.

"You crazy?" asked Chomis, indignantly. "I told you, nobody knows nobody."

"The guys from the 70th ?"[5]

Chomis pinched his mouth.

"No, no, no."

"Pierné, Longin, Lubéron," said Mathieu.

"No, no, I tell you I don't know 'em."

"Charlot, Nippert?"

"Save your breath. Tell you, I don't know 'em. You'll never find 'em like that."

"Alright, alright!" said Mathieu.

They fell silent; Mathieu reached out his hand and began to scrape the cable of the barbed wire with his nail. They turned their backs on each other, and Mathieu thought: I'll find them, I'll find them anyway. He could just see Charlot's big old smiling face, and he felt good. After a minute, Chomis put his hand on Mathieu's shoulder:

"Did you say Longin?"

"Yeah, Longin."

"And Lubéron? And Charlot? And Nippert?"

"Yeah."

Chomis turned toward the slow parade of prisoners, looked at it an instant, then called out:

"Hey, Derrien!"

A guy emerged from their ranks, followed by two other soldiers. They stopped in silence two steps from Mathieu and Chomis, and looked at them with patient, faded eyes.

"Hey, Derrien," said Chomis grandly, "listen!"

He pointed at Mathieu:

"This guy here just gets out of the hospital, right? Looking for his pals, right? Ok, so he has to run into me!"

The guys did not seem to follow.

"So I says to him, who y'lookin' for?" explained Chomis. "He says, lookin' for the orderlies. Whaddayawant with the orderlies, I says. He says sometimes they might know where my pals are crashing. So I says tell me their names already. And he says. And y'know what? It's Lubéron, Longin, Charlot, and Nippert, who I crash with at the 57th!"

They were silent. It seemed to Mathieu that they were blowing him off; he'd have to go back into the crowd, find a barracks, shout cries of joy, answer questions: too much. Around him mouths opened wide below deadened eyes; they released their laughter: always the same blind and brutal laugh that sounded like drumming.

"Shit," said Derrien.

A little shark shrugged his head:

"He can boast he's got a charmed life, this guy."

"He says I'm waiting for the orderlies, sometimes they'll know where my pals are," explained Chomis. "I says to him, what're their names. And he says, and turns out they're the guys who crash with me at the 57th."

"Brilliant!" says the shark.

"You bet," said Chomis with pride. "It's brilliant, and don't happen every day. Cause I'll tell you, this Stalag is Babylonia. You lose your division here, you'll never find it again, and this guy right out of the hospital, has to run into me."

"Brilliant!"

They turned their backs to Mathieu and laughed without paying any attention to him. He would have laughed with them, but it would have been indiscrete. He waited patiently, scraping the red rust from the barbed wire, which was both irritating and sensual, he kept thinking the flakes of rust would fall off, but they held tight, making his fingers red with rust; if I hadn't met this Chomis, I'd have stayed here all day warming myself in the sun, watching for the orderlies to come out: enough to pretty much take up a whole day. He remembered that he still had four German cigarettes, and he felt like smoking, but his pocket was impossible, so far below his sides that he'd need the arms of a giant to reach it. The urge faded: here all desires must be the same; states of mind, nothing more. His head turned about by itself, and he saw a sky that was too light, too pale, too high. Of course, skies change, they move westward; no question that the Stalag would have its own sky just for itself. Behind him the rumors and whisperings of the town, before him some shacks in open country, above him this abstract emptiness . . . He shook his shoulders, objects began returning to their normal dimensions, his arm withdrew from the barbed wire, plunged hard and fast into the pocket of his jacket, took out a cigarette; it seemed to Mathieu that for a moment he had been stretched out like a long goatsbeard flower; by contrast, he now felt himself dense and compact. He lit his cigarette, took a few puffs, and suddenly a chorus of Parisian voices rose up. He turned abruptly, and at first saw nothing but the procession of shell-less snails pulling itself through the muddy field. But then he felt himself blush: the snails were looking at him, fifty pairs of eyes had turned toward him, stupefied and scandalized. He did not understand, then he saw that Chomis' gaze was focused on his lips. He raised his hand, removed the cigarette from his mouth and let it hang against his thigh, at the end of his arm.

"I got it at the hospital," he said.

"Us guys," explained Chomis with a tone of perfect objectivity, "we haven't had a smoke since June.[6] They keep talking about puttin' in a canteen, but it's nowhere near ready."

Their eyes remained glued to Mathieu. Louder, he repeated:

"I got 'em at the hospital."

They didn't budge; they did not seem to understand French. Mathieu reached into his pocket and brought out the other three cigarettes.

"Take 'em," he said quickly, "I hardly smoke, it won't bother me."

He offered them to Chomis and Derrien. They took them indifferently. Derrien passed one on to the shark, who stuck it behind his ear. Mathieu felt the heat from his on his fingertips. He didn't dare let it fall:

"I just wanted a couple of puffs," he explained.

He stamped it out on his heel and put it back in his pocket. The looks went dark, the parade of bouncing heads with cotton eyes started up again. Derrien and the shark turned back to the crowd and disappeared into it; Chomis considered Mathieu with a wise and profound look, but did not say anything.

"So?" asked Mathieu.

"So, let's go," said Chomis.

The crowd closed about them, tossing them and carrying them along for a few minutes, then spit them out.

"To the right," said Chomis.

They set themselves to slogging through the mud between two barracks.

"To the right again."

They turned and slogged some more. Chomis turned to Mathieu:

"D'you know the camp?"

"I just got here last night."

"Ok, well, I'll take you that way there," said Chomis. "Not as quick, but it's nicer."

The ground sloped gently down to a barbed-wire fence three rows deep; Chomis made a hand gesture:

"You'll see, I'll do the honors."

He leapt between the puddles gracefully; Mathieu had a hard time keeping up. Chomis noticed, and slowed down:

"Sorry," he said, "it's because of my sea legs."

"How are the guys?" asked Mathieu abruptly. He was worried, he looked at Chomis and wondered if they had become like him. Chomis seemed surprised, but he said:

"Very well, they're all doing very well."

But the words seemed to lose their meaning as they came out of his mouth. They were close to the fence; Chomis laid his arm on Mathieu's.

"Stop," he said, pointing to a German lookout on the platform of the watchtower. "We're going to catch some crap."

They stopped; a few guys wandered around them with vacant eyes. On the other side of the fence, Mathieu saw a paved road, beyond the road a field, and far off, the top of a hill.

"This," said Chomis, "is the scenic view. Y'know what's below us?"

"No."

"Trier," said Chomis, triumphantly.

"Oh?"

"Trier!" repeated Chomis, staring him straight in the eyes.

"Sure, Ok," said Mathieu, "but I don't see anything."

"Of course you don't see anything, but there's no doubt about it. At the end of the field there's a wooded slope and a little path at the edge of the woods—if you take it down, you come out right in the town."

His eyes remained fixed:

"Seems there's a river. And some old monuments."

"Yeah," said Mathieu.

"Oh? You know it?"

"They walked us around there a little, just lately."

"See, I came in at night, and I didn't see anything at all; so for me it's a surprise. But there are some guys in our place who work down there and who told me what it's like."

He made a grand gesture and finished up:

"So there you have it. The town and the river, down there below us."

Mathieu obediently repeated to himself "Trier is down there below us," and for a moment he felt pleased: if he had to live in captivity, may as well do it at the top of a hill.

"Check that out," said Chomis.

They had started walking again and were passing by a long, resonating, singing barracks without windows, with large stable doors.

"That's the Arabs' barracks."[7]

Through the open doors, Mathieu saw dark shadows. Shapes were moving about in the dark.

"You hear the tom-toms?"

"Yeah."

"Y'd think y'were in Africa, huh? Every night they make that racket; must be like that in the Congo, sometimes y'can't even sleep. Ah," he said, "you wouldn't believe all the races and nations you'll find in this Stalag, y'll meet guys from everywhere, Belgians, Dutch, Spaniards, Arabs, Indochinese, Hindus, what a mess! Seems there's even some secret societies, some political groups, a lodge, I could write you a story: the Mysteries of the Stalag."

Mysteries! Mathieu watched the guys passing by with eyes like scars, bodies bent over, stretched out, flattened by incomprehensible habits, and they seemed to him completely without mystery. The Stalag might have mysteries for them because they recognized each other, half-understood each other, because in their eyes they made up a human society, because their faces were promising and menacing for each other, because each of them was, for each of the others, his most intimate enemy as well as his brother; later perhaps, once he'd become a prisoner, Mathieu would think about the camp's mysteries with this intrigued pride. For now he saw flat interchangeable beings scurrying about, each with the same face; they were right here, and yet he seemed to see them from far off. Ants don't have any mysteries, except maybe for other ants. Mathieu thought that it was a strange fate, for a man to be condemned to become an ant.

They passed alongside the Arabs' barracks; the drums suddenly got louder, like the flight of doves, constantly starting over, the beating of thousands of startled wings. Chomis took stock of Mathieu:

"Well?"

"Yeah," said Mathieu.

"Like you're in Africa?"

"You bet," said Mathieu politely.

He was most certainly not in Africa, not even anywhere on a human planet. He was walking, dry and crisp, between the glass panes of an aquarium. The horror was not in him yet, he could still defend himself against it: it was in things, and in the eyes of those who saw what he didn't see. But soon, because of the water pressure and the great sea-spiders, these panes would break. He made himself think about seeing Charlot, Pierné, Lubéron, again, and rejoiced: we'll be among men.

"Here's the place."

They went inside the barracks, followed a hallway; Chomis stopped in front of a door and started laughing:

"This'll be some surprise; they don't expect you."

He pushed open the door, Mathieu went in at his heels: the table, the benches, the two vertical cemeteries; sitting at the table, four prisoners were playing bridge; by the window two other guys were lying on their sides on their bunks, it took Mathieu a minute to tell that it was Charlot and Lubéron. He took a step towards them, then stopped, unsure; in a way they hadn't changed, hadn't even lost weight. But they had camp-eyes. They'd raised their heads and looked at him without recognizing him; who's changed, me or them? After a second, something clicked on Charlot's face and a surprised mouth opened up to laugh. But it wasn't his carefree laugh from before, it was the camp-laugh.

"Delarue! Shit!"

Lubéron laughed as well, and repeated:

"Delarue!"

Mathieu's heart sank as he joyfully called out:

"Hey, you guys!"

"Hey!" they said.

"So there y'are, buddy," said Charlot. "There y'are."

One of the bridge-players got up and threw his cards on the table—Longin.

"Hey there, clown-face," said Mathieu to him.

Longin gave him a serious smile, and said:

"Lucky you, it's my turn to play dead; that way I can shake your hand."

None of them seemed surprised.

"You're not surprised to see me?" asked Mathieu. "I thought you'd figure I was dead."

His voice seemed high, sounded false.

"No," said Charlot, "no, no. We knew y'weren't dead, we knew y're being patched up in the hospital."

"And now," said Longin, "you all better?"

They looked at him with a little annoyed distraction, as though he was disturbing their sleep, like kids who are dragged away from their toys into the world of grown-ups; they didn't seem all that happy to see him again.

"I'm better, yeah," said Mathieu, sadly.

"Hey, sit down," said Lubéron.

Mathieu sat.

"So where are you? Which barracks?"

"Seventeen."

"Seventeen?" repeated Longin, knitting his brow.

"Oh, yeah," said Charlot, "the way-station barracks."

"The one behind the latrines?"

"No, no," said Lubéron emphatically, "it's on the Grand-Rue; 17, just above the Krankenrevier."

"Ah!" said Longin, satisfied, "Ah, ah!"

Charlot turned toward Mathieu politely:

"And have you been in the camp long?"

Mathieu was about to answer when Chomis cut him off:

"Since yesterday," he said triumphantly. "Last night he slept in 17, then today he goes out to look around, and he had to run into me."

The guys look at Chomis, intrigued. Charlot asks:

"Do you know him?"

"Not a bit," said Chomis, "never seen this guy in my life."

"So," said Charlot, mystified.

"So, that's how it happened," said Chomis. "He's comin' towards me, he says doncha know my pals? What pals I says, he says Lubéron, Longin, and Charlot. I says all ya gotta do is follow me and you'll see 'em. And that's how it all happened."

Their cheeks showed some life, they looked at Chomis with hungry interest; Longin said:

"No kidding?"

Charlot makes himself go through it again:

"He didn't know you, he bumped into you, and he asked you where we were?"

"In front of the infirmary, yeah," said Chomis.

"As luck goes," said Charlot, "that's a real piece of luck."

"A chance in a million," said Longin.

They spoke among themselves for a minute. Mathieu lowered his head. He could vaguely hear them talking about this extraordinary coincidence, and he felt alone. Suddenly he heard his name and looked up; they were introducing him to the bridge-players.

"The dark guy down there," said Charlot, "is Garnier. He's from Marseille. The blond guy who looks like a girl is Roquebrune; the little guy is Charlier."

Mathieu gave them a wave of his hand. With interest, Garnier asked him:

"You came from the hospital?"

"Yeah."

"What do they give you to eat there?"

"That depended," said Mathieu. "Bread, soup; sometimes sausage or herring; honey sometimes."

"Greasy, fatty?"

"Yeah."

"How much bread? About 350 grams?"

"About that."

Garnier seemed satisfied:

"Same as here."

"But!" said Chomis, "they had tobacco."

They all jumped at this, and Garnier looked crossly at Mathieu:

"Tobacco?"

"No," said Mathieu, irritated. "The orderlies would slip us a cigarette if they were in a good mood."

"If that's all it is," said Garnier, reassured, "the soldiers here will slip us a cigarette from time to time."

He stopped, seemed to sigh, and repeated in a mollified tone:

"Yeah, yeah, it's the same as here."

There was silence for a minute; Mathieu finally dared to ask the question that was burning on his lips:

"So how is it, how's life here?" he asked timidly. "Bearable?"

They didn't respond right away, as though the question caught them unprepared, then Charlot raised his head and gave Mathieu a shy smile:

"You'll see," he said, "if you watch yourself, you can get by ok. It's not life in the manor, for sure, but you can have a nice little life."

A nice little life. Mathieu looked at Charlot horrified, as if he had just been turned into a gigantic cockroach. The others said nothing, faces blank as walls. Impossible to know if they felt the same. Somebody farted, a long, harsh rip. Everybody cracked up.

"It's Charlier! It's Charlier again!"

Charlier raised his finger toward the ceiling, pretending to see a rocket:

"Oh the pretty blue one!"

Chomis and Roquebrune jumped on him, laughing and punching him:

"We'll teach you not to fart when we've got visitors, that's gross! Where were you raised?"

Charlier laughed and fought back; Garnier turned to Mathieu and explained:

"It's the soup, it gives you gas. You must know, since they give you the same in the hospital."

"Yeah, sure," said Mathieu quickly.

Charlot farted next, raised his eyes and said childishly:

"Sometimes we have contests."

Mathieu made no reply, Charlot suddenly blushed. Mathieu turned away and thought, I'm embarrassing them. There was a long silence. Longin went back to sit at the table, and picked up his cards. Lubéron looked out the window. They didn't have anything more to say to each other.

"Here comes the soup," said Lubéron. They leaned toward the window, and their faces took on a fugitive air of nearly human expectation.

"Ha!" they said. "Ha, Ha!"

Charlot said to Mathieu:

"It's Schwartz, he'll be surprised. He mentions you a lot."

"Schwartz?" said Mathieu. "Our Schwartz? The guy from Sarrebourg?"[8]

"You bet, look, there he is comin' along with the soup."

Mathieu saw two prisoners carrying a large soup pot with difficulty. The first was Schwartz, looking the same as ever, except that he seemed to be asleep. The other one, skeletal and tall with yellow eyes, seemed feverish and ill. Mathieu didn't know him.

"But wait," he said, "I thought he left with the Alsacians."

"No, he didn't."

The door opened. They came in and set the pot on the table. A slosh of soup washed over the cover and splashed onto the floor.

"Have some soup," said Schwartz in a cheerless voice.

"What is it?"

"Codfish."

"Shit," said Longin, "the same thing again."

"Hey Schwartz," said Charlot. "Guess who's here!"

Schwartz raised his head, intrigued. He spotted Mathieu and his eyes shone. With a sense of hope Mathieu thought: it doesn't seem to have got him so bad.

"Little buddy!," said Schwartz, "little buddy!"

He was on him in two steps, took him by the collar, and hugged him.

"Oh, I'm so happy! In the name of God, I am so happy!"

"Me too, I'm so happy to see you," said Mathieu warmly.

They laughed as they looked each other over; Mathieu felt warmed through again; he'd just found a man who was still full of life.

"I didn't expect to find you here," he said. "Didn't they let all the Alsacians go?"

"I didn't say I was Alsacian."

"Why not?"

"That's just how it is," said Schwartz. "At the last minute, I backed down."

He twisted his mouth and went back to looking cheerless. Mathieu was going to ask him more, but a strange laughter cut off his words. The big skeleton was looking him over ironically:

"So, after all's said and done, neither one of us is dead."

Mathieu was shocked, and stared at the ravaged yellowed mask, stupefied.

"You can't see me yet?" asked the fellow.

"Pinette," murmured Mathieu grudgingly.

Pinette laughed and rolled his furious eyes. The others watched him in silence with a sort of fear. Schwartz had taken a step back.

"Pinette," repeated Mathieu, sadly.

Pinette had approached him, and breathed in his face; he smelled of fever and cellar. In spite of himself, Mathieu said:

"I thought you were dead."[9]

Pinette stopped laughing:

"No more dead than you," he said in a nasty voice. Shaking his head, he added, "They had us hands down. Unless y'were lucky."

"Lucky!" said Mathieu. "I don't think I was too lucky."

"Ha!" said Pinette, "must have been. Everybody else was killed, but not us. How do you explain that?"

"But . . . " said Mathieu.

Pinette laughed painfully:

"Either that or else there's a God looking out for assholes."

No one breathed a word. Pinette seemed like a sorcerer in the midst of his tribe. He looked at Mathieu for another minute with large fiery eyes, then turned on his heels and walked off, tossing back over his shoulder with flair:

"Besides, you'll see, we're dead anyway. All the disadvantages of the dead, but none of the benefits."

Mathieu saw him go up to the bed frame, tip up on his toes, heave himself up and disappear into the hole with the speed of a cockroach. He turned toward Schwartz, looking at him inquisitively. Schwartz seemed painfully affected. He raised his index finger and touched his forehead silently. The others remained silent, the only sound was the clicking of the cards on the table. To reconnect with them, thought Mathieu, I'll have to go through the eye of a needle. I'll have to become like them.

* * *

3. FRAGMENTS

The following fragments undoubtedly belong to a very early version of **The Last Chance**. *Many elements make clear that they are part of the story of December 1940 or January 1941, when Mathieu had been reunited with members of his regiment. The manuscript contains several variations of numerous passages; this is well illustrated in the case of Mathieu's daydream of killing (Fragment D).*

A. Ramard

The German stared at them crossly:

"The French are thieves," he said.

He looked at Pinette, waiting for a denial. But Mathieu was still holding Pinette's arm. The German began again, disappointed:

"Thieves. They steal in the camp, they steal from each other, and they try to steal from us."

"Who stole from you?"

The German nodded his head:

"It's a big deal," he said. "You'll see. The French stole from the store. A fur."

"A what?"

"A woman's fur coat."

"What was it doing there?" said Pinette.

Mathieu could see where this was going; he wanted to say, "You stole it yourselves in France." He said:

"Have you arrested them?"

The German shook his head sadly and repeated:

"A big deal! A big deal!"

He looked at his wrist and said:

"In line. Back to your barracks."

They got up like school children. On the way out Mathieu breathed to Pinette:

"It's the guys in 28 who did it, we've got to warn them."

They gathered in the courtyard of the headquarters. Ten steps away another group of prisoners waited, fifteen steps away, another. The French secretaries came to join them, the daily routine. Mathieu was in a park, a sumptuous park; he gazed at the bare branches of the trees above the wall and thought he was in a park. All the little things he was deprived of, streets, towns, gardens, he could see them there on this ransacked earth. There were some footpaths between the barracks that he hated just like Avenue La Bourdonnais. His whole universe was there. German soldiers ran toward them yelling orders. The groups of prisoners lined up together four by four; they crossed the courtyard and the door of the headquarters opened. This was the brief moment that Mathieu liked the best. The headquarters was on one side of the road, the prison camp on the other. The moment when he crossed the black infinite road, when he plunged into other people's freedom, contained all the evenings when he'd returned home from teaching, in town, while the lights were coming on. They began to march, Pinette shaking his head and talking to himself:

"Just because they beat us doesn't mean I have to lose my dignity."

"What?" said Charlot.

"Just because they won doesn't give 'em the right to see my ass," said Pinette.

"Hell," said Charlot, "if they want to see mine, they can see it, and I won't even care."

Charlot is modest, so he tries to protect himself by burying his unhappiness in old fashioned humility. He's relaxed. Pinette has a knife in his heart. There's a knot, an obscure point where his wife and his near-death on June 20, 1940 come together.[10] Pinette is resentment and recrimination. He refuses to accept his captivity the way that Pierné refused to accept the war. But since he's not in Paris, and can't live there, rejected by his wife, he's nowhere. He's just resentment, everything he sees wounds him and he hates it. Charlot is trying to get along; while Pinette's getting in line, he says:

"If you don't go having big ideas, you could have yourself a nice little life: some whale blubber, 400 grams of bread a day, we're not going hungry; we sleep on boards, but we get enough sleep, the work's not too exhausting; they hardly ever knock us around, and we get paid 30 marks a month." *A nice little life*: except that it's unlivable. We're women, slaves, dead. Fed, housed, maintained. No relationship between our work and our pay. The future has been taken away. The past is ambiguous, uncertain; defeat, like death, has taken away the meaning of everything we've lived through. The present is pure repetition, generalized. He turns around and looks at the guys: hard faces, hard eyes. Several laugh among themselves. They don't seem sad. Not melancholy. Hard but tender. They often laugh, but they never smile. They laugh in bursts. And each one confronts the same problem: how to live, what lie to use in order to live? Hunger or pain would give this existence some meaning, but we aren't hungry, and we aren't suffering. We're abstractions. They enter the camp, the German in charge of them signals the guard. They struggle through the mud in the central path (it had rained overnight); they turn left between the barracks; Feldwebel Langen approaches them; counts them. He gestures and the little group disperses. Mathieu goes into Barracks 28. He knocks on the Barracks leader's door. A nearly bald little gentleman comes to open the door: Ramard.

"How's it going?" asks Mathieu.

"Ok," says Ramard. "My leg's stiff. When it rains, the scar aches. You?" he says, pointing quickly at Mathieu's right shoulder.

"No," says Mathieu.

There was fraternity among those in the camp who'd been wounded, who'd fought. Ramard would lose himself meditating on his wound, a way to escape, his glory inscribed on his thigh by that red knife. Mathieu had a deeper subject of meditation: he had killed some men. He'd seen them crumple on the sidewalk. He carried the deaths of others inside himself. This is what separated him from the others, and what made this life livable. He went to sit on a chair. Ramard followed, and sat down too. He said:

"We hardly see you . . . "

"I work at the base," said Mathieu. He rubbed his hands together and said, "Have you heard about the problem at the store?"

"No," said Ramard.

Mathieu looked at him and said:

"Ok, well, see you."

He got up. Ramard pulled him back down.

"Wait," he said, "hold on a second."

"There wasn't any crap going on over there?"

Ramard rolled his head from side to side, hesitating. He said:

"Not that concerned us. They arrested a Jerry, I think."

"Why?"

"The Jerries were sneaking silk stockings out for their girls. They'd stick 'em in their belts under their coats, so sometimes their bellies were sticking out like they were obese."

"Are they locked up?"

"Yeah."

"They took their lumps," said Mathieu.

Ramard turned green, but said nothing.

"Expect a visit," said Mathieu.

Ramard had leaned over in his chair and was looking at his feet, absorbed.

"I've got some German cognac," he said suddenly.

"What?"

"Vienot."

"He's got German cognac?"

"Yeah. It's complicated! He stole some stuff from the store and passed it on to a guy who goes into town to work. I don't know who. And he traded it for some bottles of cognac that he sold us for French francs."

"Why not for marks?"

Ramard shrugged his shoulders:

"He wanted to be paid in francs, for after the war."

He laughed cheerlessly.

"Money changes hands in here. In the beginning we all had a little. But some of the guys have concentrated it into their hands. Y'know, I had a good bit," he concluded sadly, "but it's running out."

Mathieu smiled to himself: the story was that Ramard had been caught with his regiment's cashbox.

"There's a ringleader," said Ramard with a sort of hatred. "I don't know who it is, but there's a guy who has sworn to fleece the whole camp."

Mathieu thought: the Mysteries of Paris.[11] The camp was a mysterious immense city, but a city of dreams. There was a bit of everything: passions, projects, murders, but always dreams. Nothing counted.

"Gotta get rid of those bottles," said Ramard. He looked at Mathieu questioningly.

"How many do you have?" asked Mathieu.

"Four. Full."

"Toss 'em in the latrines."

Ramard looked at him, indignant:

"You crazy? I'm telling you they're full."

"Ok," said Mathieu, "I'll take 'em, and bring 'em back after the search is over."

He opened his coat:

"Put 'em under here."

Ramard got up. He let out a little cry of pain when his left leg hit the ground, then he limped over to his bunk.

"Don't break 'em," he said.

"Of course not," said Mathieu.

Ramard came back with the bottles:

"Or drink 'em!"

"It would make me sick."

Ramard had bent down and picked up two empty bottles:

"These I'll throw in the latrines."

Mathieu closed his coat over the bottles. He noticed the red lines on the tip of Ramard's nose.

"Looks like you're picking at your nose."

Ramard smiled wanly:

"Pick at it some, passes the time."

"I see," said Mathieu.

"That bother you?"

"Not a bit," said Mathieu, "we all do what we gotta do."

He found that perfectly natural.

He headed toward the door:

"Is it because of the fur that they discovered all this?"

"I don't know."

"What kind of asshole would steal a fur? What the fuck you gonna do with a fur?"

"Did he put it on his bed at night to keep warm?"

"Not even. You know what he does, this asshole? He walks around the camp with it on his back, showing off."

He rolled up the empty bottles in a blanket.

"You don't know if they're lookin' for 'em?"

"I don't know, but probably. It'd be better to warn 'em."

"Except I don't know where they are," said Ramard.

They went out together, Mathieu's arms crossed over on his stomach to hold the bottles.

B. Longin[12]

Sunday

Charlot said to me: "Go see Longin. Looks like he's not doing so well."

I take some books and stop by his barracks. I find him alone, sitting halfway off a bench, elbows on the table, staring, with a week's growth of beard. The feeling of Sunday sneaks through the open window on a light sour breeze. At the other end of the room, the stove snorts: Longin has moved as far away from it as he could: he's clearly in search of cold and discomfort; I can see that he's trying to push his melancholy to the point where it will be unbearable, undoubtedly to prove to God or some invisible witness that the world is evil. Deserted, the room seems like a gigantic columbarium, with its two wooden bedsteads facing each other. Not a trace of a human presence. But it's also nothing natural. These wooden bedsteads with their honeycombed cells exhibit the pitiless cleanliness and universality of utilitarian equipment. Not a speck of dust; the guy who did the cleaning must be obsessed; the guys have carefully stored their possessions at the end of their cells. Nothing human; nothing natural. Longin was in need of a *querencia*, a corner where he could be by himself, alone. He was lost here in the midst of the utilitarian, transpierced by ammonia. He has clearly added to his discomfort by being enraged at not being able to find a little space for himself alone. He's just there, abstract, in an abstract world, uncomfortable, ill at ease; he turns toward me and his eyes don't seem to see: two dry clouds in his sockets.

"How's it going?"

"It's not. Not at all."

"You got the blues?"

He shrugs his shoulders slightly, annoyed:

"No, I don't have the blues. I can see quite clearly."

He smiles weakly to himself. Obviously he's on low energy, few gestures, hardly a sign, he's circling his despair like a wolf. I sit down near the stove and we're just silent. We both have respect for great pain. Finally I say to him:

"You want to go for a walk?"

He replies quietly, with great patience, like he's talking to a child:

"No. No, I don't want to go for a walk."

For a second I want to just leave him to rot there, but I remind myself in time that these scenes are always played by someone real. He's *living* his pain, better or worse, in his own way. Pain is hard to live. I know what he's expecting, just a little warmth in my voice, a little human interest. I can't just give it to him like that; in the first place, he's not even nice to me. He keeps my company because I'm an academic, and that seems superior to him. It's his milieu: he's an architect.[13] A beginning architect. And I want him to suffer, too. I don't know why, it's a sort of fear. I have this animal feeling that there's something about him to avoid at all costs. I sense that this guy is a trap. I put as much interest in my voice as I can muster:

"Hey, man, what's the matter?"

He'd expected this slightly sing-song inflection, he looks at me for the first time, without letting up: he revels in his refusal of my kindness, in being put out by it. I'll have to try again. And I do:

"So, come on, what's the matter?"

His whole face sags, the flesh at his temples and cheekbones has slid down his jowls, so his face looks like a pear. With an air of objectivity, he offers:

"I'm a fuck-up."

I don't answer, my throat is dry, I look at him with a crisp smile, and I feel my head moving stiffly at the end of my neck. Complacently, he repeats:

"I'm a fuck-up."

A fuck-up. Yeah, last year I remember saying to myself that I was a fuck-up. Was I this repulsive? Never again, never, will I think about what I *am*—that's what I swore in the face of this caricature of what

I'd been—but only about what I *do*. He takes a pack of cigarettes from his pocket, looks at me hesitating, then lights one:

"I'd offer you one, but I hardly have any."

"It's alright," I tell him.

I wanted to smoke my pipe, but I was paralyzed when I tried to pull it from my pocket; I can't bring myself to make the gestures he's making. He takes a puff on his cigarette and repeats:

"A fuck-up."

I'm supposed to object; he wants me to object, I say

"Oh, come on."

Suddenly he holds out his calloused swollen hands with broken nails:

"Take a look at that! Just look! My hands are ruined from digging, they shake all the time. You think I'll ever be able to hold a pencil again?"

"Why not?"

"Phew!" he spews in my face. Then he smiles right away. "A pencil's so light, you don't press down, you know, you keep your wrist loose, and you approach the paper with a smile, like this!"

He gestures with his wrist, and collapses:

"I can't do it anymore! I can't do it anymore!"

He thinks he's an architect.

C. *The Newspaper Episode*

Chauchard comes in with a yellowed paper, ripped up, just the last two pages; they look like they're returning to nature, as dry as dead leaves in some spots, a kind of supple oiliness in others, evoking organic decomposition. A brown stain with a yellow halo covers half the paper; it's so deep that it looks like a watermark when held up to the light. Little black letters, so human, squeezed into aggressive columns, occupy this abandoned landscape.

"Take a look!"

Everyone gets up and surrounds him, even Pinette:

"A newspaper!" He laughs and struggles free:

"No pushing, you'll each get your turn. We've got time, right?"

"Where'd you get that?"

The guys sit back down, disappointed, eyes glued to the paper. Chauchard sits at the end of the table, his back to the window. He spreads the sheet on the table and flattens it with his hand. It's folded and wrinkled, and crinkles up into a soft pyramid when he lets go of it. With his hand flat on the paper, as though he wants to first enjoy it tactilely, he explains slowly:

"It's the guys who arrived yesterday from Rouen. I met one of 'em in the latrines. You know what he was gonna do? Wipe his butt with it! No joke. I look at him, I says to myself, that's a newspaper for Christ's sake; I was at the other end of the row, I jumped up, I got there just in time: 'You're not gonna wipe your butt with a newspaper, no!' that's what I says to him, 'not when there's guys who haven't seen one in six months!' He looked up, completely surprised, and he says, '"but it's from last month.' 'So what?' I says, 'you think we have any idea what happened last month?' So he says, 'Well, I'd like to give it to you, but I need some paper.' I didn't have anymore with me. 'Wait,' I says to him, and I runs over to the 37 and brings him back a *Trait d'union*,[14] and he growls that I made him catch a cold, but he gave me the paper. He says there's others that his pals will trade for cigarettes."

"Don't tell us your life story," said Roquebrune. "Read it and pass it along."

He settles down and reads, and we watch him impatiently. Eyebrows raised, he seems stupefied, and from time to time he bites a nail. No one speaks, the bridge players have interrupted their game, we all watch this man who, though he's in the midst of us, is now plunged into a past full of memories. Then he laughs a little all by himself, and seem to us like he's half-crazy, a half-free man, already freed. He can't keep his enjoyment to himself:

"Listen up guys: they've got velo-taxis in Paris!"

"Velo-taxis? What's that? You mean taxis being pulled by velos?"

"If you like. It's a little cart behind a bicycle I think. People get around like that."

"Like a rickshaw."

"There must be thousands of 'em."

"The races! Longchamps! Prairial won. I know Prairial, a good little horse, Rothschild's stables."

"Look at the shows," said Charlot.

"Why?"

"I dunno, just like to see what's playing."

"Ok, well, look, there's Trenet at the Alhambra."

"How about films?"

"Films . . . for films, *Bel Ami* at the Max-Linder."

"*Bel Ami*, is that an American film?"

"Idiot, how would there be any American films?"

"But I'm telling you, it's American. They couldn't show it before the war, it's about the Legion."

"No, no, you dick, that's *Beau Geste*."[15]

"Ah, yeah, maybe you're right," said Charlot, irritated.

"Trenet at the Alhambra. Danielle Darrieux. *Carnet de Bal. Pépé le Moko.* Hasn't changed," says Chauchard with satisfaction.

The others smile and say, "Nope, hasn't changed."

They're happy that nothing's changed. What lets us hold on is not being able to imagine simultaneity. Our worlds, Paris and their countryside, have been frozen in our thoughts since the day we lost them. Nothing happens there; it's a film that's stopped. It'll start up again the day we're freed and get to go home. But we don't imagine that things change there, that the women age, forget, take lovers, that new cinema and theater stars come up, that kids are being born with new destinies. If someone does think of it from time to time, he gets such a round of heartache that he just sits and stares, wide-eyed. And the newspaper makes us happy; could be a pre-war paper. *Le Matin*. Same paper, same characters, same shows. Everything the same. A world of pure repetition, soul-less, while we live, day after day, days that don't count. Time lost for everyone. The War—the main character. Turn the page, and wouldn't you know, a story about the English.

"Hey, they're talking about us."

"About us?"

"About prisoners, I mean."

"What do they say?"

"Wait."

He reads, but too quickly, raising his eyebrows. Then suddenly, in a monotone, without really understanding what he's saying:

"How will the best and most pure of us all, who suffer for our faults, judge the rest of us when they return?"

"No way!" says Charlot. "It says that?"

"I just read it."

"Well, how about . . . "

Chauchard, surprised by the reaction, returns to the text and reads it for himself. His lips move. He says:

"Shit."

"Has to be someone paid by the Krauts to say that," says Pinette. "A sell-out. No way that's how they think of us back there."

"What they think," says Chauchard, "is . . . why didn't they fight?"

The good mood is over. The guys are embarrassed, as though someone had put his foot in it.

D. The Dream

Charlot looked at his watch, winked at Mathieu, and showed the outstretched fingers of his left hand: five o'clock. The day was fading, the tall windows made bright splotches, the walls were turning grey. You could see whatever you wanted on the walls: death heads, bristling bearded men. Charlot was already bent over his writing, like a cunning student. Sure, he could have just said the time out loud, but he enjoyed acting like a student, as though he regretted never having finished his studies. The corporal yawned, sighed "Ach Gott!," pulled a packet wrapped in pink paper from his pocket, which he considered for a while, wiping away a tear from his cheek with his thumb. Mathieu had been leaning on his elbows at the long table, the dusk overtaking his eyes like a gentle fatigue; head empty. He looked out the window; German shadows passed in the courtyard, within rifle range. He looked away; Pinette was working nearby, within knife range. He said to himself, "here it comes." The air closed down, distances between men became bullet trajectories; his little afternoon obsession was starting up. It didn't worry him; he never worried anymore. He looked at the long white scar that stretched across Pinette's forehead from one temple to the other. Pinette never even raised his head, he was writing furiously, with a zeal fueled by resentment; he was copying the names of prisoners onto file cards. For a second he raised his pen and looked at his right hand disapprovingly; it was trembling. Mathieu could feel the obsession that was growing; it wasn't unpleasant, apart from a funny feeling in the pit of his stomach; it came and went as it chose, large or small, pretty small now—the larger ones came at night—and it left without ever harming anyone; his pals had never even noticed anything at all. In the courtyard, orders are being shouted in German. Mathieu knew that he'd wind up killing Charlot, as usual. Well, not really killing him, in reality all he did was look at him. But in a certain way. He looked, and Charlot became killable. Mathieu had no desire to kill him; he simply found it amusing to transform his pals into large piles of death. It was a secret he had on them, and they didn't know it. He knew that men can be crushed underfoot like ants. The end of human dignity. In all likelihood, Pinette knew it as well; he was, like Mathieu, a killer; the deaths of others filled both of them up to their eyeballs. Charlot was busy recopying an order into a register-book; he rolled his large watchful eyes, he licked his lips, with loving interest he turned his face to the card, and then, with a look of importance, to the register. He was monstrously mortal, enough to scream—and he was oblivious to it, the nape of his neck offered itself to the blade. He sighed; Mathieu slid the blade lovingly. He loved them *that much*, all the way to their ridiculous fragility. Of course, he too was fragile. Everything they were, he was too; and everything he felt, they felt. Yet, there was one thing that separated him from them: he had killed, and they had not.

* * *

He'd finished writing, his head emptied out, he began looking for a victim. In general he killed Charlot; it was more fun killing someone chubby. Vairon was too ugly, he probably had grey blood. Pinette was just a bag of bones, the blade would slip; and besides, it would be incestuous; they'd killed Krauts together. Naturally, most of the prisoners claimed to have seen action, but it was a dream, and no one believed them. Pinette and Mathieu however, were filled with death up to their eyeballs. They never spoke about it to each other, but they knew it, it was a secret between them. Charlot sat there writing, unaware of this amazing farce: being mortal. He offered the nape of his neck like a true sacrificial lamb. Between the barely visible tendons, there was a special place for the knife, a large lunar valley, butter. In the old days, Mathieu's bored gaze would undress women that he'd see, but now, it killed men. Charlot sighed, and Mathieu slipped the blade in, without hate or cruelty, with love. It was a way to make love with men. If he hadn't killed those Germans, he'd never have known how naked men are. Their mortality was a new dimension of intimacy. Mathieu reunited with them at that point, the end of human dignity; he saw the whole camp with an assassin's eyes. He got up, looked around, shook himself awake, looked over the long table, the porcelain inkwell; he wasn't upset, but still, he had to shake this obsession. At the beginning, when he got out of the hospital, it would get him three or four times a week, but now it was every day; every day, he killed either Charlot or Lubéron. It wasn't so much a game as a re-construction. To his right, like always, Pinette was smoldering; he had red lines under his eyes, from time to time he'd raise his pen and look morosely at his trembling fingers. Vairon seemed proud; it wasn't his fault, but when he relaxed, he always looked proud. Mathieu looked at the white walls, the windows, he saw German soldiers in the head-quarters' courtyard, his eyes closed and he witnessed another massacre. Posted at the four corners of the camps, the Germans began firing. Machine-guns, submachine-guns, grenades; they wanted to get rid of the prisoners because they could no longer/[16]

* * *

Charlot was busy recopying the list of new arrivals onto a register; he rolled his careful eyes, he licked his lips, he turned with loving interest toward the typed paper, then returning to the register with a look that was severe and legislative, he wrote the names stiffly, as though they were commandments: he was monstrously mortal, enough to scream, filthy mortal, real meat, full of innards to rip out, and he was oblivious to it. Mathieu stared at the nape of his neck lovingly, watching for the place to insert the blade. He loved them *that much*. He'd chop off their heads until a club cracked his own open, blurring them in a horrible fra-ternity. It wasn't sadism; he had discovered a new way to love them. Charlot felt himself watched, he started, and looked at Mathieu discon-certedly, Mathieu looked at this large sweet head that the least calamity could transform into bruises, he smiled at his atrocious fragility. He felt the same as Charlot insofar as he too could be killed, but he felt *separated* from him by the fact that he had killed, and Charlot had not. To kill was a horrible thing for a man to know, and a new love. He would probably never again kill anyone, but on June 17, 1940,[17] he had become a killer once and for all. Thirty-five years of life, and a single memory: a German, more naked than nature itself, swimming on a sidewalk. The other Mathieus, sweet and problematic, existed on the other side of that day, out of reach. Mathieu was no longer the same: the murder-obsession came to him ten times a day in the midst of this gentle unreal boredom of captivity. In a second, he'd feel himself a killer, and the others killable. Now *that, that was true*. The one thing he'd never been able to take back.

He turned his head and looked out the window. Germans were passing through the courtyard with their rifles. Three prisoners side by side: a student, a killer, a dead man. Mathieu gave no thought to the scenes unfolding in a dozen other brains. He didn't know if it was an obsession or a way to escape from the camp. In the end, he and Pinette relived that same day endlessly. But for Pinette, it had been the end of things, and for Mathieu it was a beginning. The beginning of what? He shrugged his head, and death became impossible once more. The walls returned to being opaque, and the master of life and death returned to being an employee in an office.

* * *

Human mortality blossomed forth in him, turning the skin blue like a bruise. All of them mortal. They wrote, dignified by work, and behind their backs, someone was getting ready to play a trick on them; Mathieu was in place, colluding. All it took was knowing how to look; you could see their possible deaths transparently. Not the tranquil death at home, in the midst of children, with ivory hands on the sheets. Death by massacre, obscene, half-naked, half-burnt legs in the air like pylons, black mixtures of flesh and military colors, and so many holes. All of them killable, crushable. Death by massacre. Only Pinette retained any dignity, because he was *already dead*. Mathieu played at dealing death. His gaze picked out the right spot on the nape of Charlot's neck. Charlot collapsed face down into the file cards. Mathieu became a monstrous finger that could lift itself and fall, trapping Charlot's head against the table and crushing it like a fly, sending spatters of blood across the papers. It was Charlot who Mathieu ended up killing.

* * *

Death had simplified Pinette. It turned out the Germans hadn't killed him, but they'd been wrong, and it was no one else's business anyway. As far as it concerned him, Pinette was practically dead; he'd acquired the right to live backwards, unfeeling and deaf, focused on that last morning, on that explosion where his pride and his death had become inextricably interlocked. The fleas made no mistake, and left his skeletal frame alone; the guys made no mistake either: they called him Jonah.

"Hey, Pinette!" said Mathieu.

Pinette made no reply. He liked a certain Mathieu, the one who had died with him on the bell tower of a church, whose bullet-riddled body had been found, but the Mathieu that survived rather annoyed him.

* * *

Charlot looked at his wristwatch and winked at Mathieu. The day was fading. The Germans had not turned on the lights yet, saving what they could. Charlot raised three fingers, and Mathieu understood that it was 4:45. Charlot returned to his task like a sleepy, sneaky student. In fact there was no need to be secretive: the prisoners were allowed to talk among themselves. But Charlot enjoyed acting like a student, as though he still wished he'd finished his studies (he'd quit school at 12 to work in his father's store). The German corporal yawned, and let his eyes stray for a moment along the white walls in the already darkening room. He thought for a second, leaning on his elbows on the long black bench where everyone worked, then he took a packet wrapped in pink paper from his pocket, and stared at it. Pinette had not raised his head. In child-like handwriting, he was copying the names of prisoners onto cardboard cards. His handling of the cardboard seemed childlike, as did his posture. But not his face. Outside in the courtyard of the base, orders could be heard in German. Corporal Schiler opened up his packet. He leaned toward Mathieu and said:

"It's a bolt."

He barely had an accent; he'd lived in France.

"Indeed it is," said Mathieu.

"Is 'bolt' masculine or feminine?" asked Schiler.

"Masculine," said Mathieu quickly.

The Germans took advantage of these conversations with the prisoners to get some free French lessons.

"Scharlotte!" said the corporal.

Charlot jumped. He'd destroyed his papers, and declared that his name was Charlot. While he was at it, he'd claimed he was a sergeant, so he wouldn't have to work. But work had some advantages, and he finally agreed to come to work at the base.

"Come with me," said the corporal. With deliberateness he said, "We're going to put this bolt on the door to the bathroom."

The prisoners raised their heads and looked at him with astonishment. He opened his drawer and took out a hammer and chisel. He smiled and got up. He was a large young man with a hard face, black hair and shiny black eyes. Charlot pushed back his chair and followed him, all round and chubby. Vairon smiled as he watched them leave: "Don Quixote and Sancho Panza," he said.

Vairon was a tax collector, and well-read. He ran his hand over his shaven head: "Did you see how Schiler was looking at that bolt?"

"So?"

"They're children," said Vairon. "Silly little stuff amuses them. What's so special about this bolt? Nothing. But it's new, it's shiny. They're like savages. They love things that are shiny."

He smiled and leaned back in his chair, and said:

"All the same! Savages. Barbarians."

Pinette suddenly straightened up; he looked at Vairon with unbearably intent eyes; his face looked like the flesh was missing, all the muscles and wrinkles showed and he had whitish splotches on his lips. An enormous bright red scar ran across his forehead. He'd only been in the camp for a month. Mathieu had caught him in the barracks. He often said he wanted to croak, but that death wouldn't take him. He had bad breath that was strangely cold, that smelled like a cellar. He couldn't stand others acting like they were better than the Germans. He laughed.

"Barbarians, huh? And so you're the civilized one? So tell me, why've the barbarians got the better of you?"

"Got the better of me? You gotta be kidding me!" said Vairon. He turned around and pointed at the two German secretaries peacefully writing notes, and he said with a flair, "These guys get the better of me?"

"To the bitter end," said Pinette.

"You're pretty funny," said Vairon. "These guys . . . A Frenchman can do what he wants with them. You have to know how. I'm telling you old man, Germany has always had it bad for France. Just look at history; they love our . . . our . . ."

He stops, the/

* * *

"Another one who hasn't understood," said Pinette.

"Maybe I've understood better than you have, fat head!"

142

"Dirty cunt!" murmured Pinette.

He'd pursed his lips, and his thin cheeks darkened. Faced with this smile, Longin didn't seem well either. Mathieu's eyes went from the one to the other. He watched these two deeply allied men, who enjoyed an incommunicable certainty, and who each protected his pride in his own way. He thought the only thing left was for them to kill each other. Longin kept smiling; his insipid smile was a way to kill Pinette a little at a time. Pinette had turned his eyes down and withdrawn into himself. *Maybe he's thinking of hitting him. Maybe he's understood that every one of our secret experiences calls for the death of those who don't share them; after all, he's a killer too. Mathieu looks over the fifteen amused, smiling faces, fifteen flowers. Every one of these men, at any instant, can deal or receive death. I've learned that murder is the logical consequence of everything.* They didn't kill each other; they forgot about their dispute, they both let go and fell back upon themselves, each to his own thoughts. Mathieu could not forget anything. Ever since he'd killed, he'd acquired a strange depth. Since he had killed without knowing why, nor understanding what he was doing, each of his acts seemed to him a small murder, with a secret unfathomed depth. Behind them Vairon said:

"At any rate, they aren't shits."

"Because . . . ?"

"The bolt. It's actually nice that they thought of it."

Pinette laughed.

"The bolt!"

"Hey," said Vairon, "I mean it. It's not funny doing your business in public. When I take a dump I hang on to the latch so no one comes in; it's pretty awkward."

Pinette continued to laugh.

"No," said Vairon in a firm objective voice. "That's all there is to it, it's a nice gesture."

"They can stick it up their ass."

Mathieu suddenly had had enough:

"Shut up!" he said abruptly.

They turned around towards him unsurprised, looked at him, and were quiet. Mathieu was a little surprised, but not too much: since he'd killed, he'd become a gentleman: the dead Germans had taken up lodgings in him like ancestors; they gave him rights and vague responsibilities. From time to time a command, an outburst, a cry escaped from him without his knowing quite why. Criminal or sacred? He couldn't decide. At moments like that, the other guys obeyed him without a word: to be obeyed, all you have to do is command in spite of yourself.

The corporal returned, followed by Charlot. He stopped in front of Mathieu and sized him up with an important but morose look.

"No using the bolt."

"The what?"

"The bolt. It is not to be used."

Pinette looked at Vairon, then at the corporal, with a triumphant hate.

"So then, why did you put it on?" he asked quietly.

"For us."

"You have bathrooms on the first floor."

"Too far," said the corporal. With a circular gesture he pointed to the Germans who worked in the office.

* * *

THE LAST CHANCE: CONCLUSION

Night falls. The first reflectors light up in the eyes of the detainees, two by two. Brunet yawns, sets his shovel across the wheelbarrow, and turns towards the setting sun. On the other side of the barbed wire, the earth is blue, the grass black; they've drunk up the sky. The light spreading above the pines, the open space between the trees and the field, the puddles on the road—all these are the eyes of a happy creature. Beneath its sweet natural gaze, Brunet returns to nature, bending over and straightening up, dark and mute foliage, his human anger subsiding.

Los! Los!

Brunet yawns again and takes the wheelbarrow by the handles; the sentry flutters into Black Square, good-naturedly squawking, bearing down on the detainees; they look at him with dreamy surprise, and begin to march over to the assembly point at the stables. Time to head back, return to their cells, the night, the madness.

Someone strikes him on the shoulder, and his anger awakens with a start. He straightens up and takes a good look at the guy with coal eyes who's smiling at him.

"Hi!" says the guy.

Brunet makes no reply. The guard comes up, the guy turns and speaks to him in German; he's left one hand on Brunet's shoulder, the other holds a paper. Brunet shakes himself loose, the hand falls off, the guard reads the paper, nods his head, walks off, the guy smiles at Brunet:

"Go put your wheelbarrow away."

Brunet pushes his wheelbarrow over to the shed, stows it under an awning, and comes back, taking his time; the guy is pacing up and down, head tilted to one side, hands clasped behind his back.

"So?" asks Brunet.

"So, come along."

"Where to?"

"To my barracks, Ok? I'm the interpreter for 11."

Brunet shakes his head and says, a bit confused:

"They said they weren't releasing me before tomorrow."

"The jail's full," explains the interpreter, "they need your cell."

The team of detainees starts to march away, Brunet enviously contemplates these somber heavy shapes heading back to their shells. In a voice softened by anguish, he says:

"I didn't think it would be this soon."

The detainees turn the corner at the 72 and disappear. Gone, no one left: Brunet is alone, outside. The interpreter finds it amusing:

"But he doesn't seem very happy about it! Amazing! Let's go!"

His anger returns, his cheeks burn:

"All right, let's go," he says dryly.

"We'll stop by at the prison."

"What for? Everything I have is here with me."

They walk, the anger subsides. But not for too long; in a little while he'll let it loose, and it will find its target. Tonight, I'll sleep. They cross the Grand Rue. Brunet's eyes watching out in the crowd for Chalais.

"I don't recognize a soul," he says after a minute.

"Of course not. There's ten thousand new arrivals, and the Krauts ship out the old ones to concentration camps; every day more leave. So it's simple: you never know where you are."

Brunet stops, he watches these twilight faces file by, he feels dead. The interpreter watches him, laughing with respect. Finally he says:

"Everyone's talking about you."

"Why's that?"

"About your escape. You guys got caught."

Brunet says nothing. The guy clears his throat; finally he lays out his question: "Why'd they get you?"

"Because somebody gave us up," says Brunet.

"You know who?"

"Yeah, I know who."

"What are you gonna do to him?"

Brunet smiles and clenches his fists:

"Nothing at all," he says softly.

"Wow," says the interpreter, stunned. "You don't hold a grudge."

"I'm just another Jesus Christ," says Brunet.

"But if he gave you up, he could do it to others."

"No," says Brunet. "No, he won't give up anyone else."

The interpreter takes him by the elbow, Brunet shakes loose violently, the interpreter looks at him bewildered.

"Take it easy," says Brunet. "I'm kind of spooked."

The interpreter points to a barracks:

"That's it."

A hallway, a door, Brunet goes in: silence. Guys are sitting on benches, unmoving and grey. The interpreter steps up:

"Hey!"

They don't budge. He explains:

"I bring you the famous Brunet."

Heads turn slowly toward Brunet.

"Uh huh," says a guy with a small dreamy voice. "How about that?"

"Where do I crash?" asks Brunet.

"Up there," says the interpreter. "Top row, third bunk."

"Ok, thanks."

The interpreter rocks on his heels; he hasn't chosen to leave. Brunet says nothing.

"Ok, good night!" says the interpreter abruptly.

He shoves his hands in his pockets and goes off, frustrated. Brunet closes the door after him, turns toward the guys and looks vaguely at their vacant stares. He feels empty; he hears a solicitous voice:

"Not too bad, the cooler?"

"I was better off there than I will be in this whorehouse."

All these heads seem like large birds perched on branches. Surprise travels through the branches and the birds. Brunet explains:

"There I was alone."

"Alone?" says a head, dreamily. "You mean alone in your cell."

"Yeah."

"That's incredible. Since June of '40 I haven't been alone once."

Brunet's eyes follow the swaying branches of this tree of doves. He speaks to the whole tree:

"What the fuck do you do here?"

The heads all reply with the same awful smile:

"We make ourselves sick."

"Yeah, that's how it looks," says Brunet.

"It's no worse than any place else," says a pale, fat-cheeked face. "But you know you're not staying, no point in settling in."

"Not staying?" repeats Brunet, not understanding.

"This is the way-station barracks. From here, you go straight to the camps. We've been here for two days, expect to be shipped out any minute. Y'can't do anything."

"I see," says Brunet.

He's afraid. He thinks that there's no time to lose. Anger flames up. He says:

"See you later."

He leaves amidst the rustling of the leaves; he walks quickly, he's thinking of nothing. He stops in front of his old barracks, and the memories break his heart. Anger burns them up, and when they've fallen back in ashes, he goes in, pushes open the door of his old room; his nostrils catch the smell of smoke.

"Could you knock, you hick?"

Sitting by the stove, two guys are playing chess on the wood box. Brunet's never seen them before.

"Hey, c'mon! Can't you knock?"

Brunet doesn't answer, his look races around the room from one end to the other: Chalais' not there. All these nights, once he'd close his eyes, he'd push open this door, and his nostrils breathed fire, but Chalais was never there. That would wake him up with a start. But, this time, he didn't wake up.

"Answer when someone speaks to you! You know how to talk?"

"Where's Chalais?" asks Brunet.

"Who?"

"Chalais. The interpreter."

One of the two guys turns his slender face toward him:

"I'm the interpreter."

Brunet lowers his head, exhales, and scrapes his heel on the floor. He says:

"And what about Moûlu?"

They look at each other in silence. Then, in a conciliatory voice, one of them says:

"You've got the wrong barracks."

Brunet steps toward them; they both jump up alarmed, and a knight flies off the board. Brunet sits on the bench. He puts his hands on his thighs. He says:

"This was my place, here."

The two guys exchange glances.

"Well, not any more."

"Screw you," says Brunet without raising his voice.

They're quiet. They hold themselves stiffly, on either side of the wood box, they look at their feet. The bigger one keeps a pleasant smile on his patrician mouth.

"So, Chalais never comes here at all?"

The smaller brown-haired guy shakes his head No. The bigger one continues to smile, eyelids lowered. Brunet stands up and approaches them.

"How long have you been here?"

"Will you get out once we tell you?"

"Sure," says Brunet, smiling.

"It's been seventeen days. There, you happy?"

"Very happy, ass-face!"

They say nothing. The large one smiles. Brunet laughs:

"You guys are assholes."

He looks at them, tempted; the larger one's long nose especially. A long chiseled nose like that will break like glass on the first punch. Brunet waits. But the guys don't move. They hold their breath, and their half-closed eyes give them the air of innocent pleasure. Brunet heads out, closes the door quietly and follows the corridor. At his comrades' room, he stops, he listens. He hears cries, singing, a vulgar voice singing "Le Curé de St Sulpice," other voices singing the refrain.

Brunet shakes his head and moves on, arms flailing, exhaustion crushing him.

At Thibaud's barracks, he can smell blond tobacco. Moûlu is sitting on the table, his legs dangling; he's smoking, and his lips form a lonely smile. When he sees Brunet, the blood comes into his cheeks, and he tosses his cigarette.

"No kidding!"

He leaps to the floor and runs into Brunet's arms. Brunet moves him aside gently. Moûlu laughs and throws some punches at his ribs:

"So you're out! You're finally out!"

Brunet says nothing.

"If only I'd known," says Moûlu, "I'd have gone and waited for you at the jail."

"Where's Chalais?" asks Brunet.

"Chalais? Pfft! Gone."

Brunet shivers:

"Gone where?"

"Don't know."

"And the others?"

"Gone too."

"How'd this happen?"

"One day everyone was called together at Black Square and shipped out."

Brunet lets himself fall on the bench. Forty days of anger raging around inside his chest are trying to find a way out. Abruptly he raises his head:

"Who's gone, the whole barracks, or just the comrades in the Party?"

"Only the guys from the Party. But to be on the safe side, I bolted and I've been hiding out here."

Brunet laughs. Moûlu laughs too, and asks:

"So what are you laughing about, old man?"

"It'll pass," says Brunet.

It doesn't pass right away. Moûlu crosses his arms and says:

"And so how'd this happen, that you guys missed your chance?"

"Somebody gave us up."

Moûlu throws him a quick, hard glance:

"Who? You know who?"

"Bah," says Brunet, "it doesn't matter anymore."

He shakes his head fiercely.

"Where's Thibaut?"

"He's never far off. You want to eat something while you wait?"

"Not hungry."

"Me, I gotta eat," says Moûlu. "Emotions work up an appetite."

He gets up, goes behind the stove, bends down and comes back to sit with a mug of cold soup.

"Bon appetit," says Brunet.

Moûlu lowers his eyes over the soup and stares off in space. Spoonfuls rise slowly to his lips; with each one his cheeks puff out and the soup slops into his mouth. Heavy, empty. Brunet watches him and waits. After a minute, Moûlu raises his head and looks at Brunet with kindness.

"What are you going to do now?"

"I have to fix things."

Moûlu nods his head approvingly, meditatively, then goes back to eating. Brunet adds:

"In fact, I've got to hurry up, because it looks like they're getting ready to send me to one of the camps."

Moûlu doesn't reply: he eats and dreams. When he's finished, he opens a canteen, swishes some water into the mug and puts it on top of the stove. Then he turns to Brunet, wipes his mouth on his sleeve, burps, and nonchalantly asks:

"You want to get out through the barbed wire?"

"Doesn't matter how. One way or another."

"Because," says Moûlu slowly, "I'd go with you but I gotta say the barbed wire scares me."

Stunned, Brunet sees Moûlu running in the sunlight, furious bees dancing around his ears, then he falls. But instead of blood seeping out of him, it's lard.

"You? You want to try to escape?"

"Why not? Why wouldn't I want to, just like everyone else?"

Brunet laughs. In a dignified tone, Moûlu explains:

"Sure, I'm a peaceful guy, I admit it, but there are circumstances where you have to do something different. I can't stay here with Thibaut, I'm not registered. And if I go back to my barracks, they'll have me shipped off to a camp too."

"You're as soft as a rag," says Brunet. "You'd have to get in shape."

Moûlu stares at his feet obstinately:

"Maybe I'll just come out ahead. And look, you gotta have two guys, right? So why not me as well as someone else?"

Brunet leans over, puts two fingers under his chin and raises his head: "You have a plan, eh?"

"Maybe," says Moûlu, smiling.

Brunet knits his brow; Moûlu adds vigorously:

"Just take me with you, it's yours."

He looks at him, begging:

"It's a great plan, you'd be wrong to turn it down!"

Brunet sizes him up: sure he's all soft, but that's because of life here; under that fat there's some muscles.

"Look, it's no day in the park," he says dryly. "If you run out of gas, don't think I'm gonna carry you."

"I won't."

"Cause I'll go on without you," says Brunet. "Don't say I didn't warn you."

"I won't!" repeats Moûlu in an obstinate voice.

"Ok, well, let's hear your story."

Moûlu lowers his voice:

"You've heard talk about an organization?"

Brunet shrugs his shoulders, disappointed:

"That's it? That's your plan? Try again! Your so-called organization doesn't exist."

Moûlu laughs out loud, but with no joy in it. His little eyes blink:

"Doesn't exist?"

"No."

"So, then, how is it that I know the guys who are in it?"

Brunet makes no reply. Triumphantly, Moûlu continues:

"They're clever, sure, but I wasn't born yesterday either. They've tried to go underground, but I've figured them out."

Brunet watches him, interested:

"So? They're at work?"

"No," says Moûlu in a reasonable tone, "No, you can't expect everything at once. They're not working, they're suspicious. When I talk to them, they act like they don't know anything."

He smiles indulgently:

"As if I'd be a snitch. That's a good one."

"It might be a good one, but it does us a fat lot of good."

"Exactly," says Moûlu. "That's why you've got to be in on it. Everybody knows about you since the break. Brunet this, Brunet that, you're like a star. If you talk to them, they won't be suspicious."

"Where are they?" asks Brunet.

"In the artists' barracks."

Brunet gets up:

"Let's go."

Moûlu has got up too; he's pale and his hands shake. He looks at Brunet, frightened.

"Really? You want to?"

"You're not going to chicken out now, are you?" asks Brunet.

"Listen . . . " says Moûlu.

He stops himself, startled; the door has opened. Thibaut appears, looks at them, opens his huge mouth and stops.

"Close that thing or I'll jump into it," says Brunet.

Thibaut closes his mouth. Silence.

"Have I changed that much?" says Brunet.

Thibaut shakes his head without answering. Suddenly the blood returns to his cheeks and he starts to laugh:

"But you're filthy. I'd have never recognized you. Doesn't matter. I am so pleased to see you again."

They hold each other by the shoulders and spin in the room. "Thibaut lets him go"?

"Have you eaten?"

"Yes."

Thibaut laughs again for a moment, then his laughter stops. He shakes his head affectedly:

"Poor Schneider, huh?"

"Yeah," says Brunet. "Absolutely."

Then without encouragement, Thibaut adds:

"There's a guy with some bad luck."

"Don't cry me a river," says Brunet. "I'm not his widow."

Thibaut stops, censured. They look at each other. Thibaut's mouth opens again, his jaw drops. Suddenly Brunet knocks past him and violently opens the door:

"C'mon Moûlu!"

"You're not staying?" asks Thibaut, dumbfounded.

Brunet drags Moûlu along without answering. Thibaut calls after them:
"If you come back after lights-out, you can sleep here."
Brunet runs. Moûlu begs:
"Don't run so fast!"
"I'm not running!" says Brunet.
A nice evening, a little fog. In the distance they can hear some sad, pretty music.The sky is violet. Timidly Moûlu says:
"Hey Brunet!"
"Hmm?"
"Schneider?"
"Yeah, what?"
"Did he die right away?"
"No. Not right away."
"I'd have bet he would," says Moûlu.
He clears his throat and asks:
"He knew he was dying?"
"That's enough!" says Brunet in a loud voice.
Moûlu is quiet. They walk on, the music gets louder; they go into the barracks, the music's not sad at all anymore. It hurts their ears. Moûlu says, respectfully:
"They play by heart, you know. They're star performers."
He knocks at a door, opens it, and they float into the ocean: everything is blue; the window panes are a dark black-blue, in the shadows they can make out faceless smoking entities. Brunet closes the door.
"Ho! Pinette!" calls out Moûlu.
A broken bitter voice falls on them from above:
"What'd he do?"
"It's Moûlu, hey!"
Silence. A swarming close to the ground; the ocean beasts crawling. The voice returns above their heads:
"I've told you before not to bring your shit in here."
"Pinette, I'm not shitting you," says Moûlu humbly. "I've brought a friend who wants to talk to you."
"Tell him to go fuck himself."
"Ok," says Brunet. "I'm out of here."
He takes a step back; Moûlu grabs him by the arm, and says warmly:
"It's Brunet, guys, c'mon! Brunet, whose friend got killed."

"So what?"

"Well, he's the one who wants to chew the fat," says Moûlu.

No answer. Music. Brunet would like to leave, but he's stuck in the silence; he waits. Suddenly something tumbles, and a black shape floats ahead of them. It stops in front of them, shifting, the movements of the shadows constantly changing its outline.

"So where's Brunet?" asks the bitter voice.

"Right in front of you."

"I'm the one that's Pinette. What d'ya want with me?"

Brunet won't use his fists this time either; he shoves his hands in his pockets and says gently:

"Come outside."

"Why?"

"I can't talk to you in here."

"Why?"

"Oh fine," says Brunet, lowering his voice. "So supposedly you've got some sort of plans."

"Some plans for doing what?"

"For getting away."

Pinette chuckles:

"Hey, you hear that, guys?"

They heard: the night trembles, the laughter comes from all around.

"Plans! Listen, if I had those kinds of plans, you can bet I wouldn't be here!"

"Perfect," says Brunet. "So Moûlu's an asshole. Sorry, 'scuse me, good night."

Moûlu grabs him, Brunet breaks free and goes out. He hears them laughing in their underwater cave. There's a flourish of music, and then someone touches his shoulder; it's Moûlu.

"You asshole!" says Brunet.

"Hey, don't yell at me," says Moûlu, 'cause I'm telling you it's them."

"What's them?"

"The organization, it's them."

"Maybe so, but what the fuck can I do if they won't talk to me?"

He strides away, Moûlu implores him:

"Not so fast! Stop already!"

Brunet stops.

"What?"

"You have to be patient. Have to insist."

Brunet takes him by the shoulders and shakes him:

"Patient? Be patient? For Christ's sake . . . "

The door opens again behind them, and a guy comes out running:

"Come back in, quick!"

"What for?"

"Pinette says for you to come back in."

"Tell him to go fuck himself."

"No, Brunet, no, no, no," implores Moûlu. "No, you don't have the right. I'm in this too, this is our chance, you can't refuse."

"Ok," says Brunet. "Let's go. But he better not try that crap again, cause if he starts playing games like before, I'm going to let him have it right in the face."

They go in. Black as night. They can't even make out the window anymore. Lit cigarette butts move about in the shadows.

"So?" says Brunet. "You guys decide something?"

No answer. The door slams behind them. Suddenly Moûlu moves his arm under Brunet's.

"What is it?"

"Nothing," says Moûlu. "It's nothing."

But his fingers are gripping tight on Brunet's elbow. He adds, sounding detached: "The Krauts are late tonight. Shouldn't the lights be on?"

The night turns gently around them, the glowing butts circle, a hand pushes Brunet forward.

"Have a seat."

"Where?"

"There."

Hands guide him, several, and with a light touch; his knee hits a bench, he sits down, a short breath on the nape of his neck, scent of a man. Right next to his ear a voice emerges, he *recognizes* it. Where has he heard that voice? Not in the camp, for sure. It seems to come from far away, another life.

"What do you want with us?"

"You tell me, you're the ones who called me to come back."

Silence. With his hand Brunet slashes this flower-filled night.

"Enough already! Yes, or shit, are you going to help us?"

"Help you do what?" asks the voice, and Brunet's entire life returns to him through his ears. A dead unfathomable life, through this voice of night: it's a nightmare.

"Help us escape," he says uncertainly.

"Who told you that we could help you?"

"Don't think too hard," says Brunet. "I heard it from Moûlu: I just got out of jail, an hour ago I didn't even know about you."

He's not speaking to anyone, anyone living; he's throwing words into an abyss.

"How about you, Moûlu?" asks the hidden voice.

Moûlu doesn't answer, the voice swells, Brunet loses it.

"Well, Moûlu?"

"I never heard it." The abyss closes, everything is full again. Brunet chafes under these little red bat-eyes. One eye closes, then another; Moûlu starts to call out:

"Leave me alone! Leave me alone!"

Brunet straightens up:

"What's going on?"

Suddenly the night goes out. Seated in the evening light Brunet watches Moûlu. Moûlu, alone, standing in the light, looks at his hands with a worried look. The voices are all back in their mouths, faces are all around. Everyday faces of everybody: that's all it was.

"So, Moûlu, what's the matter with you?"

Moûlu shows his hands with a muffled laugh:

"I bumped into the stove; I thought they were trying to burn me."

Brunet shudders; he expects the others to laugh. But no one laughs. The night is still there, at the heart of the light like an invisible layer of soot. Brunet turns his head and spots Schneider, against the window. Schneider is becoming a big guy with cold eyes who looks like Schneider, then the guy becomes Mathieu. It's Mathieu, thinks Brunet, disappointed. He looks like Schneider, at his worst. Brunet pretends to be surprised:

"Well, whaddya know?" He adds, like he's dreaming, "It's a small world."

Mathieu's dreaming too. He opens his mouth, talking in his sleep, he says:

"It's been more than three months ago that I spotted you."

Brunet repeats:

"Three months."

He dreams: I always said our information system was poor. He wakes up and starts: Mathieu is still there. Why does he keep looking like Schneider? He doesn't look good. Brunet runs his eyes over the other faces: none of them looks good.

"You want to escape?" asks Mathieu.

"Yes."

"Ok. We can give you a hand."

It's Mathieu's voice. Everything falls into place. Ok, yeah, it's Mathieu, why wouldn't he be here? I'm here. Brunet is surprised again: there's no time to lose.

"I want to escape as soon as possible," he says.

Mathieu shakes his head:

"There are four others ahead of you."

"That won't do me any good," says Brunet dryly.

A young tubercular guy watches him warily; Pinette's voice comes from his mouth:

"You're in a bigger hurry than the others?"

"Yes."

Two bearded guys sitting on the floor groan. Brunet looks at these pirate faces and thinks: They don't much like me. But for the first time since Schneider's death, he feels at ease, among real men. He thinks: I always made my guys shave. And our rooms were better kept. Mathieu raises his hand, and everyone stops talking.

"Maybe we'll be able to work something out," he says.

He turns to a tall bald guy with glasses:

"Anybody home in your room?"

"Nobody," says the guy.

Mathieu says to Brunet:

"Let's go to his place."

Brunet looks around at the others regretfully.

"I have to talk to you alone," says Mathieu. "I have a proposition for you."

"Let's go!" says Brunet.

Moûlu throws himself on Brunet and takes his hand:

"I'm going with you."

"No," says Mathieu gently.

Moûlu's lips are blue. He says:

"Take me with you, Brunet, take me."

Brunet hesitates. Suddenly Moûlu brings Brunet's hand to his mouth and kisses it. Angrily, Brunet pulls his hand away. The night contracts, the light is frozen darkness. Pinette comes up to Moûlu:

"Stay put. Brunet will get you on his way out."

Voices call out in the air:

"Moûlu, Moûlu! Stay with us, we'll have some fun!"

Moûlu clings to Brunet, still smiling beneath distraught eyes:

"It's just that I don't want to head back after the lights-out."

"Don't worry," says Pinette. "If you're getting out, you'll have plenty of time."

Ten pairs of hands take hold of Moûlu and pull him back. The guys' faces are all grey.

"You coming?" asks Mathieu.

Brunet shrugs his shoulders and follows Mathieu out. The music rages. Mathieu opens a door and leans back in:

"Louder!"

He closes the door again; Brunet yells in his ear:

"Louder? Are you crazy?"

Mathieu says nothing. He opens another door and flicks the switch, the light flashes on, they go in and sit down. Mathieu on a bed, Brunet on a bench. They look at each other without affection. Night has come in with them.

"So here you are!"

"Yeah, here I am!"

"You look like an assassin," says Brunet.

"You don't look so good yourself," says Mathieu.

They laugh. Laughing between clenched teeth, Brunet looks at his old friend Delarue and thinks: "How annoying, a childhood friend." He asks:

"And so what are you up to these days?"

Mathieu laughs through his nose:

"What would you like me to be up to?"

Brunet looks away, vexed. Mathieu asks, in turn, "Where were you captured?"

"At Verdelais."[18]

"Me too," said Mathieu.

"Ah!"

These words are like chewing-gum. So predictable that they're chewed in advance. Brunet yawns; he doesn't know if it's anguish or boredom. He closes his mouth, wipes the tears that have fallen from his eyes with his thumb, and asks:

"Were you in Baccarat in July?"

"No, I was wounded."

"You fought?"

"I fought for fifteen minutes."

"Were you one of those crazies shooting at us from the bell tower?"

Mathieu's face brightens up:

"Sure was!"

"Bastard," says Brunet cheerfully. "You just about got me killed!"

Mathieu smiles, eyes half-closed; he looks like a madman.

"A funny encounter!" says Brunet.

"What's funny about it?" asks Mathieu.

"In the end," says Brunet, "you're right. What's funny about it?"

Mathieu gets up absent-mindedly, puts his hand on the lock of the door and seems to be listening, then he turns around and comes back to sit down. Brunet looks at him with a grudge. He's angry with him for being there, for no longer being Mathieu, for only being Mathieu.

"Why didn't you get in touch?"

Mathieu throws him a look that's both deadly and malicious.

"What for?"

Brunet laughs, Mathieu gets hold of himself and says graciously:

"We weren't doing the same kind of work."

"So you knew I was working?"

"Well," says Mathieu in a bored voice, "you were doing your propaganda, right? Some sort of political propaganda?"

Brunet laughs again:

"Propaganda, there you go. That's ridiculous."

"You wouldn't have agreed with us," says Mathieu. "We were helping people escape, and you were against escaping."

"We were against it because it was premature," says Brunet good-naturedly. "Most guys were just worked-up. If you helped them without any preconditions . . . "

Mathieu's smile hardens:

"You'd have them take an exam first?"

"No, not an exam."

"We help guys who ask us for help," says Mathieu dryly.

Brunet wants to continue, but then he shrugs his head: what's the point of discussing this? It's like in the old days, when Brunet the communist would talk to Mathieu the professor. They were the same, equally naïve, the activist who believed in Santa Claus, and the masochistic grown-up child who put so much effort into confessing his faults and so little into correcting them. Two noble images from the Middle Ages. Here and now, they might well still be the same, but that would be exactly why they have nothing else to say to each other. And anyway, I need him to help me. He smiles:

"So, here you are, the ringleader?"

Mathieu looks at him coldly:

"I'm not anyone's leader," he says forcefully.

"Ok, Ok," says Brunet. "I didn't mean to piss you off."

Continuing to smile, he adds, "Gotta admit you've traveled quite a road since June of '38."

"Why June of '38? Oh, yeah. Haven't seen you since then."

"You were living on Rue Froidevaux," says Brunet.

"No, Rue Huyghens."

"That's it, Rue Huyghens."

A bourgeois living room, sorry lighting; fighting in Spain was going on; far away.

"You had green armchairs."

"That's right. You said they were corrupt."

Brunet starts to laugh:

"It's true, they were corrupt," he says.

Mathieu doesn't laugh, he cocks his ear, he seems concerned. Brunet stands up and walks around the room. Something's rotten in this night. From the other side of the wall a horn sounds the charge.

"Isn't that *The Ride of the Walkyries*?"

"Sounds like it to me," says Mathieu.

"God!"

Brunet paces. Suddenly he plants himself in front of Mathieu and says:

"You said something about a plan."

Mathieu shrugs his shoulders. Brunet says:

"I repeat, I'm in a hurry."

"And I repeat: not more than the others are."

"Yes, more than the others."

Mathieu looks at him attentively:

"You want to see how things are with your Communist Party?"

"There's that," says Brunet.

"Well, like I said, old pal, you'll have to wait your turn; nothing I can do about that."

Brunet begins to tremble. Luckily Mathieu isn't looking at him. Brunet gets control of himself and says quietly:

"They have such good reasons, these other guys?"

"One of them wants to get home because his family's in poverty, another one's in love . . . "

Brunet straightens up:

"And those are their reasons?"

"Who am I to judge whether yours are any better?"

"The Party . . . " says Brunet.

Mathieu says, in a quick icy tone:

"I refuse to choose. I help everyone or no one."

They exchange irritated looks, and the Walkyries leap around them in disorder. Brunet lowers his look, puts his hands together, and makes himself cool off. When he's cool again, he raises his head:

"Someone was wronged."

"Yeah? What of it?"

"I've got to fix it."

Mathieu smiles:

"Siren!"

"Siren?" repeats Brunet.

"You're singing the one song that can seduce me. You've always thought I cared more about individual misfortunes than about collective catastrophes."

Brunet shrugs his shoulders:

"I'm telling the truth."

"Maybe so," says Mathieu, "but I'm putting wax in my ears."

Brunet smiles:

"Suppose I call on your friendship?"

Mathieu bursts out laughing:

"You gangster! You'll try anything!"

He adds, still laughing:

"In '38, when I called on yours, you sent me packing."

"I was wrong," says Brunet.

He's not speaking to Mathieu; he's disgusted with Mathieu's friendship.

"No," says Mathieu, "you weren't wrong. What did we have in common? Our friendship was just words. You told me, 'My only friends are the comrades in the Party.'"[19]

Brunet repeats slowly:

"The comrades in the Party . . . "

Yeah, yeah, sure, he said that.

"As for the Party," he says, "I think I'm going to quit."

Mathieu raises his eyebrows:

"Really? So you've traveled quite a road too!"

"Yeah," says Brunet, "quite a road."

Mathieu looks at him with interest:

"What will you do when you quit?"

"I won't quit right away. There's this problem I have to fix first; which will take some time, the comrades are stubborn."

"But once you've fixed it?"

"Well, I guess I'll go retire in the country."

Mathieu keeps watching him:

"I don't see you retiring in the country."

Brunet says nothing. Mathieu asks:

"What mistake do you say the Party made?"

"Can we ever say the Party made a mistake?" replies Brunet with good humor. "The CP goes all the way, it's logical, consistent. I'm the one I blame."

"Comes to the same thing."

"Not at all."

"Yes, it does. In the old days you could never even have blamed yourself, because you weren't anybody yet. To be able to blame yourself, you had to become somebody. Which means you'd already broken with the Party before you were even aware of it."

There's a noise in the hallway. Mathieu jumps up and listens; his long eyelashes lower over his eyes, he looks like he's asleep. The noise fades, his eyes reopen, his gaze is focused on Brunet.

"You have a strange look to you," he says. "Like you've been dipped in vinegar. What did you do? What'd they do to you?"

"My escape . . . " says Brunet.

"What about it?"

"I got caught because a comrade gave me up."

Mathieu makes a face. Brunet stops suddenly:

"What is it? What do you know?"

"I'll tell you later. Go on."

"That's it."

Mathieu whistles softly:

"Here's the deal, you Frankenstein. You didn't have a self, and now your resentment has given you one, and you can't get rid of it; you can't swallow it, and you can't spit it back out. Not used to it, huh?"

Brunet shrugs his shoulders, Mathieu continues clinically:

"You just have to accept it, you never get used to it."

Brunet listens; he thinks: He's nobody, an impersonal consciousness, no past, no future. I'll escape, I'll leave him behind with his problems and his theories. He says:

"I don't have any resentment for anyone. Sure, I wanted to beat the crap out of the comrade who gave us up, but I can't say he was wrong. I just found out he's been shipped out, so that's just as well for him and for me. And, what he did—I might have done the same thing if I'd been in his shoes."

He gets up and walks. He has something he just wants to say.

"I can be completely *for* the comrades, and completely *against* our class enemies. Completely, I mean, body and soul, and all the way to the bitter end. But I can't be both *for and against* the comrades. That's too much for me."

"Who's asking you to be?"

"The Party. And it's right. The CP is a party of violence, you know. And I've never been afraid of violence. But I thought it was a necessary evil, and that you could control it, limit its use."

"And now what?"

"You can't. Once you start using it, it's everywhere—throughout the internal organization of the Party."

He stops himself; he stares at Mathieu's impassive face: I must be shocking him. Impersonal consciousness is a dream. Before him, Brunet sees a petit-bourgeois idealist, steeped in his class's prejudices. He goes on anyway, with malicious pleasure:

"You remember in '26 when you'd give me a hard time with Plato: there is justice even among thieves?"

"Yeah, I remember."

"Well here's the flip side. There's injustice even among the just. *We're* the just ones," he adds violently. "*Us*, and I'll never stop saying so, even if I quit the Party. It's us because we're the only ones that are fighting for man. And that's why . . . Well, I thought we had to tell the truth to the comrades whenever possible. But, well, that's just Trotskyism. It's *never* possible to tell them the truth, and they're the first ones you have to lie to."

Suddenly he's gripped by anguish; he looks at Mathieu like he's calling for help: "So, where are the just, and where are the thieves?"

Mathieu laughs good-naturedly:

"Man, are you naïve!" he says.

Brunet steps back. It's true that he's naïve. Ever since he stopped thinking alone, his thought has dried up, gets winded right away, gets muddled, he has weird ideas, childish thoughts; for over a month he's had the discouraging sense that he's struggling with questions that everyone else had found the answers to a long time ago. He's wearing a blindfold, and everyone else can see it, and laughs about it.

"Naïve? Apparently, to a philosophy professor."

Mathieu doesn't answer. What does he know? Can philosophy provide any answers? From *what point of view*? Brunet doesn't need petit-bourgeois wisdom. He paces, and Mathieu's eyes follow him, and understand him. Brunet calms himself; he feels better being understood by this uncharitable mind. Suddenly Mathieu says:

"Stay with us."

"With you?" repeats Brunet, taken aback.

"Yeah, there's work to do. You know perfectly well that you need to have something to do."

Brunet stops and puts his hands in his pockets:

"Well, on that point—what is it you do? You help guys escape, and then what?"

"That's it."

"That's not much."

Mathieu's eyes shine:

"It's the best thing I've found to justify my life, and you're really too much if you think it wouldn't be enough to justify yours as well."

"I'm not saying that," says Brunet. He laughs a little: "But I don't think my life is in need of being justified. Justify your life!" he repeats. "What a thing to be worried about! What for? This is just petit-bourgeois individualism."

"You've never looked for a reason?" says Mathieu coldly. "So then why did you join the Party?"

"I gave my life to the Party, that's all."

"Right, so it would give it back to you, blessed. It's a good trick."

Brunet shrugs his shoulders. Mathieu gets up and walks toward him.

"Listen Brunet, and think about it. There is nothing better to do, anywhere. With us there's no lies, no violence; we make guys face themselves, and they decide, in full knowledge of what's up. We don't force anyone, and we don't sell anyone what they don't want, but, if they decide they want to escape, we're there for them. We make it happen, we're middlemen, we don't judge them, we don't ask for anything in return, not even for them to be good republicans. We're available to everyone equally. Isn't that what you always wanted to be in the end: the means by which others could be free? The means, that's all, and you risk your skin for it, to be only that, and you save yourself in the bargain."

Brunet shakes his head: the contentment that he sees in Mathieu's eyes irritates him deeply. He's going to show him that life is not a novel. His good conscience is a horror.

"It's pointless!" he says.

"Pointless?" repeats Mathieu, astonished.

"Pointless for me," says Brunet. Paternally, he adds, "You, sure, that makes a difference for you, because you were an academic. So you find that a lot better than all your other bullshit. A little danger, some mystery, some scheming: you're all proud, to you that seems like action. But what do you know about action? And what are you all doing for the long term? Nothing at all. Some guy escapes—that doesn't make any difference. You take some guy that the Nazis oppress in a camp, and you secretly send him off so he can be oppressed somewhere else. They were prisoners, they're going to be exploited, they're going to come back to their miseries and their mystifications. All so you can puff yourself up about acting *correctly*. Maybe what you're doing is completely correct, but it's not taking action. It's a completely negative and limited operation, in a closed field, and in exceptional circumstances, and it only matters to a handful of men. It's like a psychology experiment almost.

I guess you've found a hidden exit, where you bring the guys, and then I guess you give them civilian clothes, a bit of bread and your blessing. It's just the same good old bourgeois idealism: Madame Boucicaut's good works."[20]

He opens his arms with a wide smile:

"We were risking more than that. Our conscience! I would never be one of you. I would never be able to resign myself to such little social games. What we wanted wasn't to save our own miserable existence, it was to change the world. The least of our actions would put the world in question. Help some prisoners escape," he repeats laughing, "what does that change?"

"For each of them, it changes a lot," says Mathieu calmly.

"*What* does it change?"

"Champart's going to see his wife again."

"That counts?"

"Maybe not. But then again, didn't it count that Vicarios got slandered?"

"Oh," says Brunet, "you know about that too?"

"Sure," says Mathieu, "that too. As for violence. I told you that there isn't any *between us*. But . . . "

He stops himself and looks at Brunet, no joking in the air:

"What do you think my guys are doing while we're sitting here talking?"

"Not a god-damn thing, if I know you."

"They've got Moûlu on trial," says Mathieu, "and when they're done, they'll strangle him."

"For what?"

Brunet pushes him away and runs for the door. Behind him he hears a soft voice: "Sit yourself back down—he's the one who gave you away."

Brunet turns around. His eyes hurt.

"You mean he's the one who got Vicarios killed?"

"Yes, that exactly what I mean."

Brunet looks at him uncertainly:

"Are you sure?"

"Completely sure."

Brunet doesn't move. At first he thinks of nothing, then he thinks of Vicarios. He runs his moist hands over his sweaty cheeks, the sweat mingles. He asks

"What are they playing? I know that."

"The overture from *Grottes de Fingal*."[21]

"The piano played that during silent movies."

"Right," says Mathieu, "either that or *Danse macabre*, when the bad guy was about to abduct the heroine."

"You made a good choice for the soundtrack," says Brunet.

Mathieu says nothing. With effort, Brunet adds:

"The music is to . . . "

"Yes. But I don't think he'll have time to cry out."

The orchestra has stopped. The tension grows. They wait for it, like you wait for rain. Brunet lets himself fall back on the bench: pains in his shoulder and in his back. Wearily he says:

"What if you're wrong?"

"Impossible."

"They said Vicarios was a traitor too, you know," says Brunet.

"Not the same."

Suddenly the music starts up again—it's the rain. A helter-skelter of notes, the instruments chasing each other. Mathieu raises his voice and begins speaking very quickly:

"He was always going to the Headquarters after lights-out; he saw the Commandant three times. You must have shared some inside details about your escape plans, and he passed them along."

"But why?" asks Brunet. "Why?"

"For Gold Tip cigarettes," says Mathieu.

He continues, with the same quick rhythm:

"After that, it got harder for him, because there were guys in your barracks, Chalais first of all, who began to suspect him. So he denounced them as communists."

"I see," says Brunet.

"I don't know how he spotted us, but the fact is he's been bugging us for about ten days, saying he wants to help you get out. When you got out of the cooler he must have figured that we'd trust you, that we'd arrange a long-shot escape, and that he'd get us all caught."

Brunet sees Moûlu's fat happy face against a red background; puts his hands together, cracks his knuckles, sighs. He says:

"I'll go help them."

Mathieu cocks his ear; he's gone pale, he says:

"There's no point."

Silence. Brunet doesn't budge: in his chest, the thaw, an old fury breaking apart. He breathes heavily. He says:

"You don't know . . . man . . . you don't know . . . I thought it was Chalais!"

He breathes again, he stretches, unburdened. Moûlu, well, so what? He feels empty, a big empty wooden chest, with a nice little scent at the bottom. And then, all of a sudden, anguish. It wells up from everywhere, filling the chest. He shivers and asks:

"What are you going to do with the body?"

"The latrines are just a few steps away," says Mathieu.

Brunet raises his eyes toward this childhood friend, so easily making himself into an assassin. They look at each other, but without recognizing each other. The music plays. Moûlu is dead. Brunet tilts his head and says:

"Yeah: you've traveled quite a road."

Mathieu has stayed calm, but he's ashen. He says:

"It was him or it was us."

"That . . . doesn't bother you?" asks Brunet.

Mathieu shakes his head. Brunet insists:

"Nothing at all?"

"I'm afraid the guys might get caught." He looks at Brunet, worried:

"I'm the one who made the call."

"When?"

"A little while ago, when you guys walked out. In a way, it's improvisation."

Footsteps in the hallway. Brunet hears them in his large eyes, where drops tremble with every sound. Something rattles the lock: Mathieu reaches out his hand to the doorknob. His face is blank:

"I have to go with them."

The night soars up, all the way to the ceiling, Brunet can't stop falling. He listens, he hears nothing, he surrenders to the long unmoving fall; he feels cold coming up from his stomach to his chest, Schneider and the printer—there they are.[22] Moûlu: dead. Mathieu: dead as well. The night is Truth. The world and the day are the nightmares. Night creaks, day wipes everything away, the dream starts up again, the assassin has his back to the closed door and is staring at Brunet, shaking his head. He says:

"You're filthy as can be."

Brunet starts:

"What's that?"

"You're filthy. Wasn't there any water in the prison?"

"No, there was."

"Well," he says, "you're farther gone than I thought."

And, as Brunet moves his hand up to his face, he adds:

"Don't get me wrong; you were always too concerned with being clean."

Brunet lets his hand fall back down. The guy is sitting like he's all dressed up, with his hands flat on his thighs. They're clean, but they're annoying. Brunet feels like it's the first time he's ever seen hands. They both look at these hands, and the assassin's voice, forgotten, goes on by itself:

"I've killed before."

The hands are restless, scratching against the fabric of the pants; Brunet raises his head.

"Here? In the camp?" he asks.

"No, back in June of '40. Afterwards, you're just not the same."

Brunet shrugs his shoulders:

"Well I shot at the Jerries too, if that's what you mean. It was great fun. When life had a meaning, death meant something too."

He looks, feeling slightly nauseous, at the sinister individual smoking in front of him:

"What a shabby little execution!"

Mathieu nods his head. Brunet says:

"There was an old guy, naked, in a round room."

"Where's this?"

"Oh, in a whorehouse once. He couldn't get it up, six of the whores ganged up on him. They pulled him around by his cock, fuckin' slapped him around."

"What of it?"

"It's the same kind of crap. Your guys went for Moûlu like these sluts after the old guy. And he couldn't really die, just like he could never get it up."

"That's his fault," says Mathieu. "You get the execution you deserve. The guys were just telling me they were laughing their heads off. It seemed to them like they were playing a trick on him."

"Too bad I missed it," says Brunet dryly.

Mathieu's eyes fill with smoke: "You wouldn't have killed him though."

Brunet hesitates:

"I think I would have. But in anger."

"Anger's no excuse."

"It's not an excuse, it's a right. And I'd have done it by myself."

Mathieu smiles painfully:

"Anarchist!"

"In fact, I did kill him," says Brunet suddenly. "I killed him just as much as you, because I let you do it."

"That's what I'd say too," says Mathieu.

They eye each other with the cunning hate of accomplices; Brunet looks at the trembling hands of his accomplice. An accomplice, well, it's better than a childhood friend. He smiles:

"So, got to admit, we've got a corpse between us."

They say nothing, they wait, they listen, but there's nothing else to wait for or to listen to: the night is dead. The night is Moûlu. All this darkness outside is Moûlu's body and blood. Mathieu smokes, and spits out the bits of tobacco; Brunet gets up: he'll have to open the door and plunge into the night. Tough.

"Ok, well, see you!"

"Wait!"

Mathieu takes a last drag on his cigarette, throws it, crushes it with his heel and slowly blows the smoke out his nose:

"You can get out tomorrow if you want."

Brunet throws a suspicious look at him:

"That's not what you said before."

"I told you about a plan."

"And?"

"Tell you the truth," says Mathieu, "it's not so much a plan as a deal."

"A deal? Between you and me?"

"Between you and us. But *we*, we don't lie: I'm putting my cards on the table."

A deal. Something to accept, or refuse, something to do maybe. Brunet feels himself harden, feels calm returning. For weeks he hasn't been this calm.

"I'm listening."

"Champart was supposed to go tomorrow. If you want, we'll push him off two weeks, and you'll go instead."

"That's too perfect," says Brunet. "What's the catch?"

"I'll tell you the catch! If the Jerries catch you, they'll put a dozen fuckin' bullets in you."

"I'd like to see them do that!"

They smile at each other, watching. Two suspicious merchants looking to unload their wares.

"Moûlu gave you up," explains Mathieu. "So, at 5 tonight, you're let out of jail, a few hours later, he's been strangled, and tomorrow morning when they find his body in the latrine, your barracks head will be reporting you missing. Conclusion?"

"I see it," says Brunet. "And . . . you can arrange this?"

"Let's see! The Jerries won't bother with an investigation in the camp if they think you're one who did it."

Brunet starts to laugh:

"And if they don't think of that themselves, you'll be there to help them."

Mathieu makes a vague gesture, and says nothing.

"Well, congratulations," says Brunet. "And you came up with that yourself?"

"Of course," says Mathieu.

"Between the time I left your barracks and came back? You're a genius."

They laugh together.

"And if you hear that they've shot me down, won't that stop you from sleeping?"

"It won't stop me from sleeping," says Mathieu, "because I've told you up front, and you've taken responsibility for yourself."

Slightly ironically, he adds:

"But I'd feel bad, sure."

Brunet laughs louder. Mathieu laughs too, then asks:

"So?"

"I'm in," says Brunet happily. "All too glad to oblige."

"You'll sleep here," says Mathieu.

"Perfect."

He looks at Mathieu cordially, and appreciates not having to say "thank you." I don't owe them anything. Mathieu hesitates. Suddenly, timidly, he says:

"You shouldn't quit the CP."

Brunet knits his brow, Mathieu repeats:

"You shouldn't quit."

"No, but what's it to you?" says Brunet.

"Oh right, none of my business," says Mathieu. Blushing, he adds:

"You know why I said that?"

"No idea."

"Because," he gestures at Brunet's squalid jacket and his face, "you look like shit."

"What of it?"

"For anyone who knew you before, it means something."

By the window a pocket mirror hangs by a nail. Brunet gets up and takes a look at himself. Mathieu stays put. Brunet groans and comes back to sit down.

"If you quit the Party, you're really fucked," says Mathieu.

Brunet shakes his head:

"What a joke," he says. He looks at Mathieu, dazed:

"So here *you* are—you—giving me advice . . . "

"Who do you want to get it from? Some of your comrades would be interested."

"What do you know about the CP?" says Brunet shrugging his shoulders.

"Not much. But I know you've given it your life, and that you aren't going to get it back."

Brunet gets up.

"We'll see if I can't get it back." He looks at Mathieu with irritation: "Christ, you take yourself seriously. You think because you bumped off a little two-bit informer, an irresponsible . . . "

Mathieu, with his head down, continues his point with serene obstinacy:

"You are the Communist Party. You, in spite of yourself. Your reason is what the Party calls necessary, your freedom was its will, and you see, your cleanliness itself—that was its inflexibility. It made use of you for changing the world, but you made use of it to accomplish your work on earth."

"What are you talking about?" asks Brunet. "You think I think about my work and all this silly crap? Sorry to disappoint—I did my job, that's all."

"Sure," says Mathieu. "You've had the option of being modest. When you're in the Truth, you don't need pride."

"Truth," says Brunet with a bitter smile. "Truth!"

"You without the Party," says Mathieu. "What is that? Just shit. A bit of pride and some filth. And the Party without you? What will it do? Pursue exactly the politics you want it not to follow. By quitting it, you send it in the direction you despise."

"You think there's anything at all I could stop?" asks Brunet. "You seem to think the CP is a congress of radical socialists."

"Try! You've got to try to fight from within."

"Not possible. Radically impossible," Brunet repeats, articulating the syllables.

"I know. But try."

"What good's it do to go trying what's impossible?"

"None. But there's nothing else to do."

"You talk as if you knew. You . . . you've got a reasonable enough goal, not at all impossible to attain, and you're cutting through the crap Ok."

Mathieu smiles:

"That's because I'm still not quite a man," he says.

Brunet has begun pacing about the room. He no longer knows what to reply to Mathieu or to himself:

"Besides, well, listen. You told me straight to my face a little while ago: before, I wasn't anyone. Now, at the present, I am someone. Believe me, I'm not overly proud of it, but I can't go back either. I didn't have a self. Resentment and shock gave it to me, and it's not going away. I can't spit it back up or swallow it down. Not used to it, I guess."

"Right," says Mathieu. "Not used to it. But you never get used to it."

"So you see! Even if I return to the Party, hat in hand, I won't be able to forget myself. A whole part of me will remain outside."

Mathieu's eyes sparkle:

"Exactly," he says. "Outside. Outside and inside at the same time. Completely in on it all, and out of it at the same time, wanting the impossible, and knowing you want it, and wanting it as if it was within reach—that's being a man."

He gets up and comes over to Brunet.

"Besides, what else are you already besides that? What are you today—still part of the Party, and at the same time not part of it anymore. You don't have to make it up, or change anything. All you've got to do is be what you already are. Until the point where you can't anymore."

Brunet looks at him, smiling:

"Thanks for the advice."

Mathieu goes to the door:

"No one's in the last bunk."

"Ok."

"I'll come wake you at 6 o'clock."

He opens the door and slips out without shaking hands. Brunet looks around at the room for a minute, then goes to look at himself in the mirror. He puts some more coal on the fire, he yawns, he goes up to a painted red board supported by a couple of boxes. There's a razor, a piece of soap, and two used blades. Brunet takes the razor in his hand and looks at it.

PART III

Scholarship and Analysis

CHAPTER 7
General Introduction for *Roads of Freedom*

Michel Contat

In the summer of 1938, Sartre published *Nausea* and was on the verge of finishing "Childhood of a Leader" for the collection *The Wall*, which was already under contract with Gallimard. He found himself about to embark on the third wave of the vast literary agenda he had set himself from the beginning of the 1930s. The first had been the "pamphlet on contingency," that is, the revelation of existence in *Nausea*. Then the short stories showing how existence is lived by singular individuals distinct from the author; and now the novel, a tableau of multiple personalities, as he had seen in such literary undertakings as Thomas Mann's *The Buddenbrooks*, Jules Romains' *Men of Good Will*, and Roger Martin du Gard's *The Thibaults*.

Before determining its narrative content or knowing that it would be called *Roads of Freedom*, Sartre referred to this literary cycle—far more ambitious than his previous work, not only in terms of scale but also in terms of its underlying philosophical project—as "the novel." Even at the end of his life, when he would speak about his novelistic fiction, it was always in these terms—"*Nausea*, the short stories, the novel"—which indicated three stages of a self-sufficient whole, alongside the strictly philosophical project, itself accompanied by the critical project, and more distantly, the theater. After it, as we know, Sartre was never to formulate another specifically novelistic project.

In a letter from July 1938, while Simone de Beauvoir was touring in Tignes, Sartre wrote to her, "I have suddenly found the subject of my novel, its proportions, and its title. Just as you wished, the subject is free-dom." Citing these lines in *The Prime of Life*, Simone de Beauvoir adds, "The title he sent me, in capital letters, was *Lucifer*. The first volume was called *The Revolt*, and the second *The Sermon*. The epigraph was: *The mis-fortune is that we are free.*"[1] We are not aware of any document predating this one that shows Sartre in search of a subject for his novel. The closest thing extant along these lines seems to be a letter from July 1935, in which he wrote to Simone de Beauvoir, "There are some excellent things in *And Quiet Flows the Don*, which is, however, not as good as his *Virgin Soil Upturned*. But good enough to put me to shame. This morning I tore up and threw out thirty pages about an all-female chamber ensemble, then I despaired of ever mastering my profession. Then I wisely put the question off to later. I'll start in again tomorrow."[2] The all-female cham-ber ensemble appears in *The Reprieve*; the profession that the young philosophy professor complains of not mastering is clearly that of novel-ist. Before *Being and Nothingness*, in fact, Sartre considers himself a novel-ist more than a philosopher, and Simone de Beauvoir encourages him in this, finding that he's wasting his time in philosophy. "I was always a writer first, and then a philosopher; that's how it happened," confirms Sartre in 1972; and "writer" for him clearly means novelist. The pamphlet was not, properly speaking, a novel, nor obviously were the short stories, even though the last one, *"Childhood of a Leader,"* seemed like an ironic abridgement of one. Sartre's 1938–1939 articles on Faulkner, Dos Passos, Mauriac and Nabokov[3] are enough to show that as he was about to begin his, he was working to clarify the nature and the techniques of the novel. In each of these articles, he is concerned to show how a narrative tech-nique is connected to an ethics and a metaphysics. Thus he takes up the project of his novel in the summer of 1938 with this dual preoccupation, both technical and philosophical. . . .

On December 30, 1939, Gallimard announces that *The Age of Reason* will come out in 1940, but from the beginning of this year, Sartre has hopes of publishing the first and second volumes together, so the reader will have a better sense of the direction of the novel as a whole.[4] . . .

But during the "phony war," Sartre covers a considerable amount of philosophical territory, moving from an individualistic ethics and an abstractly anarchist position to a thinking of historicity. He comes to this through an internal dialogue with Heidegger, in the face of the evidence that the war has not only changed his own relationship to the world, but has also radically penetrated the experience of his entire generation. This thought, concerning "being-for-war," inspired by Heidegger's notion of "being-for-death", is now at the heart of his reflections on ethics and freedom, and he comes to see that his own earlier failure to understand his real situation in the world and in history drags his novel backwards. The book was conceptualized before the revelation of war made him a convert to history. Indeed, the discovery of historicity is the real subject of the second volume. Sartre's problem is now to inscribe in the first volume, after the fact, a new consciousness that cannot show itself as what it is, but must make itself felt by the reader, without changing the affective tone or the economy of the narrative. The difficulty, which we think is overcome in the definitive version of *The Age of Reason*, resides for Sartre precisely in the delay between the time at which he writes, and the time of the event about which he writes; this delay will only grow after the war, and to such a degree that Sartre will be unable to bridge the gap. . . .

The German offensive begins on May 10, 1940. Between this date and June 21, when he is captured, Sartre finds himself on the eastern front, continuing to revise his novel. With any hope of imminent publication thrown aside, it is now "against the failure of democracy and liberty, against the defeat of the allies," that he engages in writing, "going all the way 'as if' everything was going to be put right again."[5] . . .

We have documents for the period covering Sartre's imprisonment, which began at Baccarat until mid-August, then continued at Treves (Trier), in Germany, until the middle of March 1941. From the letters he wrote to Simone de Beauvoir from Baccarat, she tells us that "he maintained, persistently, that our ideas and hopes would triumph in the end."[6] About August 15, he told her of his imminent transfer to Germany, almost with happiness.[7] In fact, it appears that he never lost his optimism; on the contrary, he set to work trying to encourage his captured comrades, as did a certain number of priests with whom he was imprisoned. This philosophico-moral theme of resistance through hope is central to *Bariona*, the play he wrote and produced for the camp at Christmas. It will also be found, without the Biblical trappings, throughout the second part of *Death in the Soul*, where he portrays his experience as a prisoner through the character of the communist activist Brunet, despite his ideological and psychological differences from the latter.

Sartre's experience in the prison camp is above all one of solidarity, life in common, body upon body constantly, in a sort of fusional sociality in which, according to witnesses, his general mood was one of profound happiness. . . Philosophy, however, remained central to his concerns: throughout the period of captivity, he never stopped taking notes for *Being and Nothingness*, which he began writing upon his return to Paris, after having put the finishing touches to the final version of *The Age of Reason*. He has told us he also worked on the latter from time to time in the camp. Indeed, among the reasons for which he delayed his escape until March 1941,[8] one of the most important was to first get back the manuscript of *The Age of Reason*, which had been confiscated by a German officer. . . . Once finished, however, publication was out of the question: "Sartre kept *The Age of Reason* locked away in a drawer, since no publisher would have dared to bring out so 'scandalous' a novel."[9]

According to M. Perrin, Sartre began work on the second volume, planned since 1938, in early 1941; he had decided to dedicate it to the Munich crisis, and to call it "September." Simone de Beauvoir says little about Sartre's work during the years of the Occupation, except to say soberly that she and her companion worked a great deal and without being preoccupied with immediate publication: "We had decided to live as if we were assured of victory in the end."[10] In fact, Sartre's productivity during these years is breathtaking: in three years he writes two plays, a philosophical treatise, a novel, four studies (on Camus, Blanchot, Bataille, and Brice Parain), and screenplays, all the while taking responsibility for a khange class at Lycée Condorcet. Having decided in the fall of 1941 to disband the group "Socialism and Liberty," "he set himself resolutely to work on the play he had begun: this was the only form of resistance accessible to him," writes Simone de Beauvoir.[11] He completed this play, *The Flies,* early in 1942. We can suppose that Sartre then devoted himself primarily to the writing of *Being and Nothingness*, since this was written in less than a year, between the end of 1941 and October 1942. Sartre, however, tells us that he gave equal attention to the philosophical work and the novel, going from the one to the other to distract himself, writing in cafes in Montparnasse, primarily at La Coupole and Aux Trois Mousquetaires.

The writing of the second volume is thus spread over four years; the manuscript was finished in October or November of 1944, and immediately turned over to Gallimard along with *The Age of Reason*. The two were intended to come out together in September 1945 . . . The title *The Reprieve* (*Le sursis*[12]) which replaced "September," came from a German novel by Hemito von Doderer, translated into French in 1943, *Sursis*. Von Doderer's had nothing to do with Sartre's idea: it took place in the seventeenth century, and Sartre had not read it. But he found the title irresistible for expressing both the situation of September 1938 and the philosophical idea that is a major theme of the novel: that human existence is in perpetual suspension. The choice of this title, at a moment when the outcome of the war was still uncertain, even if the Allied victory was beginning to be sensed in the distance, eloquently translates the fundamental relation of the novel-in-the-making to history-in-the-making, and the unforeseeable meaning of both: if by 1943 the Munich Accord had for all time taken on the meaning of a war which had suspended freedom, the outburst of freedom in the resistance to Nazism could not carry the day without the Allied victory, for which there was no guarantee as yet. Uncertain of the outcome of the war, on which the publication of his novel depended, Sartre works away at it like he has placed a bet on freedom, placing it in suspension, much as freedom itself is in suspension in the novel as a whole, that is to say, always put off rather than accomplished. The simple gap of time has increased: *The Age of Reason* takes place in June 1938 and was finished in 1941; *The Reprieve* takes place in September 1938 and is finished in 1944. Three years for the first, six years for the second, nine years would separate the publication of the third from the events described in it.

In the "Please Insert" that he wrote for the first two volumes, Sartre set out the time frame of the whole project: "I wanted to retrace the road traveled by certain people and social groups between 1938 and 1944. This road will lead them to the liberation of Paris, though not necessarily to their own. But I hope, at least, to be able to make it possible to sense the conditions of a complete deliverance, beyond the point at which I end this tale." The third and final volume is announced with the title "The Last Chance." It is thus to cover six years by itself, which is enormous in comparison to the first, which took place in forty-eight hours, and the second, in seven days. Given the technique adopted in the first two, which consisted of never summarizing, and omitting nothing from within the juxtaposed short temporal episodes, requiring numerous ellipses—for instance, we know nothing about what happens to these characters between mid-June and September 23, 1938—there is no doubt that a single volume would be much too brief to provide a detailed treatment of the war, defeat, resistance, and liberation. This first difficulty probably stopped Sartre rather quickly at the outset of the third volume. Had he begun this one as soon as he dropped off the other two for printing? If so, when did he finish? In an interview given just after the publication of *The Age of Reason* and *The Reprieve,* he states in October 1945 that he is working on his treatise on existentialist ethics at the same as "The Last Chance." At this time it is certain that these two are the projects dearest to him, as they extend his essential writing projects: philosophy and novel. Furthermore, he had promised them both to the public, and they were to dissipate misunderstandings. It may well be that he was in fact working on them at this point. But the manuscripts with which we are familiar date pretty certainly from 1947 for the *Notebook for an Ethics*, and 1947–1948 for the third volume of *Roads of Freedom*. The reasons for this delay are to be found in the sudden transformation of Sartre's situation around the fall of 1945.

The Age of Reason had been undertaken at a moment before the war when, thanks to *Nausea* and then *The Wall,* Sartre had achieved the kind of notoriety that is reserved for a powerful, original, young talent. To the same degree as Nizan, for example, though without the audience and responsibility that came to the latter for being a communist columnist, he was one of a small number of writers on whom the lettered public could count for producing, over the long haul, a body of literary work equivalent in importance to that of writers like Malraux or Celine who had not yet achieved the established and dominant position of Gide. This situation of being the young writer of the future had remained Sartre's throughout the war. It had not been qualitatively changed by the production of *The Flies* or *No Exit*, nor by the publication of *The Imaginary* or of *Being and Nothingness*. These new works had contributed, in the stifled literary atmosphere of the Occupation, to consolidating his reputation among a rather restricted circle, confirming promises implicit in his pre-war texts. This is undoubtedly a most propitious situation for the slow ripening of a wide-spreading corpus, conceived by its author as much, if not more, for his posterity as for his contemporaries: the expectations of a relatively homogeneous, cultivated, clear-sighted public is enough stimulation for a writer: the demands are neither so powerful nor so extensive as to inhibit him or, on the contrary, throw him into distracted or premature works.

But, in 1945, in nearly a matter of days, this situation changes completely: Sartre becomes not only a fashionable author, but steps forth as a leader of a school and is invested with the role of a master-thinker for an entire generation, before being rapidly promoted to the rank of foreign ambassador for French thought. At the same time, he is attacked from all sides: denounced by the right-thinking as a corruptor of the youth, and by the communists as a false petty-bourgeois prophet, he is accused by one after another of wallowing in the gutter. In short, he is a scandal. Sartre has explained the causes of this sudden transformation that turned him into a "public monument" after the war, into the Other with whom he had to learn to live.[13] These causes were essentially a cultural nationalism that pushes the French—who had been reduced to a second-tier nation by defeat and by a victory in which they had only a small part—to promote the writers who came through the Resistance; the development of means of mass communication that extend writers' virtual public; the opening of the borders to translations after years during which the hunger for foreign texts went unsatisfied; and finally, the incursion of politics into literature. In response to this new situation, Sartre develops the notion of "committed literature" ("*littérature engagée*"), which he understands as a way to assume the new responsibility of the writer, placed before a total virtual public of a sort that his predecessors had never had.

This engagement in the matters of the day entails that Sartre is veritably commandeered away from his own work into other immediate tasks. Apart from the theater, which is a way to reach the public directly on topical issues, he is pulled away to texts that deal with current matters, such as "Materialism and Revolution" and "What is Literature?" where he goes on the offensive and develops his ideas in response to the attacks to which he is subjected. He works on numerous fronts, firstly in his journal (the first issue of *Les Temps modernes* comes out in October 1945), but also in the press, on the radio, traveling, giving lectures and interviews, attempting at all times to state and clarify his positions, before throwing himself into a form of active politics, with the Rassemblement démocratique révolutionnaire (Revolutionary Democratic Union). He becomes a truly diversified writer, which does not mean that he abandons philosophy or literature in the sense of novelistic creativity. On the contrary, his multiple and regular interventions aim at nothing other than assuring the conditions for authentic literature and philosophy, but they require him to put off his more creative projects for the time being.

During these two or three years right after the war, it is not only his personal situation as a writer that changes, but the entire historical situation, and not only at the national level. He had intended, with the third and last volume of *Roads of Freedom*, to enter into a positive phase, in which his characters, through their role in the Resistance, would construct their project of liberation. But as time passed, he came to discover an extraordinarily blurred situation, in which the problems of freedom were no longer posed in terms of clear choices, as they had been during the Occupation: to resist or to collaborate, to take out some Germans at the risk of having hostages shot, to talk or not talk under torture, and so on. The moral problem remains the same, that of the practical implications of a choice in favor of freedom, but it has been politicized, and as a result, in a complicated and ambiguous political situation, it has lost the quality of being a clear choice between life and death, heroism or cowardice, and has become full of all the ambiguities and uncertainties of the post-war period. How, under these circumstances, can he continue a novel which explicitly announced its intention of showing how its protagonists would become heroes, without falling into a kind of edifying literature that simply commemorated the Resistance, and which was coming to be known as "*Resistantialism*"? In literary terms, how can he maintain the character of the first volumes—a fictional but concrete experience of freedom linked to contemporary events, implying a contemporaneous relationship between the writer and his fictional representative, Mathieu? In other words, how can he keep the novel open onto the present in which it is written, when the circumstances have changed so much that the nature of the choices available has changed as well?

In 1947, in "What is Literature?," Sartre defines the technique of the "situated novel," the most appropriate kind for "accounting for our times," according to him; the technique he applied in *The Age of Reason* and *The Reprieve*: "with no internal narrator or all-knowing witness," the situated novel functions on a principle of "generalized relativity" which makes it impossible for any of the consciousnesses presented in the text, one after another, to have a privileged point of view on the others, on itself or on events. This technique leaves "doubts, expectations, inconclusiveness everywhere," and obliges the reader to "make his own conjectures, making him feel that his views on the action and the characters are just one opinion among many others."[14] But in order to prevent this technique from becoming dishonest, the author must also not be in possession of the final meaning of a fixed destiny, of a contained period. As we know, Sartre was writing *The Reprieve* at a time when the struggle of the Allies and the Resistance was itself in suspense. In order to write about the Resistance in the third volume, four years after the Liberation, he has to be able to retain the open and uncertain point of view on it that will suspend it with regard to a future to-be-made. This point of view is that of revolution, socialism, to which Sartre was drawn in 1941, committing himself to a philosophical and political project linking "socialism and liberty." Under the Occupation, there was no problem: pursuit of this project necessarily entailed resistance to the Nazis and victory over the occupiers; it entailed nothing less than the project of individual heroism: to fight against the Germans was, in principle at least, to run the risk of torture and death. The choice could be more or less difficult, requiring more or less personal courage, but at any rate it was clear. Whether one sided with the nationalist resistors or with the communists made no difference. But once the Germans were defeated, the alliance between the two quickly fell apart: the world divided into two antagonistic blocks—the United States and the Soviet Union—and the class struggle of the exploited against the exploiters, suspended during the war, returned to the national stage. All would be simple, from the revolutionary point of view, if the USSR (identified with socialism) and its opposition to the Atlantic block did not mean war, and if war, given the appearance of the atomic bomb, did not mean the end of humanity altogether: no liberty, no socialism, nothing: "a bomb will have put out the lights."[15]

All of Sartre's activity and reflection now went to maintaining as a whole the requirements of liberty, of socialism, and of peace, by showing that denying their compatibility would lead the world to catastrophe. A first refusal, then: that of choosing between the two blocks, since this choice led straight to war. And a second refusal: that of joining with the French Communist Party, for in identifying its interests with those of the USSR, it had become a conservative opportunistic party aligned with the bourgeoisie while claiming to be defending the rights of the workers, and putting its intellectuals to work covering up its contradictions with a Marxism that was nothing but "an ignorant determinism."[16] But since the project for socialism, which is fundamentally that of the concrete universal, of freedom choosing itself as its goal, cannot be carried forward without the workers, and since the workers see themselves represented in the Communist Party, it is not possible to work for socialism *against* the Communist Party. Thus, in 1947–1948, for Sartre, the problem of socialism, liberty and peace is a problem in relation to the Communist Party.

Without being the adversary, the Party is nonetheless the principle obstacle to authentic socialism, and so action must be directed at the Party. But since this cannot be done directly, since the Party allows no criticism and declares anyone who is not totally on board to be its enemy, and since it stands between the workers and the intellectuals which are outside it but speaking for the workers, Sartre has no alternative but to accept his isolation, writing for readers who are just as isolated—bourgeois turned against the bourgeoisie, fed-up communists—to make them appreciate the unacceptable nature of this isolation, and invite them to invent a way out of a situation which would be completely hopeless if "clear insight into the darkest situation, were not, already, itself, an indication of optimism. It implies that the situation is thinkable, that is, that we are not lost as in a thick forest, and that on the contrary, we can get ourselves out of this by using our minds, holding it before our eyes, thereby totalizing it and forming our resolutions in terms of it, even if these resolutions should be hopeless."[17] These lines were written in 1947, when Sartre was returning to his project on Ethics. The way out, according to him, could only be found by inventing a new ethics, a "hard" morality which can find no support other than the requirement of freedom, and which must proceed through the clear insight of a consciousness that shoulders its subjectivity without any guarantee or foundation, and which can therefore only project itself a future by converting itself to itself, while knowing itself to be rigorously situated in a time that it has not chosen, but that it contributes to creating, just as do all other subjectivities.

We see that Sartre is brought back to his old problem, *Nausea*'s problem: Contingency. But he now finds it "historicized," that is, indissolubly linked to the period that gives it the form it has. At the time when he takes up the project of working on his Ethics, he does not know where he is going, and he writes something like a series of interrogations on violence, falsehood, ignorance, oppression, and so on, each organized in terms of the question of the relation of means and end. It is probably in order to avoid the trap of abstractness that Sartre decides—as he had done with *Being and Nothingness* and *The Reprieve*—to take up the task of testing his philosophical reflection in the concrete experience of the novel.

The third volume of *Roads of Freedom* represents a tentative solution, or at least a transitional one, to the set of personal, literary, political and moral problems we have just sketched out rather schematically. The constructive moment is deferred to a fourth volume, to which Sartre transfers the concluding title, "The Last Chance." For the third, which could have taken the title of one of his youthful writings, "The Defeat," or one of Zola's, "The Debacle," since it tells the story of the French defeat in June 1940, Sartre reuses the title of the pages of his war journal, published in 1942 in the journal *Messages*: "Death in the Soul." The writing of it in two very distinct styles and narrative techniques marks its transitional nature: the first part treats the characters from *The Age of Reason*, but now they are isolated and split off from Mathieu, who had been the center of gravity in the first volume, and who now finds himself at the front somewhere in Lorraine during the three days prior to the surrender. Mathieu clearly dominates in the first part of this volume. The second part seems to open up a new cycle. Brunet, the communist activist who had a secondary role in *The Age of Reason* and *The Reprieve*, takes over from Mathieu, who seems to be left for dead in the bell tower where he was shooting at the Germans who will take Brunet into captivity. The second part thus seems to be the beginning of a cycle in which Brunet, represents the spirit of the resistance in the first days of captivity in Germany. This reorientation of the novel's axis toward the communist Brunet corresponds to the reorientation of Sartre's political and moral problematic after the war, toward the Communist Party, around which it henceforth revolves.

Sartre's relation with his new protagonist has nothing in common with the relation he had with Mathieu, which was one of existential identity, interiority. Sartre no more identifies with Brunet than he did earlier with Daniel, Boris or Gomez: from outside, he observes in Brunet the development of a conflict between the existential choice of the activist, which consists of obeying the "objective" values incarnated in the directorship of the Party, and the situation of captivity where the activist is cut off from directives and has to decide what to do for himself. Though Sartre himself never lived this conflict, he nonetheless breathes into it the tension of a debate which he endured, a debate placing him in opposition to Stalinist communists at the time he was writing. On the emotional level, this debate came to a head in the summer of 1947 when Sartre called on the leaders of the Party to prove their allegations against his friend Nizan, who had died in the battle of Dunkirk in May 1940. Nizan had been denounced as a traitor due to his decision to quit the

Party because of the German-Soviet Pact. It is in *Strange Friendship*, published the same year as *Death in the Soul*, 1949, in *Les Temps modernes* as "Extracts from Volume IV of *Roads of Freedom*," that Sartre transposes his own conflict with the Communist Party into the one that Brunet lives between his friendship for Schneider-Vicarios, who represents Nizan in the novel, and his loyalty to the Party. For that to work, it is essential that it be set at a moment when the Party's position *is wrong*, that is, before it endorses the Resistance, during the period when, following the USSR's directive, it adopts a wait-and-see stance vis-à-vis the Germans, and seeks to obtain legal recognition from them—until the German offensive against the USSR on June 22, 1941 pushes it into clandestine action against the Occupation.

What is Sartre's objection to this policy? It is that it was adopted in the name of the supposed "historical process," according to which the development of history obeys objective laws of which the Party would forever be the infallible interpreter. For him, this political "realism" is the translation of a determinist philosophy that eliminates subjectivity from history and transforms the opponent into an "objective" traitor. However, this idea of objectivity, presenting itself as scientific, is inaccessible to the masses, since they have not absorbed the Marxism of which they are the bearers, and is only grasped in its truth by the intellectuals in the Party leadership. This creates a situation in which the latter have to lie to the masses, in their own interests, and present any opponent as a sell-out. Sartre demonstrates this implacable mechanism at its existential level in *Strange Friendship*, and he analyzes it at the political and ideological level, with respect to Tito, in "Faux savants ou faux lièvres?" in 1950 when he interprets Tito's dissidence vis-à-vis the USSR as the reintegration of subjectivity into history. The latter text is important, for it constitutes a link between the radically anti-Stalinist position of *Strange Friendship* and the ultra-Bolshevist position that he assumes in 1952. In it he argues that in reality subjectivity is reintroduced not as a formal ideal, in moral free will, but by the very movement of objective history, an important concession on the theoretical level, to Marxist objectivism.

Here we cannot go into a lengthy philosophical argument. But with respect to the origins of *Roads of Freedom* and the reasons for its incompleteness, we must clarify the reasons why, in 1949–1950, Sartre encounters a dead-end which makes him definitely abandon the novel, and which he gets out of in 1952 by a conversion, a philosophical *coup de force* that orients his literary project toward autobiography—prepared by the existential biographies of Genet and Mallarmé—and then leads him to the novel-biography-autobiography-philosophy synthesis of *The Family Idiot*.

The two key events that make Sartre become aware of the philosophical dead-end that he finds himself in with the Ethics project are the failure of the *Rassemblement démocratique révolutionnaire* (Revolutionary Democratic Union) and the Korean War. With the RDR, Sartre had thought it would be possible to put together the means to influence the Communist Party from the outside, toward a revolutionary politics that would be independent of Moscow. But during 1949 it becomes clear that the RDR is just a group of intellectuals, whose most active members are lining up with United States' politics as a result of their anti-Sovietism. To prevent the RDR from veering to the right, Sartre takes steps to make it fall apart, then resigns. He finds himself back in the position of an isolated writer, on his own. He understands then that the ethics he's elaborating, an ethics of lucidity above all, really only works for him, insofar as the only kind of action it implies is that of writing. It is an idealist ethics, without a grip on reality, requiring a conversion to authenticity, seemingly possible only for an intellectual. In fact, the "purifying reflection" that is the necessary condition of this conversion is understood as a reflexive and critical act requiring the intellectual instruments of an abstract critique of alienation. What is an ethics suspended in intellectual conversion? A specific ethics, a writer's ethics, but not one suited for men confronted with the realities of a concrete praxis, that of work, of material production, of class struggle. It's an ethics of a solitary man, an ethics of individual salvation. As a result, now he doesn't know what to do with Mathieu. Up until the bell-tower episode in *Death in the Soul,* he had projected his own experience onto Mathieu: the life experience of a typical intellectual who is questioning himself about himself as life goes on. Given how the novel is planned, he would now have to completely transform the character, bringing about a practical conversion within him. If he wants to keep the alter ego relationship with Mathieu, he'll have to continue to project his life onto him, paint him in the colors of his own life. But his own experience in the resistance was not that of an activist, an active resistance fighter, a hero, but that of a "resisting writer," who resisted by writing. How can he transpose this experience into that of a hero who faces torture and still maintain the relation to the novel which he has had up to this point—a relation that allows a problematic of the present to prevail through the evocation of the past?

What begins to become a problem for Sartre in 1949–1950 is writing itself: he puts his status as a writer in question insofar as this status implies a split in which he had stopped believing. The act of writing was spontaneously an act of solidarity during the Occupation: writing against the Germans and their supporters, demystifying the ideology of collaboration, like physically or morally resisting torture, posed no problem. Writing, for the writer, like refusing to talk for a resistance fighter, was the same act of freedom promoting the freedom of others at the same time as one's own, a completely unambiguous and positive act: heroism coincided with writing. But since writing had ceased to be a positive act, it was no longer possible for the writer to give writing the same meaning that a heroic act had. The Sartre of 1950 can no longer identify with the Mathieu of 1943, to whom he had long ago assigned a heroic destiny that he does not want to alter. Nor can he identify with Brunet, whom he makes follow the reverse path—in discovering his subjectivity he begins to become a lucid intellectual. In effect, it is this reciprocal overtaking of the intellectual by the activist and the activist by the intellectual—that he had intended to see incarnated in the meeting and identification of Mathieu and Brunet at the heart of the Resistance: they were both to become authentic men of action—it is this fusion of freedom and action that now appears to him to be contaminated with idealism. The spirit of the Resistance, which informed Sartre's ethics, and should have led his novel's characters to coincide with their freedom, had ceased to fit with the realities of a present that was log-jammed by the politics of the USSR-USA tensions. Thus, Sartre finds himself blocked. He has to learn the lessons of realism, and it is not through Mathieu that he can do so. The unpublished chapters of the fourth volume of *Roads of Freedom*, which we present here, show us, in fact, a Mathieu who is unrecognizable: resurrected, indeed, but in the form of a mock-up . . . We can imagine that it is because he sees what he is doing to Mathieu — making him into a fleshless image of idealism—that Sartre, as a demanding writer, saw with clarity the abstract character that his ethics was taking, and therefore dropped both of them.[18] In our view, this takes nothing away from the interest these pages will have for the reader: they are the symptomatic expression of the literary and intellectual dead-end in which Sartre finds himself in 1950.

The Korean War, which breaks out that year, disorients him even more. Suddenly the hostilities of the Cold War threaten to lead to a third world war, to a nuclear holocaust. Sartre refuses to withdraw into a silent disengagement, as Merleau-Ponty does. But, seeing no political way out of the problem, he undertakes to reflect—still on uncertain philosophical footing—upon the moral significance of the choice to write, the choice of the imaginary, in a world torn apart by the antagonistic forces of Good and Evil. This opportunity comes to him as the preface to the complete works of Jean Genet, which will take on the dimensions of a vast critical, biographical and philosophical essay, and provide the next step after the abandoned Ethics of the previous year. The conclusion of the essay is well known:

Any Ethics which does not explicitly present itself as *impossible today* contributes to the mystification and alienation of men. The moral "problem" is born from the fact that *for us* Ethics is completely and at once inevitable and impossible. Action needs to set itself moral norms in this climate of unsurpassable impossibility.[19]

It is the tension of this contradiction that we have to keep in mind in order to correctly understand the meaning of Sartre's rapprochement with the Communist Party in 1952. The reversal he forces himself to go through results from his conviction that the position of a solitary writer is no longer tenable; with the Cold War threatening to burst into flames, a choice between the two sides must be made, for to not choose, in the name of morality and freedom, is to give advantage to the camp of those who seize upon freedom and morality to extend their domination. If Sartre chooses the USSR and the Communist Party, it is solely for the reason that, taking account of the then-current balance of power, which favors the American camp, the USSR has an interest in maintaining peace. Thus it is a matter of choosing the lesser evil, rather than a positive allegiance. At the beginning, Sartre has scarcely any illusions about the nature of the Soviet regime or the democratic sincerity of the French Communist Party. However, by the logic of the theoretical justifications that he gives for his choice and of the alliances that common action imposes, he will be drawn beyond a circumstantial alliance motivated more by hatred of the adversary than by agreement with the ally—until the point when the Soviet repression of Hungary causes a moral upheaval which returns him, between 1956 and 1968, to the path of a distant and resolutely critical *compagnon de route*, and to radically independent theoretical reflection.

Could Sartre have tried out his new position, beginning in 1952, on the existential plane, in the unfinished part of *Roads of Freedom*? At first, one is tempted to say Yes. Is he not, once again, in the same relation to the Communist Party as were the non-Communist members of the resistance during the Occupation, once the Soviet Union had entered the war—a relation of political alliance and of common action? In that case, in the situation of 1942 to 1944, Mathieu would have been able to represent the position of the *compagnon de route*, and Brunet that of the non-Stalinist activist who is loyal to the Party. However, we have seen above why Sartre could no longer dream of showing the specific contradictions of the 1949–1950 situation in the framework of an unproblematic enterprise like that of the heroism of the Resistance. But there is still another reason: the Soviet camps. The simple fact of their existence—which Sartre and Merleau-Ponty denounce in January 1950 in *Les Temps modernes*—makes it impossible for him to identify the Communist Party and the USSR with the project of freedom, as had been possible during the war. The identification of the two historical periods had become radically impossible. Sartre may have been able, in 1951, to put his own conflict on stage and get beyond it through the imaginary, on the plane of myth, with *The Devil and the Good Lord*, in the context of the Peasant War; nonetheless, on the existential plane he was still not able to show the ambiguities and contradictions of his current position in the context of the Resistance. On this score, Simone de Beauvoir quotes an unpublished note of Sartre's:

> "I made Goetz do what I was not able to do." Goetz overcame a contradiction that Sartre experienced acutely after the failure of the R.D.R. and especially since the Korean War, but without being able to get beyond it: "The contradiction was not one of ideas. It was in my being. For this freedom that I was implied the freedom of all. And it was not true that all were free. I could not, without exploding, submit to the discipline of solidarity. And I could not be free alone."[20]

Not yet being resigned to abandoning his novel, Sartre has told us that he considered the idea of purely and simply leaping over the period of the Resistance, and plunging his characters into the ideological and political conflicts of the post-war period, to make them live the *divorce* from the Resistance. This would require that the readers learn only incidentally what they had done during the years of the Occupation, and at Liberation, but the story of the novel would unfold in a present that was in the neighborhood of 1950. We know nothing more of this project, which Sartre did not pursue. The last time he mentioned his ongoing work on the novel at that period seems to have been in July 1952. In an interview given to a Austrian newspaper, he describes himself as constrained by a sort of internal dictator to complete his numerous projects, and among them he mentions "The Last Chance," on which he says he is currently working, and which he anticipates publishing in October. About it, he says " 'The Last Chance' has little to do with existentialism; the novel has an almost Kantian starting point . . . I'd almost like to say that for me this book constitutes an important milestone in my work."[21] What Sartre says here about the book having the character of a moral debate corresponds to what we know from the fourth volume. In any event, the choice to abandon it comes from a later point, for Sartre has told us that at that time he foresaw not only a fourth volume, but a fifth, and undoubtedly even a sixth, all the while saving the title "The Last Chance" for the final one. As Simone de Beauvoir indicates: "Without having abandoned the idea of a fourth volume, he always found work that needed his attention more."[22]

In 1959, again, he says in an interview: "I'm having trouble finishing my novel. The fourth volume was to have been about the Resistance. At that time, the choice was easy—even if it took a lot of strength and courage to stick to it. You were either for the Germans or against them. It was black or white. Today—and since '45—the situation has gotten complicated. Less courage is required, perhaps, for choosing, but the choices have become more difficult. I just can't express the ambiguities of our time in this novel that takes place in 1943. But from another side, this unfinished work weighs on me. It's difficult to begin another one before finishing this one."[23] Like so many of Sartre's pieces, *Roads of Freedom* was thus abandoned not by a deliberate decision that can be given an exact date, but progressively, in so far as he put off completing it until he had to admit that it had been abandoned. In our view, however, it is in developing the idea, near the end of 1953, of an autobiography that Sartre decides—or rather that the decision takes place in him—to leave his novel where it is, for this new project represents a way out of the dead-end in which he finds himself with the novel. If, as in the first three volumes, he wanted to put himself in question through Mathieu, by now putting Mathieu into the historical conditions of the Cold War, Sartre would have to make Mathieu live his own contradictions. However, a whole set of reasons prevent him from doing so. Private reasons, in the first place. By this time, Sartre has become a public persona; his private life has therefore become an object of a curiosity that he has no desire to satisfy. No matter what transpositions he might bring about, no one would fail to see Mathieu as the author's double, and to attribute to him everything he has the other live through, unless he makes him so different that it would be impossible to identify him with the author. But, as we have said, their relationship, from the start, is one of identity, and it is impossible to change that if the character is to retain psychological coherence. Consequently, Sartre has to continue to lend him his being in order to give him his contradictions. But what he has come to realize is that these contradictions are not the contradictions of just anyone, but that they are linked to his status as a writer. Until now, he has not put his existence in question insofar as he is *a writer*. Writing seemed to him to be such an obvious activity, so spontaneously his, but so similar to any other, that he had been able, quite innocently, to give Mathieu the taste and the color of his life without attributing to him the same choice that he had made, the choice of writing. Because his own challenge now was about his own very being, that of a writer, he would have to make Mathieu into a writer too, and not just a "Sunday writer" as he is in *The Age of Reason*, but someone who has made the total choice of writing, who exercises his freedom completely through writing. His fame and influence have brought a responsibility to Sartre that made him realize that writing is not an innocent activity, nor of the same nature as other kinds of production. Which means that he would have to make Mathieu into himself, in other words, *nolens volens*, write a *roman à clés*. A *roman à clés* requires that fictional characters refer to real people that the readers know or think they know, that is, public figures (which is why, for every author's public, an autobiographical novel comes off as a *roman à clés*). We all know, in this respect, the misfortune that befell Simone de Beauvoir with *The Mandarins*, where readers identified Dubreuilh with Sartre, Henri with Camus, and Anne with the author. Her subsequent denials were ineffective precisely to the degree to which the novel presented itself as a piece of realistic fiction. It is enough to think of how unlikely it is that in a novel about the post-war Parisian intelligentsia, the novel's milieu, there would be no mention of Sartre,

Camus or de Beauvoir, who were in fact everywhere at the time, to understand why readers would naturally be tempted to look for them in disguise. In other words, when an author has become a player of importance in the period and milieu that his or her novel describes, he or she must be represented in it by name, as Norman Mailer will do later in *Armies of the Night*, where he has a third-person role, or else accept that the novel will be read as a *roman à clés*. And if the author rejects both, then he or she is drawn into autobiography by the very logic of literary realism.

Sartre has acknowledged all of this unequivocally but implicitly in an unpublished 1973 interview about *Roads of Freedom*:

> What is fundamentally false about a novel in which one constructs a character based on oneself is precisely that he is not *really* you. The differences you put into him, and which seem of no decisive significance at the outset, end up throwing him into falseness. In *The Age of Reason*, I gave Mathieu everything of mine—I don't mean the facts of his life, but his character—except the essential thing, which is that I lived in order to write. There is something radically false in an autobiographical novel, namely that it's straddling: it is neither completely a novel, nor completely an autobiography. But that's something I did not want to see at the time, because I did not want to abandon the novel, and I could not write without making use of my own life.

This last remark clarifies for us another motive for abandoning *Roads of Freedom*, which is that after the war, Sartre's experience becomes extremely restricted and particularized. It becomes the experience of a man of letters, a celebrity intellectual, who, apart from his old circle of friends, almost only encounters people like himself, even when he goes abroad. Sartre the celebrity becomes the Other through which all his relationships now are lived. A novel certainly can provide an account of this kind of individual experience, taking place in a milieu at once closed upon itself and visible to others, as is the Parisian intelligentsia. This is precisely what Simone de Beauvoir did with *The Mandarins*, which came out in 1954. Sartre has told us that this book somewhat cut the ground out from under his feet: "*The Mandarins* is in fact the real ending of *Roads of Freedom* as I envisaged it as of 1950, but with another point of view. From the moment that Simone de Beauvoir did it, and did it well, there was no reason to go back to it."[24] So we see that everything is coming together, around 1954, to distance Sartre from his novel, and to direct him towards an autobiography which will allow him to clarify his own relationship to writing, by putting the origin of his vocation as a writer in question and elucidating it.

To these internal and external reasons, we can add yet another motive, so far unmentioned: the tempered reception given to *Death in the Soul* by critics who had favorably welcomed the first two volumes, but now declared they were suspending judgment, awaiting the next part. Despite Sartre's belief that it was the most successful of the three volumes, *Death in the Soul* failed to provoke the anticipated and promised positive responses, as critics transferred their moral disappointment into an accusation that *Death in the Soul* represented an exhaustion of Sartre's literary creativity. Although Sartre always said that he accorded no importance to the judgments of literary reviewers, his partial failure in their eyes intimidated him in the face of the fourth volume, which he knew he would have to take up again. In 1969, when we spoke with him about a recent remark made by Mauriac,[25] who explained his own long absence from writing novels as a result of the attack inflicted on him in 1939 by Sartre, and which, he said, had not quite demoralized him, but had made him reflect, Sartre allowed that he had had a similar reaction after *Death in the Soul*.[26]

In the network of reasons we have tried to untangle to explain the non-completion of *Roads of Freedom*, the most important one seems to us to stem from Sartre's novelistic enterprise itself. From the beginning, Sartre understood his novel as a concrete test of his philosophy of freedom, placing in question the different possible existential attitudes of a given historical situation. As long as it was a matter of describing alienated freedoms and exploring the traps of bad faith, the novel developed according to a critical logic which encountered no obstacle in the literary material itself. This material, directly inspired by Sartre's own lived experience, by psychological observation, and by an imagination that was solidly anchored in the real, was like a network of meanings to be inventoried, and in which he moved forward along with his characters, without knowing what he was going to find. From that, roads of freedom opened up to be explored by the reader, who accompanied the characters, feeling their way along. Drawn by these characters' suspended freedom, the reader mobilized his or her own, and engaged it in the same contradictions. It would be up to the reader to feel the need to find a way out. Thus, in its negative, critical, and demystifying dimension, the novel functioned as a call to the reader's freedom. But Sartre's project also involved a positive, affirmative, constructive dimension: the roads of freedom should not remain a labyrinth in which everyone is condemned to wander with more or less lucidity; they should become roads *towards* freedom.[27] But we know the risks that constructive literature faces: falling into edifying literature. And in fact, in showing characters that coincide with their freedom, when the common lot is alienation, one indeed risks giving them out as exemplars and appearing to moralize from their cases. Sartre's philosophical and literary temperament is too radically critical to be able to manifest itself in such positivity. In order that freedom continue to affirm itself as a requirement rather than as a given, the novel about freedom has to remain unfinished and open, and that, no doubt, is what constitutes its disquieting force and its authenticity: the chips are not down, the game is suspended, and it is up to the reader to start it up again. Freedom is not an end to be attained; it is the road itself.

Now, leaving aside Sartre's point of view, which has guided us in reconstructing the genesis of his novel, we will attempt to take a look at each of its four parts especially as they present themselves to the reader.[28]

CHAPTER 8
Critical Note on *Strange Friendship*

Michel Contat

Readers of *Les Temps modernes* who saw the two parts of *Strange Friendship* (in the November and December 1949 issues, published as "Extracts from *Roads of Freedom*, Volume IV") may well have thought that the text follows the action of Volume III, *Death in the Soul*. *Les Temps modernes* had published the latter in six installments, from January to June 1949, and it came out as a volume in September. We had last seen Brunet and Schneider in August 1940, on a train taking them to captivity at Trier in Germany, now we find them in the winter of 1940–1941 in the Stalag. It was a logical extension, providing continuity with the whole second part of *Death in the Soul*, in which Brunet had become the protagonist. This reinforced the feeling that a second story, a Brunet story, was beginning in *Roads of Freedom*. After *Death in the Soul*, readers had undoubtedly assumed Mathieu was dead, despite the last sentence of Sartre's "Please Insert," which suggested just the opposite.[1]

In fact it would be fourteen years more before any news of Mathieu came out. And it did not come from Sartre, but from Simone de Beauvoir, who, in a passage in *Force of Circumstance*, explained why Sartre had abandoned the fourth volume and chosen not to finish it. We reproduce here the entire passage in which she provides an overview of the unfinished book:

At the end of *Death in the Soul*, we are faced with certain questions: Is Mathieu dead or not? Who was this Schneider who intrigued Brunet so? What became of the rest of the novel's characters? *The Last*

Chance was to provide the answers. The first installment came out at the end of 1949 in *Les Temps modernes* under the title, *Drôle d'amitié* (*Strange Friendship*). Chalais, a communist who has just arrived as a prisoner in the Stalag, recognized that Schneider was the journalist Vicarios, who had resigned from the Communist Party at the time of the German-Soviet Pact. The Party labeled him an informer and issued a warning about him. Chalais brought the news that the USSR would never enter the war and that *L'Humanité* had called for collaboration with the Germans. Uneasy, indignant, distressed, Brunet decided to escape with Vicarios when he learned of his intention to do so to confront his slanderers. This shared escape sealed the friendship Brunet still felt for him despite the others. Schneider was killed; Brunet was recaptured. The rest never got past a rough draft. Brunet decided to try to escape again. He learned about a prisoner who ran an escape network: he sought him out, and it turned out to be Mathieu, who was taking part in the execution of a traitor when Brunet found him. Having survived, and tired of being free "for nothing" since birth, Mathieu finally and blithely chose action. With his help Brunet escaped and made it back to Paris; he was astonished to discover—in a reversal much like that which pushes Hugo to suicide at the end of *Dirty Hands*—that the USSR had indeed entered the war and the Party had condemned collaboration. Having succeeded at clearing Schneider's name, he took up his former activism, joining in the Resistance; but doubt, scandal and solitude had brought him to see his subjectivity; he discovered his freedom in the depths of his commitment. Mathieu's road was the inverse. Daniel, who was collaborating, had been able to have him recalled to Paris to be the editor of a German-controlled newspaper. Mathieu got out of it and went into hiding. The work he'd done in the Stalag had been that of an individualistic adventurer; now, subordinating himself to the discipline of a group, he achieved genuine commitment. Starting in the one case from alienation vis-à-vis his Cause, and in the other from abstract freedom, Brunet and Mathieu both incarnated the authentic man of action as Sartre conceived him. Mathieu and Odette's love blossomed, she left Jacques, and they knew the wholeness of freely chosen passion. Arrested, Mathieu died under torture, not heroic because of his essence, but because he had *made himself* a hero. Philippe resisted as well, to prove to himself that he was no coward, and out of resentment toward Daniel. He was killed during a raid on a café in the Latin Quarter. In his briefcase, Daniel, mad from grief and anger, concealed one of the grenades Philippe had stashed in the apartment; he took it to a meeting with some important German leaders, and blew himself up along with them. Sarah, a refugee in Marseilles, jumped out of a window with her child the day the Germans came to arrest her. Boris parachuted into France to join the underground Resistance. Everyone dead, or very nearly, there was no one left to deal with the problems of the post-war period.[2]

In 1964, George H. Bauer, who was working on his book, *Sartre and the Artist*, acquired a set of 800 manuscript pages pertaining to *Death in the Soul* from a Parisian bookstore. As he examined this manuscript (handwritten except for ten typed pages), he discovered to his great surprise completely unknown pages of the abandoned fourth volume, a notebook containing *Strange Friendship* and a set of pages pertaining to the study of Genet, the essays on David Hare and Gjon Mili, several political essays, and other pieces. Apart from the notebooks which consisted of a good portion of *Death in the Soul* and the notebook containing *Strange Friendship*, the set of pages was in complete disorder.

We learned about the existence of a 223 page manuscript of material from the fourth volume that was not published in *Les Temps modernes*; it was sold on May 12, 1959 at the Hôtel Drouot. We noted this in *The Writings of Jean-Paul Sartre*, and we thought at the time that it was the manuscript that George H. Bauer had acquired. In fact it was not the same manuscript, and at the time of writing this (1981) we have not been able to consult it. On the other hand, George H. Bauer was most helpful and graciously consented to collaborate with us in preparing the notes and variations for *Strange Friendship*, himself establishing the text of unpublished passages from the fourth volume dispersed in the manuscript he owns. For this he based himself on outlines found within the manuscript. These outlines[3] show that, despite Simone de Beauvoir's opinion to the contrary, *Strange Friendship* is not the first episode of the fourth volume, but rather the third and fifth. The chapters for which George H. Bauer was able to establish the text, and which tell the story first, of Mathieu's convalescence in the camp infirmary after being wounded, and second, of the fresh encounter of Brunet and Mathieu in the camp after the failed escape attempt and Schneider's death, frame the story that is *Strange Friendship*.[4] However, since these chapters were still in draft form, Sartre preferred that we present them separately and as a single document, whereas *Strange Friendship*, which he had published, and had seen through to its final state, belongs every bit as much as do the first three volumes to the definitive, albeit unfinished, collection, *Roads of Freedom*. The latter therefore has four parts: *The Age of Reason, The Reprieve, Death in the Soul,* and *Strange Friendship*. Because Sartre was reserving the title *The Last Chance* for the final volume, and because he was not sure, when he wrote the fourth, that it would be the final one, we hesitated, despite Simone de Beauvoir's comments on the subject, to give this title to these unpublished fragments put together by George H. Bauer.

We have emphasized the variety of writing styles in the overall economy of *Roads of Freedom*; in *Strange Friendship*, as well as in the unpublished fragments, the novel is taken over by theatrical dialogue.[5] The dramatic structure of the work is that of a debate, a conflict of rights analogous to what Hegel, as Sartre noted, had designated as constituting the essence of ancient tragedy. The tone, charged with intense affectivity, is tragic as well.

As we have indicated in the general introduction for *Roads of Freedom*, the ideological intention that motivates *Strange Friendship* is to contest the Stalinism of the French Communist Party in the years after the war. This intention plays itself out through an affective motivation: Sartre's ill-fated friendship with Nizan. At the beginning of the 1920s, this friendship, "stormier than a passion," had already given rise to a novel, *La Semence et le Scaphandre*, stemming from a quarrel with Nizan, and which Sartre abandoned once the quarrel was over. We know that during the 1930's, relations between Sartre and Nizan fell off. It seems that it was Nizan's death in May 1940 that occasioned the rebirth of Sartre's friendship for him. A prisoner in Stalag XII D at Trier, immersed in a climate of warm affectivity, Sartre probably wondered what would have become of Nizan in such circumstances. How would the activist, denounced as a traitor by the Party leadership for having quit in response to the German-Soviet Pact, have been treated by the communists in the camp if they had recognized him? How would Nizan have reacted to this new situation of being an activist separated from his political family, shunned by them, and discovering the shock of isolation? This is the situation that the text brings before us in the realm of the imaginary, nine years later. It seems as though Sartre had, in a sense, interiorized

Nizan, so that he could survive within him. Through the character of Schneider (the German translation of the original Latin word for his own name, Sartor), who is really Vicarios (the vicar, Nizan's representative), Sartre brings about a fusion of himself with Nizan. The "strange friendship" between Brunet, the pure and hard activist in whom he had earlier challenged Nizan the communist, and Schneider/Vicarios, the fallen activist who brings together the conflicting positions of the isolated intellectual and the partisan intellectual—and these were the differences that had separated Nizan and Sartre in the 1930s—is a dreamt-of friendship between Nizan and Sartre, if the former had not been killed at the front, but had been reunited with Sartre in the camp, where they would have found themselves once again the same, equals, interchangeable, friends as in the good old days of adolescence. Thus, this friendship is a form of posthumous reconciliation. Schneider/Vicarios' death is Nizan's second death, but this time it is salvaged and redeemed by Sartre's friendship, by the work of mourning that the text brings about. *Strange Friendship*, where Sartre reveals his affection, without the disguise of irony, is an elegy for a dead friend, a chaste elegy, though passionate and tragic.

This is what encourages us to say, following the idea of an analogy between *Roads of Freedom* and a Beethoven symphony, that the fourth movement undoubtedly aims to be much like tragic oratory. Geneviève Idt, for her part, has justly pointed out that for the Shakespearean ending that he foresaw for the final volume, Sartre would probably have to have invented a literary form that was virtually operatic.

CHAPTER 9
Critical Note on *The Last Chance*

Michel Contat and George H. Bauer

The fourth part of *Roads of Freedom* is undoubtedly the most talked about of all Sartre's unpublished works, and the one most awaited by his public after the war. Ever since the appearance of *The Age of Reason* and *The Reprieve* in September 1945, readers knew that a volume entitled *The Last Chance* was to follow, which would lead the characters "to the liberation of Paris, though not necessarily to their own."[1] For reasons given in the General Introduction to *Roads of Freedom*, and in the Note on *Strange Friendship*, this concluding title gave way, provisionally, in 1949, to *Death in the Soul*, and was transferred to a fourth volume announced as "forthcoming." In promising this future volume, the "Please Insert" for the third volume left it vague: Sartre said only that Mathieu, having lost his problem, will find himself another. As we know, *The Last Chance* was never to see the light of day. Only two chapters, of which Brunet and Schneider were the protagonists, came out at the end of 1949 in *Les Temps modernes*, under the title *Strange Friendship*.

We will not return in detail here to the reasons why Sartre abandoned *The Last Chance*, which can be summed up as follows: how impossible it was for him to render his lived experience and the ambiguities of the post-war period in a novel that was to be situated during the Occupation and the Resistance. The sketches and outlines we have found, and which were published for the first time in the Pléiade edition of Sartre's *Oeuvres romanesques* in 1981, allow us to form a rather sharp picture of the nature of the volume's "moral debate," and of the aesthetic dead-end to which

Sartre's ideological uncertainty had led him at the end of the 1940's. Let us recall that abandoning the project was a gradual process, and that Sartre probably worked on *The Last Chance* off and on until 1952.

It is difficult to date the various fragments we have precisely, especially since we have not had access to another manuscript which may well be from a later time. Those that we have organized here, following Sartre's outlines as closely as possible, were probably written as a direct follow-up to *Death in the Soul*, the definitive version of which was completed in 1948. They are probably from the same year. It would seem that during 1949, anticipating the difficulties he would have in finishing the novel, Sartre pulled from the work-in-progress the two chapters that corresponded the best to his preoccupation at that time (his polemic with the Communist Party), to give them a finalized and publishable form. It seems as though, with *Strange Friendship*, he wanted both to encourage himself to continue, accomplishing what he could, yet anticipate the eventual abandonment of the project. A single chapter of what remains comes across as nearly polished—the one showing Mathieu at the end of his stay in the infirmary, preparing to join the others in the camp—and, according to Outline I, it precedes the episode of Brunet organizing the communist resistance in the Stalag. It thus seems to come from a phase of revision that puts it close to publication. The majority of the other fragments are not as far along, and some are doubtless first drafts.

The work of putting this text together posed delicate problems, as is always the case with drafts that correspond to no finalized version. The difficulty is increased by the fact that the manuscript contained numerous versions of several passages. Our first concern was to produce a text of maximum legibility, sometimes to the detriment of the strict rule that would forbid merging different versions. Given the incomplete nature of our information, it was impossible to tell exactly to what stage of the text the different fragments we had corresponded. Had we chosen to reproduce the succession of fragments in the initial inextricable disorder in which they were arranged in the manuscript as we found it, the result would have been a completely unintelligible text. Opting for legibility was an act of respect for the reader, not a betrayal of the author. Let us also add that Sartre had come to be aware of the work we were doing on his drafts, and that he allowed it. The texts that we present may not meet the standards that Sartre would have insisted upon for a text published by him as author, but they correspond to the documentary character that he wanted them to preserve, and they speak to the need of non-specialist readers who will find themselves intrigued by the document.

The interest of this unfinished text is, obviously, a matter, in the first place, of the importance of *Roads of Freedom* in Sartre's total body of work. To find Mathieu, who had been left for dead in the third volume, alive in the prison camp; to find Brunet, after his unsuccessful attempt at escape; to see their improbable encounter and the reversal of the situation, in relation to *The Age of Reason,* such that now it is Mathieu exhorting Brunet to not leave the Party—all this will undoubtedly be, as it was for us when we discovered this manuscript—most satisfying to the reader's curiosity. Beyond that, the intensity of the moral and political debate, its unresolved character and its tension between the register of the novel and the theatrical register, convey insight into Sartre's state of mind, which was to lead him to his pro-communist 'conversion' in 1952, and into his pursuit of a form that could elevate the realist-critical novel to the heights of contemporary myth. As for the subject of the novel itself, clearly it is the functioning of an artificial society, that of the camp of prisoners, the "Mysteries of the Stalag" aspect that especially interested Sartre. In this regard, the fragments of *The Last Chance* are a fascinating document not only on account of the failure of Sartre's great novel where "the loser wins," but also on account of the social experience that gave him so much on which to reflect, and from which *The Critique of Dialectical Reason* was derived. Thus, these fragments contain seeds of a good part of Sartre's later writing, scattered in new directions by their very failure to come together as a work.

CHAPTER 10
"Bad Faith" and *Roads of Freedom*

Craig Vasey

I mentioned in Chapter 1 that the portions of the text in which Brunet is the main character are written strikingly deliberately in the present tense. In *The Last Chance*, one might have thought this was evidence of its incompleteness, and that prior to publication, Sartre might have intended to polish it up and rewrite it by more standard literary principles. But once we realize that the entire two hundred published pages of Part II of *Death in the Soul* are also written in the present tense (with no breaks), this hypothesis loses plausibility.[1] Volume I, *The Age of Reason*, is written in standard or classic novel style as far as tense goes: the story is told by an unidentified narrator, in the past tense. Volume II, *The Reprieve*, is written in the stream of consciousness style (but using the past tense), and is such a departure from standard style that the reader often has difficulty following the action, sometimes discovering that the beginning of a sentence is about one character in one situation, and the end of it is about another in another situation. Volume III, *Death in the Soul*, is back to standard style for Part I, but limited to the present tense in Part II, where Mathieu is out of the picture. And then Volume IV, *Strange Friendship*, the story of Brunet and Schneider in the camp, is also written in the simple present tense; it reads almost like a play, with descriptions instead of stage directions. The fragments that make up the remainder of the fourth volume, *The Last Chance*, are back to traditional tenses, with the *passé simple* (the past tense used only in literature) particularly prominent—until, that is, Brunet returns to the narrative; the last twenty or so pages are once again and exclusively in the present tense. Clearly, this is deliberate, and deserves some comment.

To be represented always in the present tense is to be represented without regard to one's own past or future, as though these were not part of who one is. Whereas Mathieu is a philosophy professor, Brunet has little interest in reflective thought; even in the final conversations of *The Last Chance*, he makes fun of the idea of trying to justify your life. I propose that Sartre is codifying the character of Brunet's selfhood (how he handles the issue of being himself) in this linguistic choice.

One of the most famous, and most easily misunderstood phrases from Sartre's philosophical writing, *Being and Nothingness*, is that a person is a being who "is what it is not and who is not what it is."[2] Rather than being merely a paradox or sloppy, this formula has two very clear and related meanings. The easier one to grasp has to do with time, the issue we are addressing. This can be seen by adding in a few words, so it reads "A person is a being that is what it is not (yet), and is not (simply) what it has become." In existentialist thought, from Kierkegaard and Heidegger on, there is an important observation that a person is a project, so that who each of us is, is a function of how we are projecting ourselves from our past (our starting points) into what we are not yet. This is essential to having a self or identity, and to being able to confront (and suffer from) the question "Who am I really?"

Existentialist thinkers point out that selfhood is not something our animal friends seem to suffer from: they don't fret about the meaning of their lives, they don't contemplate suicide when the going gets too tough, and in general, they don't regret yesterday or worry about tomorrow: they seem able to live wholly in the present. To the extent to which this is possible for a human being, Brunet is such a man: he does not experience himself as an issue, as a question mark, as a problem to be addressed. He lives seriously, according to the certitudes and rules of the Party, and the Party provides his identity. In a sense, he does not have a self—until *The Last Chance*. Thus he is represented solely in the present tense.

The other meaning of the phrase "it is what it is not and is not what it is," is quite different, and has to do with the moral content of Sartre's existentialist outlook. "Bad faith" is the phrase he uses for it. To live in bad faith is to live in denial of the ambiguity of one's existence; it is, for example, to deny that one is responsible for what one is, on such grounds as that one's upbringing or conditions of birth have determined one to be thus-and-so (e.g., cowardly, generous, distrustful, selfish, lazy, etc.). For Sartre, this is a denial of how free we are, and a means for insulating ourselves from the anguish that feeling responsible for ourselves can bring. Or it can be, for example, to deny that one's past, upbringing or social starting point has any relevance at all to who one is (pretending, for instance, that being a Jew doesn't mean anything in WWII, or that having white or dark brown skin has nothing to do with who one is in US society, or that being female has nothing to do with who one is in patriarchal culture). *This* form of bad faith is not denial of freedom, but of the factuality[3] of the situation within which you project being who you shall be. In his lecture, "Existentialism is a Humanism," Sartre calls people who are in the first form of bad faith "cowards," and he calls people who deny the contingency of the human condition and of their situation—who, as he says, "try to prove that their existence is necessary"—"bastards." "Bad faith" is a sufficiently elastic category that existentialist thinkers can use it to characterize other forms of "lying to oneself" about what they see as the truth of the human condition; in some sense it always refers to a strategy of life by which one disburdens oneself of responsibility for oneself. Sartre sees religion in general as a form of bad faith, and certainly Brunet's blind adherence to the Communist Party's interpretation of reality fits in as well.

This, then, is the case for saying that, to the degree that this is possible for a human being, the character of Brunet—up until *The Last Chance*—does not correspond to Sartre's definition of a person or a man (a being who *is what he is not* and *who is not what he is*); on the contrary, Brunet seems to be (only and exactly) *what he is* and to *not be what he is not*. That is, he is a man who is not experiencing himself as having a self, as having to be himself, as making himself, or as having himself to be (From Sartre's point of view all four of these expressions are slightly different ways of saying the same thing). He is living the spirit of seriousness, and he is in bad faith.[4] Mathieu is also in bad faith through most of the story: he is a man who refuses to let himself be defined, who wants to "be free," that is, not limited by any choices or situations. This begins to change in *Death in the Soul*, and continues to evolve in *The Last Chance*, where he recognizes his experience of being with others, caught up in the world the war has brought about. The roads of freedom explored in these volumes are especially Mathieu's and Brunet's.

Notes

PART I INTRODUCTORY MATERIAL

Chapter 1

1 Jean-Paul Sartre (1981). *Oeuvres romanesques*, Paris: Editions Pléiade, Gallimard, p. 1912.
2 I have been unsuccessful in acquiring or gaining access to this TV series, and can report only what the Internet Movie Database tells us: that it aired between October 4 and December 27, 1970, was directed by James Cellan Jones, was written in part by Sartre and in part by David Turner, had thirteen episodes (six entitled "The Age of Reason," three entitled "The Reprieve," and four entitled "The Defeated"), that it was nominated for five awards (Best Script, Best Actor, Best Actress, Best Design, and Best Drama Production), and that it starred Michael Bryant (Mathieu), Rosemary Leach (Marcelle), Daniel Massey (Daniel), Anthony Higgins (Boris), Alison Fiske (Ivich), Georgia Brown (Olga), and Donald Burton (Brunet).
3 Jean-Paul Sartre (1966). *Being and Nothingness*. Trans. Hazel Barnes. New York: Washington Square Press, p. 60.
4 This means *an odd sort of war*, and is often rendered in English as *the phony war*.
5 From my experience as a teacher, I find that few young people today have any sense of the constructive or positive connotation that "communism" used to have: before being so successfully demonized in the USA by the McCarthy years, the Communist Party represented the interests of working class people against their exploitation by

209

their employers. Since the late nineteenth century, it was on the side of promoting economic revolution, to be sure, but in the direction of many of the sorts of things everyone takes for granted today: public education, health care, child labor laws, social security—quality-of-life features you could afford if you were an owner of wealth, but that the average working person could not afford. Before the geo-political situation of post–World War II, there was no ambiguity that the Communist Party stood for workers' well-being, and nearly all others stood for the interests of Business.

6 My translation of "Tu lui as foutu la mort dans l'âme," which, more literally, would be "you've fuckin' put death into his soul." Jean-Paul Sartre (1992). *Troubled Sleep*. Trans. Gerard Hopkins. New York: Vintage International, p. 373 (Pléiade, *OR.*, p. 1425).

7 Part of this passage is from the manuscript rather than the published text. See Pléiade edition, *OR.*, p. 2099.

8 Pléiade, *OR.*, p. 1426/ Jean-Paul Sartre (1992).*Troubled Sleep*. Trans. Gerard Hopkins. New York: Vintage International, p. 375/ Jean-Paul Sartre (1960). *Iron in the Soul*. Trans. Gerard Hopkins. London: Hamish Hamilton, p. 343 ("psychological balderdash").

9 Jean-Paul Sartre, *Troubled Sleep*, p. 373/ Jean-Paul Sartre, *Iron in the Soul*, p. 341.

10 "Those who aim to hide their total freedom from themselves, through the spirit of seriousness or through deterministic excuses, I will call *cowards*. Those who try to prove that their existence is necessary, whereas it is the very contingency of the appearance of man on Earth, I will call *bastards*."—My translation

11 Literally, "salaud" does not mean "bastard" in the sense of "illegitimate birth," but is built on the word for "dirt," so it could be rendered as "dirty bastard" in English; but that might seem redundant.

12 See my essay "'Bad Faith' and *Roads of Freedom*" at the end of this volume.

13 In the English translation, his French name, Gros Louis, is preserved. But this just means Big Louis.

14 This is one of the scenes Sartre speaks about in the Interview at the Café Flore with Christian Grisoli, included in this volume.

15 Neville Chamberlain, the Prime Minister of Britain, and Edouard Daladier, Prime Minister of France.

16 Anyone who attempts to read it will be in for a serious surprise! But once one understands what Sartre is up to, it becomes a very compelling text.

17 On the title page of the 1947 Knopf edition of *The Reprieve*, the third volume is announced as being in preparation, to be called *La Dernière Chance* (*The Last Chance*).

18 Jean-Paul Sartre, *Troubled Sleep*, p. 236/ Jean-Paul Sartre, *Iron in the Soul*, p. 227.

19 As indicated above, this cannot be discerned from the state of the current English-language translations.

20 See Contat's *Notice* included in this volume.

21 Contat provides a General Introduction for the entire cycle, as well as a much briefer introduction for each of the two parts we publish here (*Strange Friendship* and *The Last Chance*). I have abbreviated the General Introduction somewhat, but have included it in Part III to address the question of why Sartre never really completed the cycle. I have included the shorter introductions to the two other texts in their entirety.

Chapter 2

1 "Existentialism is a Humanism," given by Sartre at the Club Maintenant, Salle des Centraux, rue Jean Goujon, on October 29, 1945, published subsequently by Nagel (1946).

2 This theme is developed by Simone de Beauvoir in "Existentialisme et la sagesse des nations" (Existentialism and the wisdom of the world/ nations) in *Les Temps modernes* #3, December 1945 (pp. 385–404).

PART II THE LAST CHANCE

Chapter 5

1 On October 28, 1940, Mussolini ordered his troops in Albania to attack Greece. The Italian Army was quickly thrown into disarray: it fled Greece and even had to abandon the Albanian cities of Argyrokastro (December 9), Klissoura (January 10), and Tomarica (January 19).

2 The Franciste Party was founded by Marcel Bucard in November 1933, soon after the Nazis came to power in Germany. "Of all the French versions of fascism, it was the most intransigent, systematic and fascist," according to J. Plumyene and R. Lasierra's *Les Fascismes français 1923–1963* (Paris: Le Seuil, 1963). Its slogan was "France for the French," and it was a presence in most of the prison camps, with German support. Sartre has told us that in his camp, the Francistes were organized and active.

3 In *Merleau-Ponty Vivant, Situations IV*, Sartre wrote: "When I saw my officers, these incompetents, I regretted my pre-war anarchism; since we had to fight, it was a mistake to leave command in the hands of these pompous imbeciles."(See Jean-Paul Sartre (1964). *Situations IV*. Paris: Gallimard, p. 190.)

4 At the beginning of *The Reprieve* (September 23, 1938), Brunet ran into Maurice Tailleur and his wife Zézette in the Rue Royale. Maurice is a working class member of the Communist Party, Brunet a journalist for the Party paper, *L'Humanité*.

5 In August 1939, the French government shut down *L'Humanité*, the daily paper of the French Communist Party, because of its praise for the German-Soviet pact, and the first underground issue came out in October 1939. After the occupation of Paris in June 1940, several leaders of the CP petitioned the German authorities to allow the official reappearance of the paper, but this was opposed by the Vichy government, and denied. During this period, *L'Humanité* did not criticize the occupiers, but rather praised French workers for getting along with the German soldiers. It also praised the Soviet Union for having established "peace in Eastern Europe," for staying out of the imperialist war, for liberating 23 million human beings from the yoke of capitalism (referring to the annexation of Poland, Romania and Czechoslovakia), and "showing to the exploited and oppressed of the world the road to liberation, the road to happiness." (Contat, *OR*, p. 2112). This position gradually changed during the beginning of 1941, and by March, the paper was attacking Hitler and the Nazification of France. In June 1941, Hitler invaded the USSR (Operation Barbarossa), and *L'Humanité* clearly linked the liberation of France with Soviet victory over the fascists.

6 The French Communist Party was dissolved on September 26, 1939, and most Deputies of the Party were arrested. Chalais does not appear to "be" any one particular communist Deputy, however.

7 This name seems chosen by Sartre for a variety of reasons. It invokes the English word "vicarious" (suggesting a stand-in in suffering or in pleasure, as well as someone to whom one delegates work); it also suggests the role of Vicar, an ecclesiastical administrator of lands inhabited by infidels (Schneider being a heretic vis-à-vis the Party). The political reference is to Sartre's personal friend Paul Nizan: Nizan was one of the leading intellectuals of the French Communist Party, and a journalist; he quit the Party over his opposition to the German-Soviet Pact, and was immediately accused by the Party of working for the police. In an article published in *Die Welt* (March 21, 1940), the Secretary of the FCP, Maurice Thorez wrote: "The police spy Nizan has been promoting the idea of a 'national communism'—i.e., communism in words only, nationalism in reality—in the guise of a plan to collaborate with the bourgeois press to justify the censorship of the communist press." Nizan was killed at Dunkirk on May 23, 1940. After the war, Sartre went to lengths to rehabilitate his reputation in a controversy that put him in conflict with the Communist Party, and with Aragon in particular. See "Le cas Nizan," in *Les Temps modernes*, #22, July 1947, pp. 181–184.

8 Chalais seems to represent a point of view that was already falling out of favor in the Party at the time that he spoke with Brunet in the camp. It had been the Party line, but Brunet's position, ironically, was actually closer to it at that moment. This reversal makes one think of the situation Sartre described in *Dirty Hands*.

9 All of Sartre's thought in the postwar period is opposed to the notion of the "historical process," an element of the Stalinist objectivism which denied the role of subjectivity in history. Two texts especially address this: "Le Processus historique" (in *Les Ecrits de Sartre*, pp. 677–679) and "Faux savants ou faux lièvres?" (in Jean-Paul Sartre (1964). *Situations VI*. Paris: Gallimard.). In the former he attacks an article in Pravda that reproaches existentialism with disregarding the historical process; in the latter—which is essential for understanding *Strange Friendship*—he shows that the Stalinists' error is "to see in subjectivity not a certain interpretation of the objective, but

the negation or denial of this objectiveness." Subjectivity thus becomes "a constitutional blemish, a form of treason."

10 Molotov: "The friendly relations established between Germany and the USSR are founded upon the fundamental interests of the two countries." Contat cites the volume by A. Rossi, *Deux ans d'alliance germano-sovietique* (A. Fayard: 1949, pp. 166–180).

11 The printer is the French prisoner shot by the Nazis when he jumped from the train in the final scene of *Death in the Soul*.

12 For this anecdote, Sartre relied on the story that Henriette Nizan undoubtedly told him after the war, about her own encounters with Party comrades after Nizan's resignation. See Cohen-Solal, Annie (with Henriette Nizan's assistance), *Paul Nizan, the Impossible Communist*, Grasset 1980, pp. 24–247, where she tells how Leon Moussinac asked her to publicly disassociate herself from Nizan and how Ginzburger told her: "I don't salute traitors.")

13 The de-lousing barracks. —Translator

Chapter 6

1 Sartre's 1944 essay, "The Republic of Silence," begins: "We have never been so free as under German occupation. We had lost every right, and above all the right of speech: we were insulted every day and we had to remain silent; we were deported as laborers, as Jews, as political prisoners; everywhere, on the walls, in the newspapers, and on the screen, we saw the foul and listless face which our oppressors wanted to give us. Because of all this we were free." Bree, Germaine and Bernauer, George (1970). *Defeat and Beyond: An Anthology of French Wartime Writing (1940–1945)*. New York: Pantheon Books. —Translator

2 Bollard said earlier that he's from Bordeau, but Sartre now has him being from Rouen, probably for just the reason this passage invokes.

3 In *Death in the Soul/Troubled Sleep*, Sartre has Mathieu and his friends in the 61st, not the 68th.

4 A ship of the line of the French navy, damaged in June 1940.

5 The 70th was Sartre's own division; earlier Mathieu identified his as the 68th.

6 Brunet had mentioned to Vicarios about getting his new pipe at the canteen (p. 45)—this section of the story is evidently meant to precede the arrival of Chalais in *Strange Friendship*.

7 In May 1940, the French Army included ten divisions of North Africans as well as a good number of colonial troops.

8 In *Death in the Soul*, before being captured by the Germans, Schwartz pointed out that he was Alsacian, and had even said, "Better to be a live German than a dead Frenchman." Mathieu would have expected him to have gone over to the Germans.

9 Pinette was the only member of Mathieu's division who was with him and the regular French soldiers in the bell tower, firing on the Germans, at the end of Part One of *Death in the Soul*. The reader would have assumed they were both killed in the explosion of the bell tower.

10 June 18 is the date of the bell-tower skirmish in *Death in the Soul*.

11 A slip on Sartre's part? We have seen previous references to "mysteries of the camp." —Translator

12 This is the only part of the texts published in the Pléiade edition that is written in the first person. At the time of that publication (1981), *Mathieu's Journal* was not known. It seems likely that this is a fragment from *Mathieu's Journal*, since it too is written in the first person.

13 In *Death in the Soul*, Longin is a tax collector, not an architect. Sartre seems to have lost track of this earlier decision.

14 The camp bulletin.

15 A film by William Wellman, starring Gary Cooper and Ray Milland; it came out in 1939 in the US, but was banned in France because of its treatment of the French Foreign Legion.

16 End of the manuscript page.

17 The date of this event in *Death in the Soul* is June 18, 1940.

18 This is strange, because though there is such a place in Gironde, there is not in Lorraine, and Sartre makes it clear in *Death in the Soul*, that they were captured at Padoux, Lorraine.

19 The scene is in chapter 8 of *The Age of Reason*.

20 Aristide Boucicaut and his wife Maguerite (1816–1887) are well known for their philanthropic work; a hospital in Paris' XVth arrondissement is named for them.

21 In *Words*, Sartre talks about seeing a film with his mother at the cinema: "The pianist attacked the overture of *Grottes de Fingal*, and everyone understood that the criminal was about to appear."

22 The reference is to the final scene of *Death in the Soul*.

PART III SCHOLARSHIP AND ANALYSIS

Chapter 7

1 Simone de Beauvoir (1962). *The Prime of Life*. Trans. Peter Green. New York: World Publishing Co., p. 396.
2 Simone de Beauvoir, ed. (1992) *Witness to my Life: The Letters of Jean-Paul Sartre to Simone de Beauvoir 1926–1939*. Trans. Lee Fahnestock and Norman MacAfee. New York: Schribners, p. 47. Translation slightly modified. In her footnote, de Beauvoir identifies Mikhail Sholokhov as the author, and points out that he was born the same year as Sartre, and won the Nobel Prize for Literature in 1965, the year after Sartre declined it.
3 Published in *Situations I*. (Jean-Paul Sartre (1947). *Situations I*. Paris: Gallimard.
4 In reality, it was not until 1945 that *The Age of Reason* was published. —Translator
5 Letter of May 27, 1940. This one to Simone de Beauvoir is available in Sartre, trans. Lee Fahnestock and Norman MacAfee, *Quiet Moments in a War*. 1993. New York: Macmillan pp. 202–204.
6 Simone de Beauvoir, *The Prime of Life*, p. 552.
7 Ibid., p. 556.
8 Regarding the circumstances of this escape (thanks to forged documents letting him pass as a civilian), see Simone de Beauvoir, *The Prime of Life*, p. 577, and the book by one of his companions in the camp: Abbey Marius Perrin (1980). *Avec Sartre au stalag XII D*. Paris: J-P Delarge. This account confirms that of Simone de Beauvoir; Abbey Perrin himself produced the false document indicating that Sartre had been discharged because of equilibrium problems.
9 Simone de Beauvoir, *The Prime of Life*, p. 619. It is well to recall that the Vichy regime put a woman to death for providing an abortion.
10 Ibid., p. 604.
11 Ibid., p. 603.
12 "Sursis" is a juridical term used in such phrases as "suspended sentence," "stay of proceedings," "reprieve from execution," "deferment of call-up." I will use "suspension" to render Contat's meaning. —Translator

13 See "La Nationalisation de la littérature" and "Situation de l'écrivain en 1947" in *Situations II* (Jean-Paul Sartre (1948). *Situations II*. Paris: Gallimard), as well as *Sartre par lui-même* (1976, Directors: Alexandre Astruc, Michel Contat).

14 Jean-Paul Sartre, *Situations II*, p. 253.

15 Frantz' final monologue in *The Condemned of Altona,* p. 223.

16 Jean-Paul Sartre, *Situations II,* p. 235.

17 Ibid., p. 289.

18 The *Notebook for an Ethics* and *The Last Chance.* —Translator

19 Jean-Paul Sartre (1952). *St Genet: comedien et martyr*. Paris: Gallimard, p. 212. This is the reference provided in Contat's essay, p. 1877. Unfortunately, I have not been able to locate this passage in either the French or US edition. —Translator

20 Simone de Beauvoir (1964). *Force of Circumstance.* Trans. Richard Howard. New York: Putnam, p. 243.

21 Translated from Contat's translation of the German, "Besuch bei Jean-Paul Sartre," (12 Juli 1952), Wochenausgabe, No. 28. Vienna: Die Presse, p. 6.

22 Simone de Beauvoir, *Force of Circumstance*, p. 196.

23 *L'Express*, 17 septembre 1959.

24 Unpublished interview, 1974.

25 "Interview de François Mauriac," *France-Soir*, 28 fevrier 1969.

26 At this same time he also recounted an anecdote that we feel permitted to pass on. During a train ride about 1950, he was intrigued by a beautiful young woman in a fur sitting opposite him in a compartment, giving all the signs of boredom as she read a book whose title he could not see, since it was covered in a leather jacket. Finally she put down the book with an excessive sigh, and left for the dining-car. Amused at the thought of knowing which of his fellow writers was provoking such yawns from such a charming individual, he discreetly picked up the book from the bench, and discovered that it was none other than *Death in the Soul*, and that, to make things worse, the passage at which she had stopped was the one that he thought had come out the best in the whole novel, the one he had worked on the most: the scene in which Mathieu is unable to get drunk with his comrades.

27 In fact, the title has been translated in English as *Roads to Freedom*. (However, as I argue in Chapter 1 this can only be called a mistranslation—Translator.)

28 In this Continuum edition, we now reproduce just the studies of *Strange Friendship* and *The Last Chance*. —Translator

Chapter 8

1 Sartre's "Please Insert" was not published as part of either the US or the UK translation of *La Mort dans l'âme*; the title in French means "Death in the Soul," but this volume was published as *Troubled Sleep* in the United States and as *Iron in the Soul* in the United Kingdom. —Translator

2 This passage can be found in a different translation, in Simone de Beauvoir, *Force of Circumstance* (1964). Trans. Richard Howard. New York: Putnam, pp. 194–195. —Translator

3 Reproduced in the Pléiade edition, *Oeuvres romanesques*, p. 238–245. —Translator

4 In terms of this Continuum volume, this would seem to mean that the story would open with Mathieu in the infirmary and the camp (pp. 98–127) as the first two episodes. Next would come the arrival of Chalais and Brunet's fall (pp. 29–89), then the filled-out fragmentary camp material (pp. 127–143), and the escape attempt (pp. 89–97). The story would end with the Mathieu-Brunet encounter (pp. 144–174). –Translator

5 For another interpretation of the meaning of the variety of styles, see my essay at the end of this volume, "'Bad Faith' and *Roads of Freedom*." —Translator

Chapter 9

1 See "Please Insert 1."

Chapter 10

1 Again, this is something the English reader could never have realized because of the mistranslation of the third volume.

2 I am using the impersonal pronoun, "it," here, to avoid the complexity of using "he or she" twice. In referring to Brunet specifically later, I will use "he."

3 Existentialist writers call this "facticity."

4 In the Conclusion of *Being and Nothingness*, (1972) p. 796, Sartre makes the assertion that the purpose of his philosophy—and of existential psychoanalysis—is to bring us to repudiate the spirit of seriousness.

Works Cited

de Beauvoir, Simone (1962). *The Prime of Life*. Trans. Peter Green. New York: World Publishing Co.

—(1964). *Force of Circumstance*. Trans. Richard Howard. New York: Putnam.

—(1992). *Witness to my Life: The Letters of Jean-Paul Sartre to Simone de Beauvoir 1926–1939*, ed. Simone de Beauvoir. Trans. Lee Fahnestock and Norman MacAfee. New York: Scribners.

Perrin, Abbey Marius (1980). *Avec Sartre au stalag XII D*. Paris: J-P Delarge.

Sartre, Jean-Paul (1947). *Situations I*. Paris: Gallimard.

—(1948). *Situations II*. Paris: Gallimard.

—(1952). *St Genet: comedien et martyr*. Paris: Gallimard.

—(1960). *Iron in the Soul*. Trans. Gerard Hopkins. London: Hamish Hamilton.

—(1961). *The Condemned of Altona*. Trans. Sylvia and George Leeson. New York: Alfred Knopf.

—(1964). *Situations IV*. Paris: Gallimard.

—(1964). *Situations VI*. Paris: Gallimard.

—(1972). *Being and Nothingness*. Trans. Hazel Barnes. New York: Washington Square Press.

—(1981). *Oeuvres romanesques*. Paris: Gallimard.

—(1987). *Existentialism and Human Emotions*. Trans. Bernard Frechtman. New York: Citadel Press.

—(1992). *Troubled Sleep*. Trans. Gerard Hopkins. New York: Vintage International.

Index